CHRISTIANS OF INDIA

CHRISTIANS OF INDIA

ROWENA ROBINSON

Sage Publications
New Delhi ● Thousand Oaks ● London

CHRISTIANS OF INDIA

ROWENA ROBINSON

Sage Publications
New Delhi ☺ Thousand Oaks ☺ London

Copyright © Rowena Robinson, 2003

First published in 2003 by

Sage Publications India Pvt Ltd
B-42, Panchsheel Enclave
New Delhi 110 017

Sage Publications Inc
2455 Teller Road
Thousand Oaks, California 91320

Sage Publications Ltd
6 Bonhill Street
London EC2A 4PU

Published by Tejeshwar Singh for Sage Publications India Pvt Ltd, typeset in 10/12 NewCentury Schlbk by S.R. Enterprises, New Delhi and printed at Chaman Enterprises, New Delhi.

Library of Congress Cataloging-in-Publication Data

Robinson, Rowena, 1967–
    Christians of India/Rowena Robinson.
      p.   cm.
    Includes bibliographical references and index.
    1. Christianity—India. 2. India—Church history. I. Title.
BR1155.R63   305.6–dc21   2003   2003009038

ISBN: 0–7619–9822–5 (US-Hb)   81–7829–292–0 (India-Hb)
           0–7619–9823–3 (US-Pb)   81–7829–293–9 (India-Pb)

Sage Production Team: Divya Dubey, N.K. Negi and Santosh Rawat

To a woman of indomitable strength and
immeasurable grace,
my mother Marie Robinson (1921–2001)

CONTENTS

ACKNOWLEDGEMENTS

This book took shape during a three-month Charles Wallace Trust India funded fellowship that I held at the School for Anthropological Studies, Queen's University, Belfast starting February 2001. I thank the Trust for having provided me this opportunity to take a break from teaching and prepare the manuscript for this book.

I thank my colleagues and friends at the School for their warmth and encouraging attitude and for their helpful comments and suggestions made at the seminar I presented at the School, based on the first chapter of this book. I also thank the staff at the University Library for their help in accessing various materials. Hazel and Valerie at the School's office were extremely helpful with all administrative matters (including the parcelling and despatch of books and papers!).

I would like to thank my colleagues in sociology at IIT Mumbai who filled in for me during my absence, taking on the extra burden cheerfully and without complaint. Four doctoral students of the Department of Humanities and Social Sciences at IIT Mumbai helped me. I thank Anoop Sarbahi for preparing the diagrams for this book and Samit Roy for help in the final stages. I also thank Bidhan Chandra Dash for assistance with the bibliography and K. Omkumar for help with the map.

I thank Omita at Sage, who is always pleasant, efficient and wonderful to work with. The anonymous reviewer of the manuscript provided several useful suggestions.

I would like to record that the simple title of the book was inspired by both Susan Visvanathan's path-breaking anthropological work on Christianity in Kerala titled *Christians of Kerala: History, Belief and Ritual among the Yakoba*. J.P.S. Uberoi, long ago and in a different context, had made me sensitive to the distinction between 'of' and 'in'. As this book will reveal, I argue the case for speaking of Christians *of* India, not just Christians (who happen to be) *in* India. Veena Das' recent work on contemporary

India, *Critical Events: An Anthropological Perspective on Contemporary India*, reveals anew the enduringly unique worth of anthropological endeavour. André Béteille taught respect for the comparative perspective which inspires this text, and has, from time to time, administered the injunction to *keep on writing*.

I thank the friends and colleagues who have encouraged me and have provided shelter and support and, often, more direct inputs for this book, either through guidance towards relevant materials and references or by helping me to work out my arguments through discussion. I would like to mention Nilika Mehrotra, Soumendra Patnaik, D. Parthasarathy, Sharit Bhowmik, Meera Warrier, Robyn Lim, Tracey Heatherington, Paloma Gay y Blasco, Suzel Reily and Sathianathan Clarke. They all helped in different ways. My sisters have always been caring and supportive. My mother passed away before the manuscript of this book could reach the stage of publication. With maternal disregard of the level of achievement, she was always immensely proud of all her children's creations. If heaven is and has an address, she's sure to order a copy.

1

INTRODUCTION: FROM PERIPHERY TO CENTRE

TOWARDS AN ANTHROPOLOGY OF INDIAN CHRISTIANITY

I have written this book for scholars of the anthropology of religion in India at different levels, for specialists as well as for students and for others with some interest in the field. It appeared to me in the course of drafting a short piece on 'Christianity in India' for the *Oxford India Companion to Sociology and Social Anthropology* that there is need for an introductory book in this area. This is not to say that literature on Christianity as such is completely unavailable or very meagre. There are a number of published and unpublished ethnographic and historical accounts of different communities and regions. I will be drawing on many of them for my description and analysis.

However, accounts are scattered, their quality varies and they do not give us a general perspective on Christianity in India because their focus is usually more fixed and concentrated on a particular small region or a specific group. My purpose in this book is different. It is precisely to bring together a number of ethnographic and historical accounts that are otherwise dispersed but also aims at the thematic integration of the ethnographic material. This would enable us to study comparative trends, particularly where material is richer. We would get a glimpse of the many 'Christianities' in India! This is something that has not been attempted so far.

A HISTORY OF NEGLECT

While anthropological or sociological and to a much greater extent historical materials are beginning to accumulate in the field, till very recently (and, in fact, even now) writing on Christianity in India suffered from enormous neglect. I will try and outline here the root of that neglect because it tells us something about the story of sociology in India in general and it also defines the possibilities and limitations of what the literature on Christianity has to offer.

It is not scholarship on Christianity alone that has faced neglect. This neglect has extended to the study of all non-Hindu communities (for want of a better term at this moment) in India. What material was available often lacked richness and depth and, sometimes, analytical rigour. This fact is not surprising once we begin to look at the historical roots of disciplines such as sociology, anthropology and history and the pattern of their development in India. The Dumontian perspective,[1] in sociology and anthropology, for instance, which dominated the study of Hinduism for so long, gave centrality to an upper-caste, essentialized version of Hinduism and treated it as synonymous with India. The study of India therefore was and has been for a long time, the study of 'Hindu' India. This notion led both to the reification of Hinduism and the marginalization and neglect of non-Hindu groups and communities.

The dimensions of this neglect are manifold and are only now in the process of being analyzed systematically. Work is now being initiated for the rectification of the bias in the literature. In fact, it must be stated that the roots of neglect go back to the roots of sociology and anthropology, in general, from the moment that these disciplines came to India. It needs no reiteration of course that these disciplines came to India from outside. The tremendous impact that the manner in which the disciplines came has had on their growth and development could do perhaps with some elaboration. In this context, it is useful to look at some of the literature that has begun to look critically at the anthropological work done in India, particularly during the colonial period, by European scholars.

Edward Said, in a pioneering work, spoke of what he called 'Orientalism' (1995). It is worth quoting him at some length to understand what he means by the concept (Said 1995: 3):

Taking the late eighteenth century as a very roughly defined starting point Orientalism can be discussed and analysed as the corporate institution for dealing with the Orient—dealing with it by making statements about it, authorising views of it, describing it, by teaching it, settling it, ruling over it: in short, Orientalism as a western style of dominating, restructuring, and having authority over the Orient... My contention is that without examining Orientalism as a discourse one cannot possibly understand the enormously systematic discipline by which European culture was able to manage—and even produce— the Orient politically, sociologically, militarily, ideologically, scientifically, and imaginatively during the post-Enlightenment period.

Briefly, therefore, Orientalism refers to the literature and knowledge generated by European colonialists about non-European societies. The argument is that all orientalist literature is somehow unreliable because it is knowledge produced by societies that exercised control and power over non-western, colonial territories. It was the political and economic interests of colonialism that produced certain kinds of knowledge about the Orient and this knowledge must therefore be looked at with suspicion. Orientalism, as Inden (1990),[2] Trautmann (1997) and Thapar (1997) point out, includes both the knowledge produced by European scholars and the European representation of the Orient. These interweave to form certain kinds of patterns.

One of the dominant and best-known paradigms that such Orientalist knowledge generated was the Aryan theory. It appears to me possible to argue that the search for the mythical Hindu Arya has had widespread ramifications for social science discourses in general and those on religion, caste and community, particularly. It is possible to trace directly or in a more winding fashion, many of the taken-for-granted ideas and viewpoints in Indian sociology or anthropology to this paradigmatic, overarching myth. I would include among these ideas the definition of India as 'Hindu' India and the understanding that a central position has to be accorded to caste as the most important social and cultural marker of India. Concomitantly, one might also trace the marginalization of the study of other 'communities', whether Christian or Islamic, to the Aryan myth. The myth also has its reverberations in contemporary politics of identity and religion and on popular discourses in general. Van der Veer (1994: 23) has in fact pointed out that Orientalism created Muslims as the other for Hindus, just as Muslims and Islam were historically the 'other' for Christianity in Europe.

If we accept Edward Said's argument elaborated above, we find traces of the Orientalist myth of the pure Aryan race and all the ideas that grew and emerged out of it in all kinds of places. One is reminded sharply of his words (1995: 6):

> I myself believe that Orientalism is more particularly valuable as a sign of European-Atlantic power over the Orient than it is as a veridic discourse about the Orient (which is what, in its academic or scholarly form, it claims to be.)...[A]ll academic knowledge about India and Egypt is somehow tinged and impressed with, violated by, the gross political fact...*that is what I am saying* in this study of Orientalism.

Let me elucidate a little about the origin and growth of the Aryan myth. The work of an entire body of Indological scholars and administrators came together in the construction of the racial understanding of Indian civilization that was established with the Aryan theory. These scholars included William Jones, H.H. Wilson, Henry Colebrooke, Charles Grant, James Mill, Max Müller and others. Ancient Indian textual evidence was sought to support the theory: the *Rgveda* was referred to constantly. According to the myth, Indian history was said to have its roots or its point of origin in the conquest of the *dasas* by the Aryas. The Aryas came with their superior language (Sanskrit) and culture and they dominated the rest of Indian history.

Dravidians too came to be defined by a merging of the markers of language and race. Thus came the idea that Dravidian speakers were an indigenous race and their subjugation by the Aryans created India's most distinctive, unique and defining institution, that which sets it apart from the British and by extension the west, caste. Can one not see here roots of ideas that were to find their way later into a mature, full-blown scientific structural discourse on the radical difference between India and the west? Do we not find here the same distinction as that made between *homo hierarchicus* and *homo equalis* in Dumont?

Projected onto this set of ideas was another set of ideas by which a link was established between race, language and nation. In the context of the emergence of nation states in the course of the nineteenth century, this became a critical concept, and language and race came to be seen as vital elements of national identity (Thapar 1997: xii). Why was this link so important? As Thapar (ibid.: xii) argues eloquently in her introduction to Trautmann's work on the Aryans, the link was vital to the task of differentiating the indigenes from the foreigners, the rightful owner/inheritors of the land from the mere arriviste, the parvenu, so to speak. This theory has had enormous implications for India's political history. Let us see how.

The Dravidian anti-Brahman movement, Sri Lanka's ethnic violence and last but certainly not the least, the politics of religion and religious communities in India have employed its ideas. For the Dravidian movement, it is important to prove that they are an indigenous 'race' that was conquered by the Aryans, who came from outside their land. This idea is overturned in contemporary discourses of the Hindu Right, which need to prove that the *Aryans* are indigenous to India. Thus, they follow attempts to view the Indus Valley Civilization as an *Aryan* civilization, rather than as one that pre-dates several waves of Aryan invasion.

Indological and administrative discourses ran parallel and merged very substantively at times. The need to map the colonized territory, its land, its natural resources and its people led to immense efforts in the areas of cartography, economics, linguistics, legal studies, zoology, botany, epidemiology and, certainly, anthropology. This project of mapping was directly related to the exigencies of rule, the necessity of proper administration and of establishing 'authority' over the Orient. Questions needed to be addressed. What were the structural principles of India? Where did traditional authority lie? And hence, though linguistics managed to prove the 'kinship' of Europeans and Indians through the Aryan theory; once incorporated into colonial administrative discourses, this became the kinship of the unequal. The right to rule and the legitimacy of the Empire could only be defended by such a hierarchical model.

As Thapar (1997: xiii) elucidates, even the discovery of the pre-Vedic Indus Valley Civilization did little to dislodge the Aryan theory. Rather, as I have tried to show above, various elaborate efforts were made to contain the Indus Valley Civilization within the confines of the myth of the Aryan race. The people of the Indus Valley Civilization were sometimes treated as non-Aryans who were conquered (as were the Dravidians) by the Aryans. Otherwise, attempts were made to redefine the Indus Valley Civilization as an Aryan civilization!

Various groups have taken up the Aryan theory to suit their own political interests. For the upper castes, the idea that they were lineal, biological descendants of the Aryans, made good sense. It enabled them to appropriate Indian civilization and then the Indian nation. The homeland of the Aryan 'race' was located somewhere between the Arctic and Iran. It was believed that the Aryans who came from there and 'conquered' India were the most civilized of all Aryans. This idea merges neatly with Dayanand Saraswati's and the early Hindutva argument that the Vedas were the source of all knowledge and that modern India should emulate Vedic society.

Other strands were interwoven to consolidate the myth. It was not long before the Aryans came to be regarded as specific people, a race or ethnic group set apart by their use of Sanskrit and its accompanying culture. In the Hindutva construction, as already noted, the requirement that the Hindu Arya be indigenous leads to a denial of the Aryan invasion. It would appear clear though, that historical and linguistic evidence points to the imported roots of Sanskrit and even if an invasion by Aryans were to remain unproved, certainly the language *had* to be brought by a migrant people. However, and this cannot be stressed enough, *this does not mean that they had to be a distinct race or ethnic group*. The Aryans were migrant people, probably many diverse groups. The idea that they were a single, pure race remains a myth that historical evidence does not support.

Hindutva ideology may not necessarily insist upon the racial integrity of the Hindu Arya. However, there is always a need to stress on ethnic identity. As Thapar (1997: xv) points out, this assertion of an indigenous Aryan identity forms the root of the notion that only the Hindu Arya is indigenous to India. Christians, like Muslims are alien, since they cannot prove that India is either their *punyabhumi* (sacred territory) or their *pitrbhumi* (land of their ancestors). This view confounds biological descent and conversion to another religion (from outside India) and bases itself on the absurd assertion of straight biological descent from the people of early times. It disregards entirely the fact that Christians or Muslims lay rightful claim to Indian ancestry.

Once the Hindu Arya has been given an indigenous ancestry, it is but a short step from there to claim that the Indian territory and by conflation the Indian nation, belongs as a right to the descendants of the Aryans. When even the Indus Valley Civilization is equated with the people of the Vedic corpus, the Hindu Arya is endowed with an unbroken lineal ancestry going back several millennia and the Vedic corpus, conveniently, re-emerges as the foundation of Indian civilization (Thapar 1997: xv). These ideas repeat themselves everywhere and as Fanon (1965; 1967), Chatterjee

(1986), Pandey (1993) and others have argued, they get taken over by the ruling elite in the colonized countries as well.

These ideas, therefore, keep recurring in different places. One variation on the theme, which has now become commonplace of Indian political and public discourse, can be traced to Nehru, though he insists simultaneously that he does not see India as a Hindu land (1981: 75). This is the view expressed in *The Discovery of India* of the powerful, synthesizing Indic civilization which has taken in and assimilated 'foreign' elements at various times without giving up its own 'essence':

> We see in the past some inner urge towards synthesis, derived essentially from the Indian philosophical outlook, was the dominant feature of Indian cultural and even racial development. Each incursion of foreign elements was a challenge to this culture, but was met successfully by a new synthesis and a process of absorption. This was also a process of rejuvenation and new blooms of culture arose out if it, the background and essential basis, however, remaining the same (1981: 76).

In Nehru, the Hindu and the Indian are kept in somewhat uneasy separation, but other politicians, lesser mortals and many many scholars (see Ghurye 1969; Karve 1961 and others) have easily conflated the two, using almost the same language. It has been easy for those who subscribe to this kind of view, and there are many, the Hindutva ideologue included at the extreme end (Nehru remaining at the benign end), to collapse the 'Indian philosophical outlook' with a Vedic/Hindu/Aryan/Brahmanic one and then to argue that this culture forms the basis of Indian civilization. From here, there are two paths. One talks of the assimilative power of Hinduism and how it has absorbed many foreign elements, which have contributed to its growth and development positively. This is the good view, the nice view, the 'secular' view. The Hindutva ideologue, however, would argue that though Indian civilization has taken in and given shelter to many alien elements, these remain foreign to the land ('descendants/sons of Babar, remember?') and are here at the sufferance (if not the mercy) of the descendants of the ancient 'Hindus'.

Some of the unhappy implications of the variations on this idea even get articulated in the Constitution and in formal law (see Conrad 1995). This makes for inequality and discrimination between communities at this level itself. Thus, though minorities are given rights in the Constitution and these are articulated in the Preamble and in Articles 15, 16, 29 and 30, there are also certain other areas, where definitions themselves give rise to problems.

The Preamble to the Constitutions resolved itself to secure to all its citizens social, economic and political justice and provide equality of status and opportunity. These provisions are further reinforced with the help of the Articles mentioned above:

Article 15—Prohibits discrimination on grounds of religion, race, caste or any other such grounds.

Article 16(2)—No person can be discriminated against in matter of public employment on grounds of race, religion and caste.

Article 29(1)— Any section of citizens of India having a distinct language, script or culture of its own shall have the fundamental right to conserve the same. This means that if there is a cultural minority which wants to preserve its own language and culture, the state would not by law impose upon it any other culture belonging to the majority of the locality. The promotion of Hindi as the national language or introduction of compulsory primary education cannot be used as a device to take away the linguistic safeguard of a minority community as guaranteed by Articles 29 and 30.

Article 29(2)—Guarantees no discrimination in state educational institutions. It protects not only the religious minorities but also local or linguistic minorities and ensures that there is no discrimination against any citizen on grounds of religion, language, race or caste.

Article 30(1)—All minorities whether based on religion or language shall have the fundamental right to establish educational institutions of their choice.

Article 30(2)—Guarantees that the state shall not in granting aid to educational institutions, discriminate against any educational institution on the ground that it is under the management of a minority, whether based on religion or language.

Though the minorities have been given rights and safeguards against discrimination, we find that there are legal inconsistencies in the Constitution itself. There are certain Constitutional definitions and provisions that act in a discriminatory manner towards minorities. The Hindu Code Legislation of 1955–56 divided the nation by categorically stating that the meaning of Hindu was:

1) A person who is Hindu by religion in any of its forms or developments including Virashaiva, Lingayat or a follower of Brahman, Prarthana or Arya Samaj.
2) Any person who is Buddhist, Jain or Sikh by religion.

3) Any other person domiciled in territories to which this Act extends who is not a Muslim, Christian, Parsi or Jew by religion unless it is proved that any such person would not have been governed by Hindu law or custom.

In other words, all Indians are 'Hindu' *other than those belonging to religions originating outside India*. The definition of Hindu therefore embodies the well-established principle that application of the term Hindu is not confined to persons actually professing or practising Hindu religion in any form but extends to all persons except those belonging to religions coming from outside Indian shores. The Hindu Marriage Act introduces a uniform matrimonial system for all castes and classes of Hindus, namely monogamy with a possibility of judicial divorce. Accordingly, a Hindu may marry a Buddhist, Jain or Sikh but cannot marry a Christian or Muslim under the Act. A later conversion by one of the Hindu spouses to another religion within the range of what has been defined as Hinduism would have no effect on the status of the marriage, *whereas conversion to any 'alien' religion would constitute sufficient grounds for divorce*.

There are other provisions which show even more clearly the character of their being a sanction against anyone leaving the Hindu community. For instance, all claims to maintenance under the Hindu Adoption and Maintenance Act 1956 by spouse, children or parents are lost upon conversion to any non-Hindu religion. A wife may have grounds for separate residence and maintenance, but loses both if she is unchaste or ceases to be a Hindu (note the unhappy correspondence drawn between the lack of chastity and conversion) by conversion to another religion. The discrimination becomes even more unreasonable when we see that a married Hindu does not need the consent of his spouse to either adopt or give in adoption a common child if the spouse has ceased to be a Hindu. Even children of former Hindus born after conversion 'to another religion' are disqualified from inheriting property from Hindu relatives. Legal disabilities do not arise in case of conversion between the Hindu religion 'proper' and Jainism, Buddhism and Sikhism (Conrad 1995: 324–25).

The attention of the law appears to be exclusively directed to conversion from one of the indigenous religions to 'alien' religions like Christianity, Islam, Judaism or Zoroastrianism. This is clearly discrimination based on religious identity and, in a secular state, is extremely dubious. It actually accentuates the differences between religious groups within the country and creates divides on religious grounds. It provides further, grounds for privileging the 'indigenous' religions and treating them as a community (Conrad 1995: 326).

I hope I have been able to demonstrate to some extent at least, the complex interlinkages that occur across a variety of discourses and articulate as well as express the idea of India as a Hindu nation, a civilization synthesized by Hinduism and critically, by caste. Once this synthesis between the ancient and the modern is woven around the idea of 'the caste Hindu', little historical support or exploration is considered necessary. Hinduism emerges full-blown and complete, transcending time, capturing space, suppressing difference and variation.

The modern anthropological and sociological discourse on religion in India had another Godhead and trajectory different from Indological and administrative writing. Yet, somewhere along the way, the links with colonial administrative and Indological frameworks took place empirically and theoretically. Indology was the father of the colonial scholarly discourses. The work of Hutton and others in colonial administration resulted in a collection of vast amounts of data on India and Indians and added the necessary empirical substance. For anthropology, fieldwork, deriving from the school of Malinowski and inspired by the work generated in Africa, was the basis of the discipline. The 'text', that constant of Indological knowledge was eschewed in favour of the 'context', the field.

One may like to discern in the early structural–functional approach and the folk-civilization continuum model used in the study of religion (Marriott 1955; Radcliffe-Brown 1922; Singer 1972; Srinivas 1952), the merging of anthropological and Indological traditions. Tribal and village community studies had their separate and merged, complicated and intricate intellectual trajectories in African village studies, legal and Indological discourses on India and Marxist writings of a very long period. They linked the empirical field-based data including lists of castes and communities, which derived further legitimacy from constructions made popular by census procedures, with the textual tradition. Thus, one had the 'great' and the 'little' traditions, the 'civilizational' and the 'folk', the 'universal' and the 'parochial'.

The overarching frame appears to have been provided by some attempt to search for the unity of the 'east' as it were, or the principle by which the entire civilization was structured and the logic according to which it functioned. Indology provided that principle in the pairing of caste and Hinduism. Caste became the major link bonding the little field studies with the textual models; even the centrality that the village community got in the studies of the 1950s linked the village to the 'great' Sanskritic tradition. India was Hindu, Hinduism was caste and despite the fact that Aryans are brothers and the British and Indians, therefore, mythical patrilateral cousins, 'the East is East and West is West and never the twain shall meet'. *Homo hierarchicus* stands in unique contrast and, indeed, opposition to *Home equalis*. Dumont again.

It is clearly very difficult to understand Christianity or Islam in this model. Where was the great 'Indian' tradition to which these could be linked? The difficulty of absorbing everything into the great 'civilizational' model though, showed up in the cracks. Some things refused to be easily assimilated. One sees this with tribal studies: Verrier Elwin's *Saora Religion*, for example. It may not be coincidental that as Dumont's model surfaced and then began to arch over all things anthropological and sociological, tribal studies suffered in silence. Apart from Walker's work on the Todas, Vitebsky's on the Saora again, Troisi's on the Santal religion and a few studies here and there, that silence is yet to be broken.

From the fieldwork tradition established in the 1950s, the major shift came with Dumont's highly influential work, which certainly opened the way for a new type of study. Dumont clearly saw the study of India as lying at the confluence of Indology and sociology and returned to the text as the source of indigenous categories of meaning. The notion of subjective meaning entered the field. It was not just ritual that was important but ideas of karma/dharma known to the villagers from wandering priests, bards and the like (Mathur's work on a Malwa village, for instance).

Veena Das' *Structure and Cognition* and *The Word and the World*, R.K. Jain's *Text and Context*, Khare's *Hindu Hearth and Home*, Madan's *Non-Renunciation*, Heesterman's *The Inner Conflict of Tradition*, Pocock's study of religious beliefs and practices in a Gujarat village, Fuller's work on temple priests in Madurai, Parry's *Death in Banaras*, Diana Eck's work on the Hindu cosmos, Susan Wadley's work on *Shakti*, Ann and Daniel

Gold's works on Hindu pilgrimage, chart the course of this opening up. Hindu cosmic thought and structure was at the centre of studies in the sociology and anthropology of religion. Fuller's book *The Camphor Flame* summarizes some of these trends very well.

Dumont's work threw wide open the text/context debate, but he privileged the text and cognitive models derived from them, thus centring an upper-caste, essentialized version of Hinduism, and treating this, as already noted earlier, as synonymous with India. It has been suggested how this tradition, grounding itself in the belief that the spirit of India is essentially Hindu, has not only led to a reification of Hinduism itself but also to the marginalization of non-Hindu groups and communities.

Again, the India versus the west debate that Dumont launched, opposed the two without any hope or possibility of comparative study. A historicized and grounded approach to the study of religion did not obviously develop because India was the static land of religion, where the play of power and the dynamics of change were, with pun intended, immaterial. A living culture is thus rendered still. No sense emerges of the development of religious faith or practice. Hinduism (and then other religions as well) is discussed as a mature, full-blown faith originating in a single (textual or Brahmanic) source rather than embedded in social, material and political contexts.

Finally, the way in which non-Hindu communities were brought within the boundaries of study was by viewing them through the lens of caste, that essence of Indian social structure. So, we have studies framed by the question: is there caste in non-Hindu communities? Certain forms of ritual such as life-crisis rituals, for instance, came in for a good deal of attention because they could be captured through the conceptual category of 'syncretism'. When the study of caste among Christians, for example, became one of the main problematics, it allowed the idea that Christianity in India was somehow not quite authentic. It furthered the impression that the most important feature of Christianity in India was its syncretic character, exemplified by the 'adoption' of caste by Christians.

Thus, while Hinduism received attention in the sociology of religion in India, this was not the case with the other communities, their religious practices and their social organization. The tools for the analysis of these communities have not been sufficiently developed to take account of the complexity of issues relating to the practice of religion in India. View, for example, the inadequacy of the sociology of the relation between text and practice. One of the problematics in the study of Christianity or Islam in India became that of seeing the variation between text and practice, but the text was seen here as something that was in no need of definition. It was static and ahistorical like Hindu texts but also, here, universal. An elite and priestly understanding of the text was privileged. All everyday practices of Christians and Muslims, therefore, that did not fit the universal textual tradition were viewed as deviant. The framework of the ideal versus the deviant dominated the studies for a long time.

Many practices, thus, were not even seen as worthy of attention—because they were viewed as being the same everywhere universally and therefore, not exotic enough to be considered worthy of anthropological interest. The services in the church for Christianity for instance, the sermon or the idea of prayer, all suffer from inattention due to this understanding. The specific expression that a particular idea or set of texts from the classical tradition was given in a definite historical context and circumstance, the shifts that the expression took over time and the critical relation of these to questions of identity and the contests over identity definition between different groups have not received the attention that they deserve.

Concepts such as 'fest' (feast) or 'Maataa' (Mother Mary) used by some Christians , for example, are not taken up for analysis, even though these are also 'indigenous' concepts and partake simultaneously of 'local' and 'classical' traditions. Such concepts rarely mimic, in a simple fashion, classical or textual traditions. Rather, they play with the latter, add to them perhaps, select from them, redefine and reconfigure them to fit their own social and historical circumstances. We need to understand these transformations and the agency and contextuality they involve.

It is interesting, though perhaps not inexplicable, that interest in many minority groups in India—Muslims, Christians, Sikhs—has developed in relation to their importance vis-à-vis Hindu society, usually due to conflict. Hence, studies of Muslims mostly figured in the area of politics, partition and communalism. As we have seen, when ethnographic studies began these emphasized caste using the syncretic model to synthesize Muslims with

'Hindu' India and simply ignored what was specifically Islamic about them, because this was non-Indian, universal and could, anyway, be studied elsewhere. It was not unique to the east and could not constitute the 'essence' of India.

Studies on Sikhism emerged prominently in the context of the politics of identity in Punjab, including those of Harjot Oberoi and Joyce Pettigrew. Christianity has been viewed through the lens of conversion (*from* Hinduism) as Sikhism and Islam were viewed through the lens of communalism or fundamentalism (*in opposition to* Hinduism). This does give rise to further problems in studying these communities because of the politically sensitive nature of issues related to such a perspective. We have only to remember the controversy over conversion to Christianity in 1999 and the virtual stifling of voices of objectivity that resulted to understand this.

These trends in the study of religion in India have led to problems in the understanding of the interaction between the different religious streams and in the developing of concepts to discuss such interaction. The terms 'syncretism' and 'composite culture' which, as has been suggested, have been freely employed, have their limitations and assumptions. They typically view the interaction between different religious streams and traditions as being an essentially harmonic, non-conflictual one. In fact, they are also imbued with an essentialist view of religion. They locate religion firmly within a notion of culture typically secure from the mediation of troubling questions of control or conflict. By viewing religion as a closed, self-contained corpus of ideas, such concepts are unable to incorporate the correlation or connections between religion, social and material processes and relationships of power and hierarchy.

While teasing out some of the implications of the concept of syncretism, it may also be possible to perhaps delineate a way out of its limitations. Kalpana Ram (1991) has dealt with some of these issues. While most Christian communities live in worlds permeated with 'Hindu' norms and ideas, as Ram has argued, it is facile to view the retention of Hindu elements among Christian groups as a sign of the lack of authenticity of their faith or to assume that converts always have an easy and harmonious ('syncretic') relationship with all strands of Hinduism. Second, as we have said, we need to bring a much greater degree of complexity into our understanding of the 'interrelationship' between communities. In an analysis of these interrelations and interactions, what is being taken and/or exchanged needs to be historicized.

We certainly need, therefore, to historicize popular religion and ground it in regional, spatial and temporal realities. We also need, simultaneously, to historicize and put in an anthropological perspective, the history and culture of the west. While we speak quite legitimately of religion full-blown, we end up with a reification of the west, if we do not enquire more closely into the kinds of knowledge and cultural information different groups had during the periods they came and interacted with south Asian societies (see Dube 1992; Robinson 1998; Webster 1976). We also need to enquire into the social roots of groups and individuals.

Conversion is an issue fraught with all sorts of difficulties. For one, the assimilative model used to study Hinduism pre-empts any efforts to analyse reconversion movements or to understand the ways in which Hinduism 'converts' and to compare and contrast it with models of conversion from other traditions. The idea that certain religions such as Islam and Christianity have an internal drive to convert also prevents us from understanding the historical circumstances of conversion, the various different strategies adopted and the ways in which religion articulates with power in certain regimes, which cannot be replicated elsewhere.

It is issues of this sort that we will attempt to highlight in the course of this book. I turn now to a documentation of the different denominations of Christianity available in India and offer some understanding of the periods when they came in and spaces where they are prevalent. Then an outline of this book follows and I put forward the kinds of questions that are of central concern here.

THE FIELD

Christianity in India offers a fascinating field for study. Denominationally, we are speaking of a range that includes Syrian Christianity, Roman Catholicism and various forms of Protestantism and Evangelicalism. Ecologically, one covers pockets of concentration in the north-eastern region, the central plains, the coasts (and some inland areas) of southern and western India. Both caste and tribal communities have been drawn into the fold of Christianity in different places, and among the former both the highest and lowest groups. Some Christian communities have existed for hundreds of years, while others have not completed a century in the faith.

According to the 1991 census there are 19,640,284 (nearly 20 million) Christians in India, who constitute 2.34 per cent of the population. The uneven geographical spread of the Christians is brought out by the available statistical data. Kerala has 28.62 per cent of Christians, 16.18 per cent to Tamil Nadu, 4.37 per cent to Karnataka and 6.19 per cent to Andhra Pradesh. These four states account for 55.36 per cent of the total Christian population. In the northeast, the states of Assam, Arunachal Pradesh, Nagaland, Meghalaya, Mizoram and Manipur together have 21.67 per cent of Christians.

In Goa, Christians constitute 29.86 per cent of the population. Elsewhere, Christians are much more scattered. Just 0.44 per cent of Gujarat's population is Christian, 0.10 per cent of Haryana's and 0.09 per cent of Himachal's. In terms of actual numbers though, the population may well be quite significant. For instance, while they only constitute 0.98 per cent of Bihar's population, there are over 800,000 Christians in the state. Over 31 per cent of the Indian Christian population is an urban one, the rest rural.

Intertwined with demographical distinctions and the rural/ urban divide are also distinctions which are of denominational and temporal significance. Not only is the greater part of the Christian population found in these regions, but the south and west of India were also home to Christian traditions very early on: the Syrian Christians of Kerala, for example, trace their origin to A.D. 1, while Catholicism in Goa is no less than 400 years old.

Thus, even at the end of the eighteenth century, most Christians were to be found in the southern part of the country. The places where the Christian influence was embedded most strongly were the western coastal belt including Goa, Mangalore and Kerala. Tamil Nadu had a large number of Christians. Christian groups had been established in parts of Kannada and Telugu speaking areas. A number of Christians were also to be found in

Mumbai and its neighbouring districts and in Daman and Diu (see Menachery 1982).

Most of these were Catholic communities and there were Orthodox Christians as well, as in Kerala, but the Protestants had not until then made any great efforts at conversion in this region. Chaplains had, of course, been around, but they were there mainly to serve officers and men of the Company. The first organized Protestant mission in the south was launched in 1706 at Tranquebar by two German Lutheran pastors, Ziengebalg and Pluetschau (see Hudson 1993). They had come to Tranquebar in order to 'address "pagans" and "moors" with the protestant message and were the first Europeans sent to India for that express purpose' (ibid.: 39). They succeeded, if in a small way, helped no doubt by the fact of learning and using Tamil and even translating the Bible in that language.

On the whole though, individual conversions were few in this entire period. By far the most intriguing effort was made in Tamil Nadu by the Jesuit Robert Nobili, who explicitly attempted to enter into dialogue with Brahmanical Hinduism. Nobili adopted the attire, diet and lifestyle of a Brahman *sannyasi* (renouncer). He studied Tamil and Sanskrit sacred scriptures and entered into discussions with Madurai's priests (Bayly 1989; Neill 1984). His converts were high caste men who individually affirmed their belief in Christ.

It was only at the end of the eighteenth century, during the period of the spread and consolidation of British rule, that the north of the country witnessed a significant growth in Christian mission activity. A few efforts predated that period and there were small groups of converts here and there. The mid-eighteenth century conversions to Catholicism in Bettiah, where the local ruler patronized the mission, is an interesting case (Sahay 1986). In the north-eastern region, where Protestantism dominates, Christianity is largely the product of nineteenth and twentieth century conversions.

The British period also saw a number of individual conversions, one of the more interesting and well-known being that of Pandita Ramabai of Maharashtra. There were others. Among them were the conversions of Narayan Vaman Tilak, Krupabai Satthianadhan, Nehemiah Gore, Madhusudan Dutt, Cornelia Sorabji, Kali Charan Chatterjee and Gopi Nath Nundi.

In terms of social background, there were certain similarities between these individuals drawn to the Christian faith out of deep convictions and a re-orientation of their inner selves. They belonged in general to the urban literate higher caste groups. Educated and discerning, some of them contributed to the making of Indian Christian theological discourses (Webster 1976). It would be too easy, however, to argue that all individual conversions came from among the upper castes based in cities or towns. This would simplify a more complex reality. There were others, from more humble backgrounds, who were also drawn to Christianity through considerable internal negotiation. In this connection we have the interesting cases of the *Isa faqirs* in Uttar Pradesh (ibid.: 125) and the Sabarkantha *bhagats* of Gujarat (Boyd 1973: 89).

The Indian census collapses Christians into a single, undifferentiated category, but they belong to distinct persuasions, churches and sects. A church is 'an institutionalized organization of people who share common religious beliefs and practices. A church has a stable membership and formal bureaucratic structure with trained clergy and other officials' (D'Souza 1993: 15). A sect, on the other hand, is defined as a small group that has 'broken away from a parent church often with a call for a return to the old ways' (ibid.:16). A third type of organization is cultic. A cult is the most loosely organized and temporary of these religious groups: it generally forms itself around a charismatic leader who calls for a completely new and distinctive life style (ibid.).

Catholics form the largest Christian group in India, nearly half of the total population. Another 40 per cent are Protestants, while 7 per cent are Orthodox Christians and 6 per cent belong to indigenous sects. What are the more clear marks of distinction between these various groups? Catholics regard the Pope as the supreme head in all religious affairs and are organized according to a well-defined hierarchy. Protestantism includes many distinct denomination and churches. Orthodox groups, such as the Syrian Christians, are affiliated to one of the Orthodox churches of eastern Europe or west Asia or to churches dependent on these. Most Indian indigenous sects arose through separation from mother churches in the west, though some have broken away from Orthodox churches (D'Souza 1993:16–17).

As we examine in the text, while the popular image of Christians as descendants of low-caste, low-status converts stretches reality, it is true that over half of all Christians are from the Untouchable castes. There are 15 to 20 per cent tribal in origin, while the upper caste Christians, largely from Kerala and the Konkan coast, constitute a quarter of the total (Tharamangalam 1996). They are considerably represented in the priesthood and exercise an influence and authority far in excess of their numbers. There would be great differences between them and, for instance, the Santal converts of eastern India.

Christianity is often associated in the popular imagination with British colonial rule and the process of westernization. But its appearance in India preceded the British by several hundred years. Indeed, one might say that Christianity in India is as old as the faith itself. Historians agree that there was a Christian community in Kerala in the first century A.D. Though it maintained links with Chaldea or Persia, it remained relatively isolated from western Christianity at least till the sixteenth century. Kerala Christianity was linked to west Asia, not western Europe.

Apart from being interesting in itself, this rich complexity described in the preceding paragraphs seriously subverts all academic (and indeed, political) efforts to unify the Christians as 'community', 'minority' and the like. It also raises a host of questions, which I would argue are best addressed in a comparative mode.

OUTLINE

The first set of concerns are centred around the sociology of conversion, the dynamics of interaction between missionaries and indigenous populations in different parts of the country, the varied modes of the constitution of identity and the drawing of boundaries consequent upon these diverging forms of social and religious interaction. Within each of these one catches the murmurs of other queries. The original question is of course that of origins: where did Christianity come from, at what points in history, from which parts of the world and out of what impulses or motives. In a word, why? Is mission activity, as it is popularly treated, an undifferentiated category, an essential force which is understood merely in the naming of it? For instance, what were the meanings and implications of missionary activity in the sixteenth century? Did these remain the same, for example, into the nineteenth century?

The sociology of conversion in India has not yet been written, though limited efforts in this direction have been made. One finds early and more recent accounts providing details about conversion movements in different regions (see Devapackiam 1963; Frykenberg 1981; Richter 1908; Sherring 1875). As yet there has been no collation of these materials or their overall anthropological or sociological interpretation. The existing efforts are, from various points of view, incomplete (Houtart and Lemercinier 1981; Neill 1984). Neill's is a historical (and theological) compilation, while Houtart and Lemercinier give an overly materialistic explanation of conversion to Catholicism.

Early accounts such as that of Sharrock (1910) on the south Indian missions or Pickett (1933) on the mass movements to Christianity provide much demographical and descriptive material. There are numerous others, mostly from a historical and principally, theological perspective. (A few of these largely theological accounts include Capuchin Mission Unit 1923; Castets 1925; Clark 1907; Clough 1914; Corbet 1955; Cronin 1959; Da Trinidade 1954; Estborn 1959, 1961; Fishman 1941; Gibbs 1972; Grant 1961; Juhnke 1979; Kaye 1859; Paul 1958; Plattner 1950; Warren 1965; Westcott 1897). From such accounts we can glean some material useful to understand the dynamics of conversion to Christianity in India, though the accounts themselves are by and large, written within a theological framework and need to be read somewhat critically. It was in 1977 that Oddie raised the issue of conversion to religions such as Buddhism, Islam and Christianity in south Asia, posing the problem in these words (1977a:1):

> We know something about the origins of these religious communities in South Asia; yet, in spite of the way in which their subsequent growth and interaction has affected the region's history, we still know very little about how and why they developed in the way they did, how they attracted or enrolled adherents, why they experienced different rates of growth and why some of them are larger and more influential than others.

Could we say the same of just the different denominations within Christianity itself? Oddie's book provides accounts of a few movements in order to 'shed light on the conversion process in general' (p. 11). Focusing on the literature on Christianity, we find that most historical and anthropological/sociological accounts of particular groups or specific regions, some of which have been mentioned above, sketch in some detail the processes of conversion that were involved. What we lack is a general and comparative picture, drawing out similarities, relating differences and attempting to understand both.

Not only has Christianity come to India at different points of time and from different regions of the world, it has made its impact through a variety of means and approaches. India has been witness to Christianity as a religion of conquest (in Goa), Christianity as the religion of groups that negotiated their status through political alliances with local rulers (Syrian Christianity) and Christianity brought by missionaries with only the indirect and not always unequivocal support of colonial authorities (as in parts of British India).

A theme of significance that requires some exploration therefore is: what was the relationship between religion and politics, the church and the state under different colonial regimes? This involves analyzing the kinds of support various missionary groups had or could garner. Implicated here is the study of how this plays a role in defining and informing the modes and strategies used by missionaries to convert.

The greater stress on the use of force and disprivileges seen in Goa may be compared and contrasted with Nobili's conscious efforts to forge linkages with Brahmanic tradition in Tamil Nadu and the contradictory position of particular missionary groups in central India, who combined a certain paternalistic attitude towards their congregations with a participation in idioms of domination characterizing the colonial cultural construction of the Other. A comparative analysis could bring out these distinctions meaningfully. It is these concerns that form the subject of the next chapter.

From here we turn, in the third chapter, to a consideration of patterns of hierarchy, of ideas of class or status differences and of gender inequalities within different groups. It does appear that wherever land is an important resource, particular patriarchal tendencies seem to remain entrenched. Caste and other modes of configuring difference retain their relevance because of the stress on descent and the culturally felt need to retain and ensure the purity of descent. The Christian churches are rarely innocent of the markings of status and gender inequalities. Though they fight against the worst features of caste, they often remain complicit in perpetuating various kinds of hierarchical differences.

The early missionaries, such as the Catholics of the sixteenth century, came with ideas of hierarchy influenced by the 'estate' order of their own society. Their attitude to 'casta', as the Portuguese were to name it, was one of much greater tolerance. Nineteenth century missionaries coming out of Europe (or America) in which the ideas of 'equality' and 'individuality' had come to prevail, viewed the disabilities of caste with much more horror. With their male dominated authority structures and patri-centric notions, the different churches sometimes clashed with more equitable tribal customs, while the gender norms of caste society were not countered.

A view of church centred ritual as well as social and cultural practices of different Christian communities reveals an astonishing degree of consonance with local custom. The shared cultural world of Hindus, Christians and others within particular regional boundaries manifests itself in these practices. Nevertheless, several points need to be stressed. For one, hierarchy may determine the extent of participation in such shared worlds. Moreover, it is sometimes likely that the relationship convert groups have with 'Hindu' traditions, for instance, might not be completely harmonic or unproblematic.

What one might like to stress is that conversion, when perceived anthropologically or sociologically, rarely emerges as a change in the realm of ideas or beliefs alone. Other areas of social and cultural life are invariably transformed. In the process of evangelization in different parts of the country, Christianity has articulated and often clashed with prevailing patterns of ritual, kinship, marriage and patrimony, sartorial codes and even food conventions. An examination of some of these issues, in particular the organization of kinship and the norms of inheritance, forms the subject of the fifth chapter.

Demonology is our final subject, though it is not an end in itself but leads to the analysis of expressions of resistance against hierarchy and the retrieval of power through alternative modes.

Thaumaturgical discourses within popular Christianity offer a challenge to the authority of the church, its patriarchal ideology and its hierarchical organization. The challenge was contained, until these discourses became a part of millennial and fundamentalist Charismatic and Pentecostal Christian cults, which offer an alternative to the mainstream churches themselves.

The last chapter draws together the various themes and issues, in the context of the agenda and ideas formulated here. Questions are raised and problems identified for future scholarship. The bibliography for this text has focussed on sociological and cultural materials, but has also tried to include several works of historical interest as well as some theological accounts of Christianity in India. It cannot claim to be exhaustive, but it does bring together many early and more recent works and, therefore, acts as a significant starting point for anyone intending to do research in this area.

NOTES

1. Louis Dumont's work, particularly his monumental *Homo Hierarchicus*, was very influential in promoting the view that Indian sociology must be Indological in its approach. It needs to take into consideration ancient Indian textual materials. Most of the material that Dumont had in mind was Brahmanical, Sanskrit literature. Relying on this literature, Dumont constructed a static picture of Indian society dominated by caste. Many scholars have argued that Dumont focussed only on a Brahman-centred Hindu version of Indian society, to the detriment of other groups. Dumont also ended up making a radical distinction between the west and India. The first he saw as the space of equality (*homo equalis*); the latter as the quintessential home of hierarchy, exemplified by the caste system (thus, *homo hierarchicus*).

2. Inden is critical of Orientalist literature in his work *Imagining India*. However, in his reformulation of the best way of doing social science and history, he also ends up constructing a 'Hindu' India.

Fig. 1 **Density of Indian Christian Population (1991 census)**

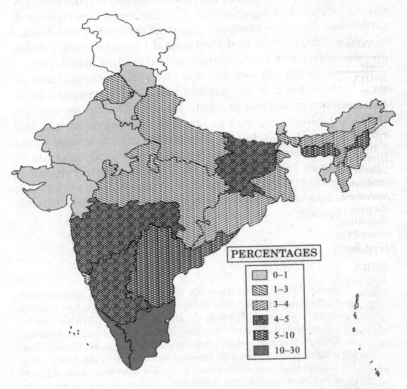

PERCENTAGES

- 0–1
- 1–3
- 3–4
- 4–5
- 5–10
- 10–30

This figure excludes Jammu & Kashmir, where 1991 census was not undertaken.

Table 1 **India: Religions (Based on 1991 census)**

Religions	Population	Percentage
Hindus	687,646,721	82.00
Muslims	101,596,057	12.12
Christians	19,640,284	2.34
Sikhs	16,259,744	1.94
Buddhists	6,387,500	0.76
Jains	3,352,706	0.40
Other religions	3,269,355	0.39
Religion not stated	415,569	0.05
Total	838,567,936	100.00

Table 2 **Statewise Indian Christian Population in Per cent**

State	Christian Population in %
INDIA	2.34
Bihar	0.98
Chandigarh	0.78
Delhi	0.88
Gujarat	0.44
Haryana	0.1
Himachal Pradesh	0.09
Lakshadweep	1.16
Madhya Pradesh	0.64
Maharashtra	1.12
Punjab	1.11
Rajasthan	0.11
Uttar Pradesh	0.14
West Bengal	0.56
INDIA	2.34
Andhra Pradesh	1.83
Assam	3.32
Dadra & Nagar Haveli	1.51
Daman & Diu	2.86
Karnataka	1.91
Orissa	2.1
Pondicherry	7.22
Sikkim	3.3
Tamil Nadu	5.69
Tripura	1.69
INDIA	2.34
Andaman & Nicobar Islands	23.95
Arunachal Pradesh	10.3
Goa	29.85
Kerala	19.32
Manipur	34.11
Meghalaya	64.58
Mizoram	85.73
Nagaland	87.47

Fig. 2 **Statewise Distribution of Christian Population (%)**
(Lower than 1.5%)

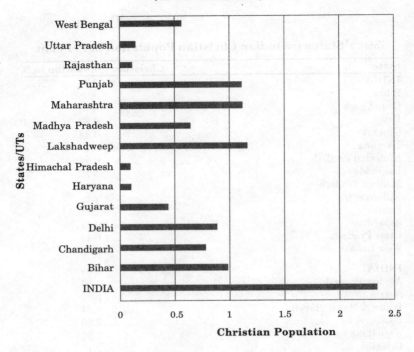

Fig. 3 **Statewise Distribution of Christian Population (%)**
(Above 10%)

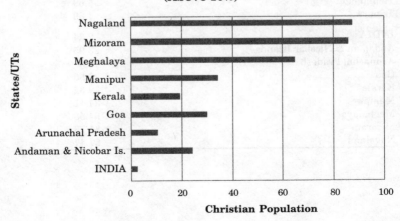

Fig. 4 **Statewise Distribution of Christian Population (%)**
(1.5% to 10%)

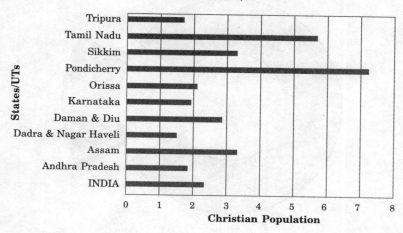

Table 3 **Distribution of Population by Religion, India, 1991**

Religious Community*	Per cent of Population
Hindus	82.00
Muslims	12.12
Christians	2.34
Sikhs	1.94
Buddhists	0.76
Jains	0.40
Others	0.44
Total	100.00

* Excludes figures for Jammu & Kashmir where 1991 census was not conducted.

Fig. 5 **Percentage Distribution of India's Population by Religion**

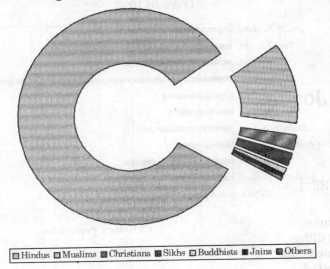

Hindus · Muslims · Christians · Sikhs · Buddhists · Jains · Others

2

JOURNEYING THROUGH THE SOCIAL WORLDS
OF CONVERSION

PRE-BRITISH PERIOD

Christianity has come to India from different parts of the world,
at different historical moments and out of different impulses.
One finds it crucial to differentiate between the British and pre-
British periods, and within both further distinctions become
necessary. These distinctions are important because the modes
and strategies of conversion are, I would argue, crucially linked
with varying political regimes and historical junctures and the
possibilities and limitations they hold out.

THE SYRIAN CHRISTIANS: HIGH CASTE CHRISTIANITY

The earliest and, perhaps, best known Christian community of
India, is that of the Syrian Christians of Kerala. Their history
has been documented in several early accounts (see Arayathinal
1947; Ayyar 1926; Brown 1956; Mathew and Thomas 1967;
Podipara 1947; Tisserent 1957). The traditions of the Syrian
Christians attribute the origin of the community to the evangelical efforts of Saint Thomas, who is believed to have arrived
on the Malabar coast in A.D. 52. The Syrian or Thomas Christians regard themselves as the descendants of the high caste
Nambudiri Brahman converts of Saint Thomas (Bayly 1989: 244;
Visvanathan 1993a).

Literary evidence on Saint Thomas coming to India is absent.
However, the possibility may not be completely far-fetched. There

is a great deal of evidence available to demonstrate the strength of commercial links between India and the western world during the period that the saint was supposed to have arrived here. Gold and pepper were central articles of trade. Knowledge of the monsoons was available, and the possibility of more rapid journeys to India was now very real.

Malayalam versions of the legend of Saint Thomas converge with an early west Asian hagiography, the 'Acts of Thomas'. This work was most probably written around the third century in Syriac. It describes the travels of Saint Thomas in a setting that appears to be based on the Indo-Parthian kingdom of Taxila. This was apparently a cosmopolitan kingdom where Greeks, Bactrians, Scythians and Indians interacted. It may well have been a centre for a good deal of intellectual activity as it was for commerce. Perhaps the tradition of the saint came to the south coast through merchants who were part of the already thriving trading networks of the time.

Whatever the case may be, the Syrian Christians of Kerala contradict all popular theories about the low-caste origin of Christian converts and their dependence on western political and religious authorities (Bayly 1989: 243). The Syrian Christians are far from constituting a low-status group, which owes its origin to European missionaries or is reliant on the colonial state. Rather, they have a long history of prestige and privilege, enjoyed under the regimes of different local rulers. Neither conquest nor colonization is written into the social history of the Syrian Christians. Saint Thomas is believed to have travelled through the Malabar country evangelizing and building churches. It was when he moved east that he is supposed to have met his death and (martyrdom) at Mylapore, near Madras.

While the Saint Thomas tradition is an important part of Syrian Christian lore, it slides in with another Thomas tradition, that of the merchant Thomas of Cana. Thomas of Cana is said to have come to the Malabar coast in A.D. 345 with a number of Christians from Jerusalem, Baghdad and Nineveh and to have received the right to trade in one of the ancient kingdoms of Kerala (see Ayyar 1926; Brown 1956; Fuller 1976; Visvanathan 1993a). There appears to have been mercantile and spiritual integration between the indigenous and immigrant peoples, though they remained separate endogamous groups.

Among the churches that Saint Thomas is supposed to have founded are those of Palayur, Quilon, Kotamangalam, Paravur, Niranom, Kokkamangalam and the site at Cranganur-Malankara. It is significant that these include Kerala's most important precolonial export nuclei as well as localities that served as critical centres for internal trade and transport. None are far from the coast and all are in areas that even today have large populations of Christians. Syrians have been linked with maritime trade and commerce for centuries. They also have a history of warrior service and clientele under the region's chiefs (Bayly 1989: 246).

Syrian holy places were incorporated into the network of shrines and temples which comprised the ruler's domains and to which he made benefactions. Outright conquest by local chiefs was rare during the period we are talking about. Political authority was legitimated by endowing sacred sites in the area one wanted to control. It is through their warrior and mercantile skills and tradition of rendering service as pepper brokers and revenue officers in the Malabar, for which they received honour and social privileges from the regional rulers, that the patrilineal, prosperous Syrians established themselves as a high status group within the indigenous hierarchy (Bayly 1989). They negotiated their position through alliance with the local rulers and maintained their status by adhering strictly to the purity–pollution codes of regional Hindu society.

Sradhas were performed by the Syrians for many centuries and their life-cycle rituals, including the terminology applied to them, were virtually identical with those of high-ranking Hindus. Adherence by the Syrians to these traditions ensured their status within the sacred and the moral order. Proof of the high standing of Syrians within the regional social order is received from the fact that they were accepted as patrons and sponsors at Hindu temple festivals and shrines. Temple and church were often located cheek by jowl and occasionally even shared the same 'processional regalia' (Bayly 1989: 252–53).

PORTUGUESE STRATEGY: CONQUEST AND CONVERSION

Our next major encounter with Christianity comes in the sixteenth century. At that time, the Portuguese came to India bearing

Catholicism. Trade, conquest and Christianization went hand-in-hand for them; the sword accompanied the cross in the search for spices. Goa, which the Portuguese first gained control of in 1510, formed the Asian centre of their overseas activities. The Portuguese viewed theirs as a commercial and maritime empire cast in a military and ecclesiastical mould (Boxer 1969). Religion and trade were indistinguishable. The king was aligned with the Papacy in what was termed as the *Padroado* form of jurisdiction (Ram 1991: 30; Roche 1984: 41–42). A series of Papal Bulls passed between 1452 and 1456 gave the king the authority to 'conquer, subdue and convert all pagan territories'.

To control Asian trade routes, the Portuguese were in need of particular key posts along the coast. Goa was one of the main ones, and it was here that political and military rule was established. However, there were also tinier trading bases along the southern coastal belt. To establish themselves in Goa, for instance, the Portuguese required the support of the local people. Since they defined themselves primarily in religious terms, their typical mode of incorporating local populations into their political body involved converting them to their own religion. Mass conversions were, hence, linked to the need to create social allies (Houtart and Lemercinier 1981).

CONVERSION AND THE CONSOLIDATION OF THE *JATI*

Thus conversions took place between 1527–49 among castes with fishing and boat-handling skills such as the Mukkuvars and the Paravas along the southern coast of India, where trade and proselytization were carried on in conjunction in the shelter of the forts. Available literature on the Paravas shows them to have had a corporate caste structure. The *jati* enclosed their world economically, politically and socio-ritually. The Paravas also had a grip on the profitable pearl fishing industry. The Mukkuvars, fisherfolk, had a more precarious material existence. Association with the Portuguese helped the Paravas, in particular, to develop considerably in terms of economic strength and occupational diversification (Ram 1991: 31; see also De Silva 1978; Fernando 1984).

For both these groups, Christianity became a means of strengthening their *jati* or community identity. Whatever the Portuguese interests in conversion, for the Mukkuvars and the

Paravas, association with Christianity facilitated the marking out of corporate identity. For these castes, involved in occupations considered low and ritually defiling, conversion served not to climb up the status ladder but to heighten a sense of distinctiveness and difference from the agrarian caste world. Their *jati* identity was strengthened and religion became the axis around which, through a merging of indigenous and Christian elements, this more secure identity was woven. For the Parava pearl fishers, moreover, alliance with the Portuguese yielded a range of economic and political benefits. The latter sought to cream off easily, the returns of the pearl trade by patronizing and consolidating the authority of the Parava caste leaders (Bayly 1989: 325–27; Ram 1991: 30–32).

Goa: Conversion through the Interlock of State and Church

It was in Goa though, that the interlock of religion and politics, of the state and the church, was uniquely manifest. The state actively espoused mission: successive viceroys communicating the progress of conversion efforts to the king. Not all the missionaries were Portuguese, but they functioned under and by the orders of Portugal's king. What Diffie and Winius have to say about Jesuit missionaries applies equally to the other orders which worked under Portuguese rule in this period (1977: 405).

> Xavier was a Navarrese, Valignano an Italian, and Frois a Portuguese and so the Society'd dream was not primarily a Portuguese one. But Portugal was the patron, the transporter, the financier, and the licensing agent of the Society in Asia, and it backed Jesuit projects with its money, its personnel, and its prestige. Xavier's mummy lies today in a silver tomb in Goa. The apostle of the Indes and his men, if not all Portuguese, thoroughly represented the Portuguese cause and became its spiritual mercenaries.

There are primarily four missionary orders which functioned in Goa during this period. The Franciscans arrived in 1517 and their mission field was Bardez. The Jesuits, who arrived in 1542, were responsible for the conversion of Tiswadi and Salcete. The other two orders of some significance were the Dominicans, who came in 1548, and the Augustinians, who came a few years later. The orders were not without their differences, but it could be said with some assurance that they functioned in similar ways in their missionary activities during this period.

The missionaries could rely on access to state forces to remove temples, overcome resistance to conversion and quiet the defiant. The operation of such a regime made mass conversions, of both the high and the low castes, almost inevitable (Robinson 1993, 1998). A number of laws were enacted against the Hindus, particularly against those with socioeconomic and religious dominance—the high caste *gauncars* (village landholders and administrators) and the priests. These laws included the banishment of Hindus from the Portuguese terrain if they did not convert. Banishment meant, of course, that those who had to leave lost their property. Other laws involved the banning of the performance of Hindu religious rites, festivals and ceremonies and the prohibition of the religious activities of Hindu priests.

Hindu *gauncars* were forbidden from convening a general council unless the *gauncars* who had converted to Christianity were present. Disobedience invoked a fine. It was also declared that if they did convene a council without the presence of the Christian *gauncars*, the decisions of that council would be considered null and void. In villages where there were more Christian than Hindu *gauncars*, the latter were not permitted to enter the assembly and when the decisions were recorded, the names of all the Christian *gauncars* had to be written first (Wicki 9). Artisans who served the village *gauncars* and fashioned the objects of worship required in temple rituals could not be employed to produce any objects of Christian worship unless they converted.

The regime was concerned with eliminating at least the substance if not the form of indigenous culture and religion. This was typified by the Inquisition established to prevent recourse by converts to non-Christian customs. Its range of prohibitions covered a large number of socio-cultural practices. It was also evident in the interaction between Portuguese missionaries and the Syrian Christians in south India, which culminated in the not uncontested establishment of Portuguese ecclesiastical dominance by the Synod of Diamper of 1599. The Synod's decrees aimed both at the correction and systemization of the Syrians' rites and doctrines and the weeding out of Hindu ritual influences (Visvanathan 1993a, 1993b).

The Inquisition was established in 1560 in Goa and completely withdrawn in 1812. It must have been quite effective (Subrahmanyam 1993), for novices of various religious orders kept an eye on the people and state forces and prisons were used to detain those who disobeyed the laws. They could be fined or face jail sentences. While death at the stake was the most severe punishment available, it appears to have been more rarely enforced. It is possible though, that a number of people died imprisoned without ever having had their cases come up for trial (Neill 1984: 231).

As I have noted, a system of disprivilege and constraints was central to the strategy of conversion in Goa. Jobs and offices were reserved for those who converted and denied to those who did not. Places of worship were converted into churches, sacred images were removed and the public practice of Hinduism was prohibited. The landed upper castes were threatened with the loss of their property if they did not convert. Artisans who had not converted could not be employed by the landowning patrons, or to create articles of worship for Christians.

Hemmed in by such compulsions, few options were available to people. Fleeing from the territory or resisting with violence were among the more drastic responses to the intrusive regime. There were those who chose these responses. Violent resistance to conversion came in the form of attacks on missionaries. In 1583, five Jesuits were killed in Cuncolim village (De Souza 1990:103). Though the come back was swift and repressive, such acts of resistance make it difficult for us to view the Hindus as completely passive. Even when people did get converted, some means of purification and re-entry into Hindu society may have been possible.

Kulkarni (1992) records that the situation of mass conversions called for hasty measures. The Brahmans of the sixteenth and seventeenth centuries devised various simple methods of purification such as bathing in the sea on the occasion of particular festivals or being sprinkled with water from the sacred river Ganga. According to him, the Christian missionaries retaliated against this move by erecting crosses at various points along the sea front, driving the Brahmans to look for places for the mass bathing ceremonies further along the coast.

However, the success of Catholicism, witnessed by the fact that by the turn of the sixteenth century the entire area of the original Portuguese conquests had been converted (D'Costa 1965), seems to suggest that people did accept conversion in many cases. We should try to understand the motives of those who converted. Let us analyse how the *gauncars* of Carambolim discuss in 1560 the situation arising out of the increasing influence of Christianity.

One spoke up and argued thus: 'We are caught at a tough time because what we have is sown and cast into the land. If we go to the mainland, the Muslim land on the other side, we have to leave our property and if we stay we will be forced to become Christians. We should take mature counsel and give thought to the future to prevent what might happen. We should go with our families to the mainland and live under our laws because...it seems to me that it is better to lose our property than our souls'. Another responded thus: 'I do not think that the fervour of Christianity will last beyond the reign of this viceroy because it is his zeal that has led to all this. It appears to me that we should wait till he leaves and in the meanwhile sustain ourselves as best as we can in Goa'. Finally, the seniormost, to whom the rest gave great due, raised himself and said: 'I do not think it good to calculate when the viceroy Dom Constantino is going to leave for Portugal but rather when the fathers of the Company of Jesus are going to leave. And it is clear that they will never leave or stop making Christians. It will not end with this viceroy but will carry on with all the others. Therefore, let us commend ourselves to God and become Christians'. As a result of this resolution, fourteen *gauncars* with their families became Christians (Wicki 4: 658–59).

It could be argued that this decision by the *gauncars* to convert was totally pragmatic. They did so to avoid losing their lands and their sown crop. Yet, there may have been other reasons. By aligning themselves with the new rulers through conversion, the *gauncars* could hope to re-establish their position, which had recently been encroached upon by the Muslim military. Again, the *gauncars*, like other Hindus, faced the realization that since the missionaries would not leave, access to their own deities would remain cut off by the displacement of temples and images and the prohibitions mentioned above. In such a situation, they had little choice but to adopt the new religion. It may be possible that some time later such converts began to perceive that the new religion could be adapted to their own social and religious needs.[1]

According to (Silva Rego 1: 343), in 1543 in the village of Daugim in Tiswadi, a church was built on the site where a temple had previously stood. The latter was pulled down by the Hindus themselves, who asked for a church in its stead. We know that the Portuguese had already decided to remove the temples around this time and that this process had already commenced. Idols were being removed and laws had come into force making the open practice of Hinduism virtually impossible. Under such circumstances, how might we understand the suggestion in the literature that the Hindus 'asked' for a church; volunteered, as it were, for conversion?

We have other instances of Hindus themselves apparently asking to be converted. For example, (Wicki 4: 342–43) tells us:

Near the church of Saint John...dwelt an honest pagan man who out of fear of shaming himself in front of his relatives could not say that he wanted to become a Christian. He knew that one of the provisions of the king was the prohibition of the celebration of Hindu festivals under the threat of punishment. One of these was the festival of Shigmo. The man contrived to make it appear as if he was celebrating the festival, and then went to Father André Vaz and asked the latter to behold his action and, accordingly, arrest him and give him the punishment he merited. He asked Father Vaz to charge him before the Vicar General for his breaking of the law, so that he could then become Christian without fear of his relatives.

How are we to read such a narrative? Similar stories are to be found about the celebration of other festivals such as Ganesh Chaturthi and of ceremonies such as marriage. Those who had attempted to perform such ceremonies or to celebrate such festivals in hiding proclaimed their desire to convert when caught in these prohibited acts. Why? Of course, there is an easy explanation: they wished to escape punishment. But our examination should go deeper rather than stop at the first available, easy and pragmatic answer.

We need to locate such stories within the context of the prohibitions placed on the practice of Hinduism. The option to convert can be appreciated if we view it against the increasing furtiveness that had to accompany any attempts at maintaining prohibited rites, which, in their basic form, were being rendered less and less *available*, less and less recoverable. In parenthesis, I would like to suggest that the only mode of recovery, if partial, to become possible was within the context of the new religion, and perhaps, soon enough the converts were to realize this. The expediency that appears to underlie the simulated celebration of Shigmo must also be viewed in the light of the fact that the fitting modes of ritual observance were already increasingly inaccessible. I would argue, therefore, that the Hindus did not act either solely out of pragmatism or completely out of a sense of helplessness. A choice was clearly being made to adopt Catholicism. Let us try and comprehend this more clearly.

It appears that the Portuguese had gained some idea of the centrality of the temple in the life of a village community. They were aware that lands were kept aside for those who served in the temple and of the link between agricultural processes and religious celebrations. In this respect, the agricultural societies of Europe and India were similar. Indeed, wherever agriculture is important in Europe today, the same similarities are found. Local churches played and still play an important role in village life in Portugal, as in other countries of Europe.

Fairs are celebrated around the feasts of local patron saints and agricultural festivals are a part of the local calendar (Marques 1971:184). In fact, the Catholic calendar moves in consonance with the seasonal changes in Europe. Of course, Goa's indigenous seasonal changes are very different from the European ones, but these factors do suggest why the Hindus may have perceived Catholicism as not an altogether alien religious tradition. Further, the missionaries also soon tried to learn Konkani, the local language, in order to communicate Christianity to the local people.

Missionaries encouraged the celebration of feasts of various saints and higher and lower social groups hosted such celebrations separately. In the Hindu pattern, the lower castes had access to their own deities within the Hindu pantheon but in temple-centred ritual, where the higher castes were privileged, they probably had a more peripheral role. The high castes did not lose such ritual privileges after conversion. Does this provide some inkling as to why they asked to be converted? For the lowest castes, conversion provided a more positive position in that while they were still not as privileged as those above, they now had their own church cult centred around a particular saint.

Clearly, the missionaries were not ill-disposed to the privileges of social rank. Many of them came from the top ranks of a hierarchically organized society themselves. This explains why they made considerable efforts to convert the high castes such as the Brahmans (D'Costa 1965), why they incorporated Brahmans into priesthood and why they granted administrative posts and offices principally to those of high caste. They also allowed the converted high-caste *gauncars* a variety of honours and privileges in the church-centred Catholic ritual cycle that came to exist in the villages where the new religion was established. In different ways the missionaries and the local people, especially those of high social status, seem to have colluded in a process whereby the church itself could become an instrument for the expression (and maintenance) of relations of hierarchy.

There is another important aspect to the acceptance of conversion by the Hindus. The Portuguese required conversion as a basis for recognizing various groups within their political body. Accepting the new religion signified willingness on the part of the converts to come to terms with them and negotiate with them within the changed environment. It opened the way for the high castes in particular to gain access to new administrative jobs and offices generated by the Portuguese regime. As some writers point out (Arasaratnam 1977; Ifeka-Moller 1974), Christianity was the religion of the rulers and conversion was often viewed as the first step towards acquiring some of the superiority of their position.

Let us now turn to look at the ways in which the Portuguese intervened in the socioeconomic and kin relations of the local Hindus. We begin with the example of commensal relations between castes. The Portuguese were aware that eating food with strangers defiled the Hindu. It involved a pollution so great that the person found guilty of it was rendered an outcaste and no social relationships could be entered into with him (D'Costa 1964: 25). The *Documenta Indica* (Wicki 4: 345–46) tells us the story of a woman who, when she found that her son had eaten beef at a Christian's house, went to a priest and told him that she wanted to be converted because her son had eaten beef and already become a Christian.

The boy who had eaten food (and that, beef) at a Christian's house had, in effect, lost his caste and his place in the circle of kinship. For his mother, little remained but to follow suit. In this way, not just individuals but whole families, kin groups or local caste groups could be converted. We do have evidence that meat eating was not taboo among the lowest Hindu castes (Azavedo 1890: 37). Their deities were often honoured with animal sacrifices. For them the adoption of a meat-centred diet would not have been a wrench. This may have been another reason why the idea of conversion might have appealed to them. In our story, however, we are probably meeting a Brahman woman or one from another high caste.

What is interesting to note is that among Catholics today, beef, and even more particularly pork, is the festive food par excellence.[2] Moreover, the consumption of these is a sign of social status. 'To cut a pig' for a feast is a matter of pride and invokes the admiration of others. It is possibly only for the wealthy, and they are more often than not of high caste, to do so. Yet even the lowliest Catholic will try to purchase at least a kilogram or so of pork for a feast day. It is clear that the consumption of beef and pork (*mas*) are associated with the Portuguese. It is said that they brought the mass and meat (*mis ani mas*). No wonder that the mass and the feast centred around *mas* are the principal activities of a festive celebration.

In the period of conversion, it is probable that accepting *mas* became a crucial way of aligning with those who ruled. Fiddes (1991: 22) argues that in medieval and late medieval Europe, meat was the food of the rulers and the wealthy and powerful. Their diet was heavily meat-centred. Beef and pork, along with goat and mutton, were staple foods. Vegetables were the food of the poorer folk (Marques 1971: 22). According to Fiddes (1991), meat has, in western thought, always been associated with ideas of power, control or status.

Braudel (1973: 67; 1981: 105) mentions that the Europeans attempted to establish meat-eating civilizations in the new territories taken over by them. In these regions, as the food of the rulers and the rich, meat was clearly associated with status and authority. As he says, 'the European, true to his long-established tastes, regularly and promptly demanded that they be catered for when he was overseas. Abroad, the lords and masters ate meat' (Braudel 1981: 105). It is, therefore, possible to argue that the converts, who associated meat with the Portuguese rulers, may have adopted their meat-eating habits as a means of aligning themselves with them and gaining access to some of their superior power.

In some cases, the network of social relations in the village communities may have been used to bring about conversions. The *Documenta Indica* (Wicki 4: 753) tells us of a priest who came to a village to pray over a Christian. When he had finished praying, the priest asked the man, a *gauncar* and village leader, to call together the Christians of the village so that he could talk to them about God. When they had come together he gave them a lecture which pleased them very much. He then told them to go and gather together all the *'gentios'* so he could talk to them and make them Christians.

The priest initially used the man to approach the people of the village because, according to him, he was their 'leader'. Does this speak of a missionary policy to convert the lower castes through their patrons and 'leaders', the land-owning *gauncars* of the village? It may be so because there are other cases where the missionaries first persuaded the 'elders' or leaders of the village to convert. Such conversions were followed by conversions of other groups (D'Costa 1965). The vertical ties of socio-economic dependence which bound the lower-caste groups to their higher-caste land-owning patrons may have been utilized in order to convert them.

This is the 'downward percolation' technique of conversion that Forrester (1977: 36) and Oddie (1977b: 94) refer to as being used in later periods by missionaries in other parts of India. Those who did not convert could, in any case, not be employed by the Christian *gauncars* and landowners. From the point of view of these groups, taking on Catholicism was probably both a way of aligning themselves with the new rulers and re-establishing their relationship with their patrons within the terms of the new regime.

Conversion of the lower castes may, however, have also come about in a different way; one which undermined rather than re-established the village patron–client relationships. The entry of the Portuguese and the establishment of the church in Goa gave rise to certain new occupations such as wine-selling and baking. The products of these trades would be essential to Catholicism because they were used in the sacrament of the mass. It is probable that many of the lower castes converted because they saw as distinctly positive, the option of taking up occupations associated with the Portuguese regime in comparison with their position in Hindu caste society. It is true that the extent of such mobility was not very great. The groups remained at the bottom of the social hierarchy, only losing their earlier 'polluting' occupations. However, the expectation of change may have been an important factor in their conversion.

Thus, for the upper castes conversion meant alignment with the rulers and the protection of their economic, social and ritual privileges. For the low-ranking, there may have been the expectation of social mobility; for instance, through movement into non-traditional, pollution-neutral occupations opened up by the new regime. In many cases, though, it is likely that things worked differently. Patron–client relations were employed to bring about conversion. The village elders were converted and they in turn influenced the other caste groups, which were bound to them by ties of socioeconomic dependence (Robinson 1993).

PROSELYTIZATION IN THE INTERIOR

Proselytization did not remain altogether confined to the coast in the centuries after the Portuguese came to India. Incursions into the interior were made by Jesuits and other missionary orders. Conversions were made in inner Tamil Nadu and Karnataka, and in Bombay, Daman and Diu. Then there is the case of three successive waves of Catholic converts from north Goa, who fled to Mangalore and its nearby areas, due to the Inquisition, famine and political upheavals (D'Souza 1993).

The Portuguese came to Salcete, now part of Bombay, in 1534. Cultivating and fishing groups, more particularly, formed the bulk of the population in this region. It was the Jesuits who ruled and administered over the area for the next two centuries or so (see also Borges 1994; Godwin 1972). The use of sermons, instructions and catechisms in the local language fostered conversions. The schools and orphanages run by the missionaries offered spaces for propagating the message of Christ. Here again, mass conversion was enabled in part by the support and backing given the missionaries by the state. Higher castes were offered grants in land and education and employment opportunities opened up. These may have served as incentives to conversion.

PONDICHERRY: CONVERSION THROUGH ECCLESIASTICAL AND POLITICAL CONTROL

Another area, apart from Goa, where the convergence of ecclesiastical and political domains managed to produce the conditions favourable for cross-caste mass conversions in large numbers, was Pondicherry. Pondicherry was a small town with a population of Hindus and some Muslims, when the French arrived there in 1672–73. It was to remain the headquarters of their possessions in India until 1954. Caste was an important basis for stratification already in the seventeenth century and each group had its own locality in the town.

The local rulers of Pondicherry allowed the French to establish themselves on the condition that they would not interfere with local cults and the activities of local merchants. The condition was not, however, met. The Jesuits, who led the conversion drive, employed a combination of ecclesiastical and political control to achieve their ends. As in Goa, a conjunction of benefits and deterrents was central to conversion strategies. Employment and economic benefits were restricted to those who converted. A number of high-caste Hindus converted possibly to retain the favours shown to them by the French or to extract more favours from them. Charitable activity during famine and epidemic drew converts among the lower castes.

There were, on the other hand, also measures to inhibit the practice of Hinduism and Islam. All their religious ceremonies were prohibited during Easter and on Sundays. There was the destruction of temples and people were prohibited from working on Sundays. Finally though, the French East India Company keeping its commercial interests in mind, directed that Hindu festivals should be allowed and the missionaries should be cautious in their dealings with the Hindus. The threat of the Hindu merchants and others to leave the town in the face of the prohibitions imposed was, no doubt, responsible for this decision (More n.d.: 18).

CONVERSION THROUGH DIALOGUE AND ACCOMMODATION

Individual conversions were fewer in this period. The endeavours of the Lutherans Ziegenbalg and Pluetschau in the Danish colony of Tranquebar in the early eighteenth century are of some interest in this regard (see Beyreuther 1955; Gensichen 1967; Hudson 1993; Lehmann 1956). Ziegenbalg was a mere 24 when he set foot on Indian shore and Pluetschau was 29. Theirs was the first effort at conversions to Protestantism directed towards non-Europeans in India. They had to negotiate with a complex environment, culturally and socially, in which Tamil and Telugu speaking Hindus and also Muslims, Portuguese and north Europeans participated in varying measure.

Ziegenbalg, in particular, studied Tamil and made special efforts to translate doctrinal and liturgical material into that language. He also wrote tracts and held talks on religious matters in Tamil. He solicited written responses to Christian thought from the 'pagan' Tamilians of the town (Hudson 1993: 41). He deliberately used familiar, prosaic Tamil in his writings rather than the poetic, refined forms normally employed. Documents for distribution to all interested Muslims and Hindus were copied laboriously by hand before the first printing press arrived from Germany in 1713.

Ziegenbalg's efforts call to mind the most intriguing attempt to bring about individual conversions made—again in Tamil Nadu—by a Jesuit, who separated himself from the strivings of the *Padroado*. Based in Madurai in the late sixteenth and early seventeenth century, the Italian Robert Nobili explicitly attempted to enter into dialogue with Brahmanical Hinduism. The *Padroado* had, on the other hand, linked itself with south India's low-ranking maritime communities. Nobili adopted the attire, diet and lifestyle of a Brahman *sannyasi*. He learned Tamil and Sanskrit and studied the sacred scriptures in these languages. He held discussions with the Brahman priests of Madurai (Bayly 1989: 390; Neill 1984: 299). In the context of the strong influence of *bhakti* cults in south India during the period it is not surprising that Nobili was also identified, quite simply, as offering a new *margam* (path) to enlightenment.

Nobili created a Christian vocabulary employing expressions from sanskritic Hinduism. Terms such as *veda, mantra* and *prasatam* were centrally located in this novel and accommodative religious discourse. Nobili's converts were high caste men. They wore the sacred thread and received the sacraments from select priests who, like their leader, maintained a Brahmanical lifestyle and called themselves *sannyasis* (Bayly 1989). From the viewpoint of the converts, receiving baptism was akin to being initiated by a *guru*. They did not associate with lower-caste Christians and, for them, Catholicism denoted membership of a particular kind of sect, which forbade their taking part in idolatrous rites but allowed them to live with their families and retain their caste ideas and symbols (Neill 1984: 283).

UNDER THE PATRONAGE OF RULERS

In the north of India and east of India, conversions prior to the end of the eighteenth century, the time that the British were consolidating their rule, were rare. Where they took place, this was usually due to the patronage and individual regard of particular rulers. The Mughal Emperor Akbar, invited Christians theologians from Goa to his court. The King showed a great interest in Christianity and the Portuguese missionaries were permitted to live and propagate their faith within the empire, though the number of conversions they made was not large (Das 1974). Nevertheless, it was their efforts that gave rise to small Christian communities in Bengal and in different parts of north India.

In Bettiah, the local ruler, Raja Dhurup Singh, patronized the missionaries. The Capuchins under the leadership of Reverend Joseph Mary were invited to set up a mission within his territory. Christians from different castes converted, and the ruler granted them land in a special mission compound that was created and that formed the 'Christian Quarter' of the town. *Kayasthas, Sonars, Lohars, Kumhars* were among the castes in which conversions took place. It is possible that individuals or families associated with the court or reliant on its patronage came under the influence of the missionaries (see Sahay 1986).

THE BRITISH PERIOD

The British period did not see the kind of relatively unambiguous bond between religion and power that characterized the *Estado da India*, the areas under Portugal's imperial control. The linkages between missionary activity and British colonialism were complex and intricate. The English East India Company, though it employed chaplains for its own servants, merchants and soldiers, was at first hostile to missionary activity. This hostility stemmed from the fact that, as a commercial enterprise, the Company could only hope to succeed by accommodation to indigenous social and cultural traditions, including religion. It feared that brash evangelical efforts might give rise to violent reactions, creating political instability and threatening vital commercial interests (Kooiman 1989).

A change came about in the early nineteenth century after pressure was put on the British government by missionaries and returned civil servants such as Charles Grant, who argued that the propagation of Christianity, far from endangering British interests in India, would produce obedient citizens and strengthen the foundations of the empire. The motifs of civilization, paternalism and moral improvement woven into the missionary enterprise thus potentially facilitated the forging of linkages with the project of colonialism (see Dube 1995, 1999; also Hollis 1962; Studdert-Kennedy 1998).

The Company had itself not followed the practice of complete neutrality in religious affairs. Accommodation to indigenous religion meant that large sums of money were donated for the maintenance of temples and priests and Company officials attended the more important sacred celebrations with a view to manifesting their respect for native traditions (Kooiman 1989; Oddie 1991). It was partly this participation by Company servants in Hindu rituals that provoked the missionaries to complain to the government. Following the shift of policy then, the Charter Act of 1813 directed that missionary efforts be permitted, if not actively supported.

A fairly cautious attitude towards the missionaries resulted. In the decades which followed, their work began to be viewed with increasing favour, though at no point was a missionary-cum-imperialist drift completely dominant (Kooiman 1989). In the case of conversions in the tribal areas of west, central, east and north-east India, there is clear evidence of official patronage extended to the missionaries (see, for instance, Minz 1962; Seybold 1971; Thomas and Taylor 1965).

Conversion in the north-east had begun to advance while the British were in the process of shedding the role of traders to assume that of rulers. Annexation brought the British into contact with the tribal people of the hilly regions, whom they considered unpredictable, primitive and difficult to deal with (Natarajan 1977: 58–59). It was hoped that missionaries, through evangelization and education, would be able to civilize and domesticate the unmanageable tribes in terrain hard to administer and govern directly. Hence the support for the mission project.

Among the missionaries who worked in the north-east, the Presbyterians and Baptists were prominent, though Methodists, Catholics and Anglicans were also present (see Downs 1981, 1994; Eaton 1984; Mills 1926). The government took an interest in the educational activities of the missionaries and funds were donated for the purpose of building and maintaining educational institutions. This interest increased in the latter half of the nineteenth century. In 1854, the Governor General Lord Dalhousie took an interest in the work of the Presbyterian mission and instructed that an amount of Rs 50 a month be donated for its educational work. In 1867, this grant was increased 10 times with the *proviso* that the schools run by the mission would be inspected annually to report on their progress by an inspector chosen by the Presbyterians with the approval of the government (Natarajan 1977: 66). Thus, schools in the area were often financed by the state even though they were managed by the church and the textbooks included those of Christian theology. Churches were also built with viceregal support and that of the administration and local converts.

Attempts at conversion of the Santals by the Baptists had commenced during the first half of the nineteenth century and a few schools had been opened. The Santal rebellion of 1855–56 drew attention to the problems of the tribe and conversion efforts increased thenceforth. The British commissioner at Bhagalpur, Yule, noted that the Santals who had attended the missionary schools were not among those who participated in the rebellion. Therefore, the government co-operated with the missionaries in the establishment of more schools in the area and gave grants-in-aid to those already in existence (Troisi 1979: 263).

At all times, individual officers with an interest in ideas of reform and civilization could support missionary efforts. For instance, the missionaries of the Gossner Evangelical Lutheran Mission were invited in 1845 by Captain Hannington, Commissioner of Chotanagpur, to preach among the Oraon. In 1844, four of these missionaries had come to work in India and had landed in Calcutta. On learning about them, Captain Hannington wrote to the Secretary of the British and Foreign Bible Society in Calcutta asking him to send them to Chotanagpur to work among the Oraon (Sahay 1986). Again, the work of Oscar Lohr of the German Evangelical Mission Society was patronized by Colonel Balmain, the Commissioner of the Chhattisgarh Division. Balmain invited Lohr to work among the Satnamis. He advised him to secure a site for a mission station and even informed him of a stretch of wasteland that was up for auction in the area (Dube 1995: 172–73).

The Bhils and other tribal groups of Gujarat and western India also posed administrative problems for the British because of their perceived insubordination. The mission project was again visualized as a critical tool by means of which they might be pacified and converted into submissive subjects of the Raj. Hardiman (n.d.) quotes Sir Lepal Griffen's pronouncement on the Bhils.

> I believe that it would be an immense advantage if the Bhils could be converted to any form of Christianity by missionaries, either Catholic or Protestant..It is obvious that the inconvenience and even danger which attend proselytising enterprises in Brahmanical and Muhammadan States which possess a creed as dogmatic and systematic as Christianity itself, do not exist with reference to a people like the Bhils, who have no dogmatic theology, and who would accept with very little difficulty the civilising creed which would be offered to them (ibid.).

As a result of pressure put on them by the colonial state, the local rulers permitted missionaries to enter these regions in the nineteenth century. The scope of their civilizing presence included the spread of the new faith and moral values, and the provision of educational and medical facilities (Hardiman n.d.: 4). The Bhils, proud rulers of the terrain, barely acknowledged the missionary message, though there were some conversions among the much more inferior *adivasi* groups.

What were the associations between colonialism and the mission project? Missionaries were associated with the colonial order in several respects. Though they interacted very closely with local people, often ate Indian food, learnt Indian languages and visited Indian homes, their separateness was highlighted through their distinct lifestyle or leisure patterns. In fact, missionaries believed in maintaining this separateness—their particular approach to dress, time or the organization of domestic space—for they perceived it as being a necessary part of Christian upbringing and western culture and civilization. The mission project therefore involved, as part of the same deal, the civilization of the converts through their initiation into particular practices that centred around, for instance, clothing or building (Dube 1995; see also Skaria 1999).

Through their participation in and upholding of this distinct lifestyle, the missionaries constructed a sense of belonging to the community of white settlers. They reinforced a particular civilizational model that merged almost imperceptibly with the ideology of colonial rule. Nevertheless, the links between mission and state were never entirely untangled. Evangelical missionaries in Chhattisgarh did tend to describe their converts as children and always retained a certain paternalistic attitude towards them. They had to be cared for and disciplined by the 'adult' missionaries. In this as in certain other respects, the missionaries clearly participated in the idioms of domination that characterized the colonial construction of the non-western Other (Dube 1995, 1999). However, they also viewed the converts as equal in the Kingdom of God and invoked the principle of self-determination to assert the convert's religious freedom. Thus, within the colonial culture of order, the evangelical enterprise may be viewed as having been paradoxically rather than simply located.

Apart from the mass conversions of Untouchables in certain parts of the country, the bulk of converts made during the British period were located in more outlying regions at the margins of the agrarian plains, as in particular north-eastern tribal pockets. It is suggested that the conversion of tribal groups such as the Nagas may be explained, in part at least, as a function of the larger process of social transformation. Isolated as they were in geographical terms and in religion from traditions with a wider literary base such as Islam, Buddhism or Hinduism, these groups retained elaborate but highly parochial belief systems (see Eaton 1984).

The opening up of the hills under the British brought about several material and economic changes. It integrated the hitherto insulated Nagas with the rest of the subcontinent and led also to an erosion of traditional village institutions and forms of authority. The cognizance of these rapid shifts and the broadening of the horizons of the social world required something other than the existing localized belief systems, which had, in any case, been greatly dislocated by the changes taking place. Thus, entire groups caught in a fluctuating social, cultural and political environment could become amenable for conversion (Eaton 1984).

Mass conversions in the British period, took place largely among the low caste groups from the middle of the nineteenth century. In the north, Chamars (leather workers), Chuhras and Lal Begis (sweeper communities) in the Punjab and the United Provinces were drawn into such movements (see also Mullens 1848; Whitehead 1913). Conversion among these groups was, generally, a result of group decisions and followed kinship lines (Webster 1976). In the south of India, among other such movements, the mid-nineteenth century saw a mass conversion movement among the Nadars, a caste located on the borders of the boundary of pollution (Raj 1958). In Telugu country, groups of Malas and Madigas converted *en masse* (Forrester 1980; see also Gladstone 1976, 1984).

Mass movements of this type indicated a growing discontent among the depressed classes, which may be related to the extensive disruptive effects wrought by colonial rule in many parts of rural India (see, for instance, Bugge 1994; Pickett 1933). A dual effect resulted. Traditional relations of production and distribution were undermined rendering the lowest castes extremely vulnerable. At the same time, there were new opportunities opening up for such groups to enhance their social position or to acquire new skills, new patrons and new religious attachments. A product of this immense disquiet and change, thus, was the attempt by the most lowly groups to disengage themselves from caste structures. Christianization, and this must be emphasized, was *one* among a number of potential means available for this purpose. Conversion to Islam, Sikhism or the reformed Hinduism of the Arya Samaj were other modes, adopted by some (Forrester 1980).

Christian missionaries did not have at their disposal, the means to enforce conversion. Particular benefits could, however, be had from association with them. And these may have served as incentives to convert. For the low castes, these included intercession with the government, protection against moneylenders or exploitation by the high castes and perhaps, educational and employment opportunities. Many tribal groups also viewed the missionaries as mediators with the courts and colonial administration. The fact that often missionaries actively took up the defence of tribal interests, particularly in connection with their rights regarding land tenure and services to landlords, may have done much to contribute to their attraction (Sahay 1986).

Mass conversions may be viewed, in part, as movements for improvement in social and material conditions, but they were also movements for dignity and self-respect. Groups in a condition of social and religious disadvantage may have perceived that they had much to gain by adopting Christianity: the satisfaction of receiving instruction from educated and sympathetic white clergymen and of obtaining new skills and educational opportunities to be able to pursue a better life along with others of their caste (Webster 1976). It is true that the higher castes did not change their attitude towards converts of the lowest social groups and that, in the end, their situation, in all cases, did not significantly improve. The expectation of change, however, would itself have been a powerful catalyst for conversion (Forrester 1980; Oddie 1977).

Thus, whatever the missionary agendas, the converts appear to have usually had their own. Social mobility was often part of the low caste convert's agenda. On the other side of the picture, in Goa, the higher groups sought to keep hold of their caste privileges. In a somewhat different vein, particular tribal groups in some parts of India had the expectation that the missionaries would undertake to stand up for their rights and protect them against oppressive tenancy laws. They were looked upon as intercessors in the negotiations of the tribals with the law courts and the British-introduced judicial system.

ISSUES IN THE SOCIOLOGY OF CONVERSION

A number of themes arise that are relevant in the construction of a sociology of conversion to Christianity in India. We need to look more closely at questions of motivation and the understanding of what constitutes conversion or, for that matter, mission. Themes regarding the 'agency' of converts and the ways in which they sometimes redefined the terms of evangelical interaction are of great interest. Moreover, we need to try to sort out particular patterns and strategies of conversion and attempt to analyze the conditions under which they become possible. This section raises a host of queries regarding conversion and examines various issues of concern from a sociological and historical perspective.

Misunderstanding, subversion, compromise and negotiation were all part of the narratives of conversion that I have attempted to chart above. Though the missionaries were sometimes complacent enough to believe they 'knew' what was going on, they were actually often apt to make blunders or profoundly misconstrue the manners and motives of converts. One recalls the classic case of the missionaries who got involved in the Nadar 'breastcloth' controversy (see Hardgrave 1968, 1969; Hospital 1979; Yesudas 1975). The Nadars of Tamil Nadu were a group whose social position lay at the boundaries of the line of pollution. Throughout the nineteenth century, Nadars were engaged in a struggle for social upliftment. Conversion was, for some of them, part of the attempt to attain upward social mobility.

By caste rules, Nadar women were not permitted to cover the upper part of their bodies. The upwardly mobile Nadars petitioned the courts for the right of their women to cover their breasts after the custom of the high castes. The missionaries supported their case, couching their arguments in the language of Christian modesty and womanly decency. The missionaries won for the Nadar women the right to wear upper garments, but not to wear the particular item of clothing used by high caste women. The Nadars continued their protest. Clearly, while the missionaries had been acting merely in the name of Christian virtues and morality, the Nadars were playing an altogether different game. For them, engaged as they were in a movement for social uplift, the issue of covering women's breasts was less important than that of covering them in the manner of the high castes (Hardgrave 1968, 1969).

In Chhattisgarh, Oscar Lohr went to work among the Satnamis, the largely Chamar members of a sect initiated by Ghasidas, who began a hereditary *guru* tradition. *Satnampanth* involved the belief in a formless god (*satnam* means true name) and the abstention from meat, liquor, tobacco and particular vegetables (Dube 1992: 114). In 1868, Lohr visited the Satnami *guru* on the occasion of *gurupuja*. He was seated next to the *guru* and served refreshments. He was elated by the warm welcome he received from the *guru* and all present. He used the occasion to assert that the real *satnam* was Jesus Christ.

It has been suggested, however, that it is possible that Lohr's visit to the *guru*'s residence on the day of *gurupuja* unintentionally signified to the Satnamis, his endorsement of and affiliative assimilation into the *guru*'s domain of authority. In any case, hopes for a mass conversion movement among the Satnamis were belied. A few conversions did come about as individuals, who survived with the help of mission medicine, long illnesses that had brought them close to death, decided to embrace Christ. In other cases, it was ties of kinship, to an initial convert, that proved critical for the growth of the community (Dube 1992: 103). Clearly, interpretations often clashed and missionaries were not always the ones in control!

Whatever the circumstances, the Word had come to India to stay: its particular modes of revelation and interpretation framed by the specific conditions of its entry and penetration. Literacy, education, translation, writing and the introduction of scripts were all also clearly implicated in the story of the spread of Christianity. Conversion in Goa brought the printing press and the creation of works such as the *Krist Puranna* and the *Puranna of Saint Peter*, texts in vernacular verse detailing, respectively, the life of Christ and that of Saint Peter. In Kerala, the missionary effort relied on Nambudiri and Nair translators.

In Gujarat as in other regions of the country, tracts in indigenous languages were distributed to spread the faith (Boyd 1973: 84). Though a lot of early Protestant literature displayed little understanding of the Hindu faith it sought to replace, some later texts attempted to project Christianity as a fulfilment of certain prophecies available within Hinduism. A little book *What is in the Veda* published in Gujarati and Marathi in the late nineteenth century put forward the view that animal sacrifices in the Vedas were a foreshadow of the true sacrifice of Christ. The *rishis* rightly emphasized sacrifice, and it is in the Cross that one finds the true fulfilment of their vision (ibid.).

The need to translate the Bible to disseminate the Word led to the development of scripts by missionaries for tribal and other languages. Particular, and sometimes, peculiar, kinds of dialogue resulted. The missionaries used the Ao Naga word for spirit without attributes, *tsungrem*, for God. *Tsungrem* could be applied to all levels of the Ao pantheon, from the more vaguely conceived supreme deity to specific, jungle ghosts or even house spirits. By translating *tsungrem* as God, the missionaries could draw what the pantheon had in common—spiritness—and suffuse the concept with the transcendental power and universality of the Biblical God. Perhaps *tsungrem*, reconfigured by Christianity, answered the Ao Naga need for a powerful deity who seemed more in command of the much larger universe in which they found themselves with the breakdown of their isolation under British rule. Certainly, the number of conversions was phenomenal (Eaton 1984).

Translating the Bible and Christian literature into Tamil in eighteenth century south India, German missionaries used the word *ajnana* (ignorant) for heathen. Interestingly, the Shaiva response to this usage was to re-apply it to the Christians and to assert from within their religious system that those who did not wear the ashes of Shiva, did not rely on Shiva's five-syllable chant for ritual purposes, did not make offerings or fast and were without mercy, love, humility and patience were the real heathens (Hudson 1993).

The attempts at translation of Ziegenbalg and Pluetschau, despite the overturning they received, give us some understanding of the ways in which individual conversions proceeded. These relied a good deal on painstaking persuasion, through some effort to come to terms with the existing faiths and to 'answer' them with what the missionaries believed were Christian 'truths'. Without reliance on colonial authority, the peculiar nature of the regimes seen in Pondicherry or Goa, geared towards mass conversions, could not be easily replicated.

Nevertheless, I am making no easy dichotomy between 'force', however defined, and persuasion or mapping this unequivocally on the distinction between mass and individual conversions. However, I am arguing that the shape of conversion strategies acquires a different dimension when the relationship between state and religious authorities is relatively less ambiguous. This was the case in Goa, though even there the two often came into conflict and the King, ironically both monarch and patron of the faith, was resorted to for a decision between them.

For instance, in the 1590s, the then Viceroy of Goa wrote to the King of Portugal that while he agreed that all the temples of Portuguese India should be destroyed, this could not be done in Diu. 'If it were all the vanias *would* leave, and commerce at this most lucrative fort would grind to a halt' (Pearson 1987:122). Political and commercial realities could soften the conversion effort, despite the explicit mission enterprise.

Sustained attacks on religion though, could usually only be reproduced in small, confined territorial regimes, where the authorities could and did act in tandem. It is in such cases that we find simultaneous low and upper-caste group conversions becoming feasible. Elsewhere, the situation usually differed a little and took an either/or route. Conversions limited to a caste (the Mukkuvars, the Paravas or the Syrian Christians) took place, or more often, one finds the divide between the generally (but not exclusively) urban-based, individual conversions among upper castes and mass-based conversions among the lower social groups in rural, hill or tribal regions; at the margins as it were, of Empire.

Further, what becomes evident is that debates regarding the temporal *versus* the spiritual motivations for conversion (D'Costa 1965; Heras 1935; Priolkar 1961; Rao 1963; Pereira 1978) raise a false problem. From a historical and sociological perspective, it appears that for the converts everywhere, the two seem to have been largely inseparable. The converts must be said to have perceived the missionaries' offerings as an undifferentiated package deal. Acquiring dignity or maintaining privilege, achieving social and economic mobility or retaining status—depending on where one's position in the hierarchy lay, conversion was usually bound up with a complex of such motives.

Conversion certainly involved more than only a change in religious beliefs and ideas. Apart from the fact that it was often motivated by concerns more entangled than those arising from religious disposition alone or that it was sometimes part of larger social processes of transformation that could not be traced back solely to the realm of ideas, it is also perceived that missionaries almost always required of their flock more than just a change of heart. In the case of Goa, this requirement instituted through the Inquisition is notorious. It was not only that recourse to Hindu sacred rites and modes of worship were prohibited. The Inquisition also viewed with suspicion a variety of indigenous cultural practices and sought to eradicate them.

These practices included ceremonies in honour of ancestral shades; the maintenance of Hindu sacred rites, festivals, fasts and holy days, and the use of the *tulsi* plant or of rice-flour, oil, flowers or leaves for ceremonial or ornamental purposes. The use of betel leaves and areca nuts in ritual exchanges or as marks of social precedence was also prohibited. The singing of celebratory verses at marriages and other festive occasions and the employment of traditional musical instruments were forbidden. The use of garments such as the *dhoti* and the *choli* was frowned upon. Such prohibitions did not apply only in Goa. Missionaries in other parts of the country, Catholic or Protestant, demanded from their converts various outward signs of religious change.

In south India, Protestant missionaries wanted their converts to shave the *kudumi*, the tuft of hair which signified high status, to refrain from chewing betel nut, having oil baths, expressing relationships of honour through the use of sandalwood and flowers or maintaining puberty rites (Visvanathan 1993b). Hudson (1982: 249) also describes how missionaries in the late nineteenth century in Tamil Nadu opposed expressions of Hindu identity among the Christians. The expressions cited included the public announcement of puberty for girls, the smearing of cowdung in houses, the painting of designs in doorways for auspicious occasions, the manner of washing with water after excretion, the practice of daily bathing, of bathing in the river, of taking oil baths on particular days of the week, of chewing betel and showing reverence to others by using words in the plural form and offering items such as sandalwood, flowers or betel. Christian missionaries working among tribal groups objected to their participation in New Year or harvest celebrations, drinking of rice beer or dancing and attending indigenous dramatic performances (Nongbri 1980: 113, 224; Troisi 1979: 126, 267). They had objection to the use of traditional instruments of music (Troisi 1979: 265).

These injunctions differ little from the prohibitions of the Inquisition, if they do not in fact rival them in detail. It seems clear that missionaries everywhere, across temporal and denominational boundaries, sought visible signs of religious transformation from the converts, though the conditions under which they functioned would ensure that they differed significantly in the degree to which they could enforce their directions. Conversion nowhere remains only a transformation in the system of beliefs. It always involves social and cultural changes. It will be perceived that there is accommodation and negotiation though, rather than a simple elimination of indigenous ways.

A further question that one might think of addressing is that posed by the idea of 'mission' itself. It becomes clear that mission is not a simple category. The motivations and ideas which imbued mission activity in the sixteenth century had much to do with notions of 'conquest' and building a Christian body politic in the conquered realms. There was no ambiguity about the state's interest in supporting mission activities, which were, in fact, viewed only as an extension of its economic and political goals. Mission was necessary for and in fact, integral to the whole project of the consolidation and maintenance of rule.

Christian mission activity in the nineteenth and twentieth centuries was infused with ideas of reform and civilization of the 'natives', bringing it into harmony with the ideology of racial superiority held by colonial rulers. Nevertheless, mission was never an arm of the state in any unequivocal fashion. In fact, far from believing that mission furthered the colonial project, the state looked upon it with a great deal of suspicion. This was the post-Reformation period and religion was no longer as entangled in the construction of statehood or political identity as it had been in sixteenth century Catholic Europe. The location of mission in colonial enterprise inflects missionary activities in particular ways, as we have tried to uncover in the course of this chapter.

NOTES

1. This cannot be proved but we know that it is likely that the annual cycle of church festivities has over time been adapted to suit the Catholics' own needs. This process may have been helped along by the missionaries. Through the use of the Inquisition, the converters prohibited access to Hindu deities and temples, the celebration of Hindu festivals and the use of Hindu forms and items of worship among the converts (Priolkar 1961). Yet, adaptation

was also possible. The converters were apparently prepared to allow church rituals to be adapted to local custom as long as the object and means of worship were Christian in content. The *Documenta Indica* (Wicki 4), for instance, gives an example of how the harvest festival might have come to be incorporated into the Catholic calendar in Goa. The people and *gauncars* of the village of Diwar in north Goa requested the priest to come and bless their harvest as the Hindu priest had done in the past. They went to the field carrying a banner with the name of Jesus and Saint Paul on it. The priest came carrying his stole and surplice. When they reached the field, the priest blessed them with holy water and blessed the sheaves. These were carried back to the church, where the priest laid his on the steps of the altar, followed by all the others laying theirs. The people of other villages such as Navelim, Malar and Goltim did the same. One might argue that it is from beginnings such as this that the Catholic calendar came to be adapted to indigenous social and religious needs. I am not saying that conversion came about because people immediately perceived the possibility of such adaptations, but after taking on the new religion they may quite soon have found that they could adapt it in such ways. The missionaries may have been amenable to such adjustments because the incorporation of agricultural festivals, for instance, was not unknown in the European Catholic calendar of that period.

2. Braudel makes the statement that Europeans populated the New World with 'herds from the Old' (1981:105). There is no evidence that the Portuguese brought pigs to Goa. Wild and domesticated pigs were found both in north and south India. While all Hindus in Goa, including Brahmans, always ate fish (Mascarenhas-Keyes 1988), except on ritual occasions, the meat of pigs may have been consumed only by the lower castes. In south India, swine-herding was the occupation of certain very low castes (Srinivas 1965). Muslims would not touch pig meat because of the Islamic injunction against it.

3

PATTERNS OF INTERNAL DIFFERENTIATION: CLASS, STATUS AND GENDER

THE VEXED ISSUE OF CASTE

It goes without gainsaying that most of the literature on Christian communities in India in identifying and discussing modes of internal differentiation highlights, if not isolates, the 'caste' configuration of these groups for special focus. Material on gender inequality is less easy to find and one has, sometimes, to dig for it. The same goes for class and economic groupings. Caste itself has to be spoken of with caution, for it is the subject of debate and controversy as to whether the pattern of stratification found in many Christian communities fulfils or does not fulfil the criteria of what goes under the label of 'the caste system' among Hindu groups. This chapter will delve into the available literature in order to explore the differing structures of internal organization that characterize different groups. While the caste debate is by no means peripheral to this purpose, other structures of differentiation will also be discussed, such as class, gender and distinctions within tribal groups.

The understanding of 'status' and 'class' that undergirds this chapter follows Weberian definitions. He argues that (see Gerth and Mills 1981: 405) 'classes' are groups of people who, from the standpoint of specific interest, have the same economic position. Ownership or non-ownership of material goods or of definite skills constitute the 'class-situation'. 'Status', on the other hand, is a quality of social honour or a lack of it and is in the main conditioned as well as expressed through a specific 'style of life'. Status is not directly determined by economic considerations though people of a certain status have a particular elite style of life that makes them 'prefer special kinds of property' and certain kinds of 'gainful pursuits'.

Caste is usually discussed in the context of 'status groups' as I conceive them, though the whole point really is to understand whether a 'caste system' can be said to exist among Christians. The presence of 'caste-like' differences is perceived everywhere, though the mode of their articulation differs considerably (see, for example, Bayly 1989; Behera 1989; Caplan 1980a; Forrester 1977; Robinson 1998). Some groups, such as the Syrians for instance, found their place as a relatively high caste within the overall regional social order. They were located on a par with the Hindu Nairs and may even, at one point of time, have intermarried with them. They were considered 'clean' or *suvarna* and had right of entry into Hindu sacred precincts and places of worship (see next chapter). On the other hand, the Goan Catholics have a system of stratification on a par with the Hindus around them, but the two orders exist *separately* and are not integrated with each other ideologically or in terms of systems of exchange and interaction (D'Costa 1977; Robinson 1998).

Caplan's Madras Protestants (1980) also have some ideas of caste identity but are not incorporated into the system of Hindu castes. The Catholics of rural hinterland Tamil Nadu, however, described by Diehl (1965) or Mosse (1986, 1996) live and work alongside Hindu kin and caste fellows. Christians and Hindus, therefore, share caste identities and are assimilated into a single system of hierarchy and ritual exchange. There are Hindu and Catholic Vellalars, Utaiyars, Pallars and Paraiyars. As Mosse puts it (1996: 463):

...while sharing in many exchanges, Christians and Hindus do not intermarry, either because they belong to different sub-castes (as in the case of Vellalars and Paraiyars), to different religions (in the case of Utaiyars and Pallars) or to both. Religious affiliation merely re-enforces existing rules of sub-caste endogamy or imposes further rule. Religion is thus of wholly secondary importance as a principle of social organization in this part of south India, where Hindus and Christians live as members of rural village communities primarily organized around *caste* rather than religion.

Caste shows up everywhere: in marriage and sometimes commensal patterns, in the organization of church celebrations and in the division of labour. The extent to which it does so and the areas in which caste shows up has some links to the historical development of Christianity in those areas, the period in which conversion took place, the groups involved and their motivations and the role the missionaries played in negotiating with the prevailing social order. Broadly, it may be argued that conversions that took place in the nineteenth and early twentieth centuries came about because of the converts' desire to move out of the inegalitarian caste society of the Hindus into a religious community where they were treated equally (see Bugge 1994; Forrester 1977; Oddie 1977b; Pickett 1933). Most of these conversions were among Dalit groups. Oddie (1977b: 73) quotes a missionary as saying:

> The Malas and the Madigas, as members of the Hindu social system, are deliberately kept in a state of ignorance, poverty and degradation. When they become Christians they are treated as human beings, their children are educated, the men and women are taught the truths of the Christian faith and...meet together for worship.

Forrester and Oddie, among others, suggest that conversions during this period came about because of the decision of various groups to opt out of the indigenous social order—the order of caste in Hindu society. This was a time when conversions took place within an atmosphere that emphasized individualism and egalitarian values. Like Caplan's and Webster's Christians, converts from this period show relatively fewer traces of adherence to caste values, especially in places where individual conversions took place. With group conversions though, one thing often remained true. Despite the attempts of convert groups to shed caste, society refused to let them. Converted Christian Dalits faced the same humiliating disabilities that they had intended, perhaps, to flee (see, for instance, Japhet 1988; Karnanaikal 1983; Koilparambil 1982; Koshy 1968; Ponniah 1938; Singarayar 1978).

Catholic missionaries, by not discouraging group conversions, quite frequently ended up working within the framework of caste. Protestants seem to have much more consistently regarded the caste system as an obstacle to evangelization and attempted to foster individual conversions. Forrester argues that:

> On the whole the Roman Catholics have all along been fairly consistently favourable towards group conversion and have seldom put

as much emphasis on the values of individualism and equality as the Protestants. This has meant, of course, that they have tended to be very much more tolerant of the caste system... (1980: 39)

While it is certainly true that missionaries came to terms with the existence of caste under certain conditions, it should be recognized that the attitudes of different denominations towards the caste system could change over time. Catholic and Protestant missionaries played important roles in fighting against some of the most severe caste disabilities, while Protestant evangelists struck a balance with caste when they entered the field of group conversions in the latter half of the nineteenth century.

Conversions which took place during earlier periods often tell another story: of how converts themselves resisted any missionary efforts to establish egalitarian relations. There are telling instances of particular castes fighting to defend the maintenance of status distinctions, with or against missionary effort. Bayly (1989), Robinson (1998), Roche (1984) and Visvanathan (1993a) have shown that during the sixteenth and seventeenth centuries conversion maintained and sometimes, paradoxically if you like, even reinforced corporate caste identities. Bayly (1989: 7–8) argues with regard to Syrian Christianity and early Catholicism in south India that 'Indian Christians did not opt out of the indigenous moral order; on the contrary, the behaviour and social organization of these converts continued to reflect perceptions of caste rank, honour and ritual precedence which were shared throughout the wider society...'

Moreover, the church itself was not innocent of notions of hierarchy. The Christianity that entered western and southern India in the sixteenth century incorporated within itself a hierarchical vision of society. According to notions extant in Catholic Europe at the time, the clergy, knights and labourers constituted the three main orders of the social whole. Common worship and sharing in the Eucharistic body of Christ brought the different groups together but they remained in a relationship of inequality. It is not surprising that status differences expressed in the idiom of caste were maintained among Christians of Goa and the Konkan region. In Tamil Nadu, ideas of servitude and respect, purity and impurity continued to inform the relations between castes among convert communities. In both regions, a structure of rights and honours based on caste developed around the celebration of feasts in village churches, analogous to the pattern existing in Hindu temples.

THE MANY FACES OF CASTE: CASTE IN THE CHURCH

In some communities then, the church became the centre for the manifestation and maintenance of status differences centred around caste. Church celebrations and processions began to express and articulate relations of rank and status, hierarchy and honour in particular local contexts. On a par with Hindu temple celebrations, most Christian feasts find the distribution of rights and honours on a caste basis. Elaborate rules of rank and precedence order the pattern of participation of different castes and social groups in such celebrations. In the south Goan village of Cuncolim, described by Newman (2001), at the church dedicated to Our Lady of Good Health, it is the high-caste, landowning Chardo *gauncars* (male descendants of the original settlers of the village), who are members of the 'red and white' fraternity who organize the religious festivals and lead the processions. The colours refer to the capes that the *gauncars* wear at such processions. The non-*gauncars* of the village including members of all castes, particularly the lower-caste Sudras, are distinguished by their blue capes. They have no right to administer feast-day celebrations and have to walk behind the high-caste *gauncars* at festive processions. They are also not allowed to touch any of the processional regalia or distribute candles at the celebrations.

In Goa as in some other parts of India, the churches replaced temples as the focus of the socio-religious life of the village communities following conversion. The converts were able to reconstruct their socio-cultural system around the new places of worship. Indeed, from the very early period of conversion, the missionaries themselves allowed the Catholic high-caste *gauncars* a variety of honours and privileges in the church-centred Catholic ritual cycle. In the village studied by Robinson (1998), the church is at the centre of the relations of power and hierarchy within the Catholic community. While these relations are based on caste status, the ownership of land or control within the local village panchayats, the church maintains and articulates them. Honours in church ritual are important in themselves *and* because they signify authority and stature in the community.

The privilege of hosting the celebrations for the different feasts belongs to the two Catholic lay associations in the village. These are the major and the minor confraternities. The major confraternity (*confraria maior*) is *Confraria de Santissimo e Nossa Senhor de Socorro*. Only the high-caste Chardo *gauncars* may be members of this confraternity. The confraternity enjoys the privilege of organizing the harvest feast celebrations and those centred around Good Friday and the feast of the patron of the village church. It is the minor confraternity (*confraria menor*) to which the other groups in the village belong. Non-*gauncar* Chardos, Sudras and other lower-caste groups are members of this confraternity. This confraternity organizes the feast of Saint Sebastian. In the processions on the harvest feast and on Good Friday, the Chardo *gauncars* play a major role. They lead the procession and, on Good Friday, used to carry the large cross. On the feast of the patron of the village church, Our Lady of Perpetual Succour, the *gauncars* carry the image of Our Lady.

Processions start at the side door of the church, which is to the right of the altar. The participants circumnavigate the square in front of the church and enter the church again through the main doors. The image is taken and placed on the main altar. The organizers or main celebrants carry the image, leading the procession. Behind them usually come the women and children, followed by the lower-caste men. On the feast of Saint Sebastian, the Sudras generally lead the procession and carry the image of the saint. High-caste *gauncars* generally walk at the back, keeping some distance between themselves and the lower-caste celebrants of the feast. Sometimes, they do not join the procession at all, indicating their reluctance to participate actively in a celebration which is organized by those lower down in the social scale.

The main privilege that is important in these processions is that of carrying the image and leading the procession. Other rights though, are also involved. It is the members of the major confraternity who have the right to dress and decorate the image of Saint Bartholomew (in whose name the harvest feast is celebrated) or bathe the body of Christ before mounting it on the cross during Good Friday celebrations. They also have the right to decorate the altar during the feasts. On the feast of Saint Sebastian, the high-caste Chardo *gauncars* remain in the background. It is the minor confraternity that organizes the celebrations and decorates and dresses the image and the church. The processions and the practices related to them clearly serve to symbolize status within the community. The church has become a part of the local social system of the Catholics.

Church feasts in south India manifest a similar pattern. In Alapuram, described by Mosse (1994c), the rights to carry the saints and chariots in the procession associated with the annual feast of Saint James, the patron of the village church, were restricted to the high castes. The participation of the low-caste Pallars in the festival was limited to contributing to the festival fund and receiving the sacrament. Rank manifested itself here as well. Up until the early twentieth century, communion was brought to the Pallars at the back of the church at a separate rail, after it had been received by the high castes. In the south Arcot district of Tamil Nadu, Dalit Christians and the 'clean' caste Malaiman Udaiyan Christians occupied clearly differentiated places in the church until the 1950s (Wiebe and John-Peter 1977). Pulaya and Paraya Christians in Kerala worshipped in separate churches from the Syrians (Alexander 1972, 1977). It was not until 1914 that, in one Catholic church, the low-caste Christians were allowed to attend worship together with the Syrians (Fuller 1976).

Caste issues like this could become very complicated. In Alapuram (Mosse 1996), caste conflicts arose over the question of funeral biers. Until the 1970s, two biers had been in use. One was used exclusively by the high castes and was kept inside the church, the other was for the use of the low caste Pallars and it was kept outside the church. In 1979 or 1980, the Pallars took the bier from inside the church by force and used it for a funeral. After this, the high castes not only did not touch the bier, they refused to allow it to be brought back into the church. Instead, at each funeral they would bring a bier from a neighbouring village: one which was used exclusively by the high castes there. These disputes continued into the 1980s until the priest refused to bless the biers at all.

The classic case of castes fighting for special concessions in the church comes from the Tamil Nadu village of Vadakkankulam.

The case highlights the fact that, quite often, missionaries and priests were but pawns in elaborate games played by various castes against each other. Even if they wanted to prevent the church from becoming a site fought over, they had a hard struggle. In Vadakkankulam, Vellalars and the more lowly Shanars were in constant dispute over rights and honours in the celebration of the main feasts of the Holy Family Catholic church. The priests were wittingly or unwittingly drawn into these battles. It was quite interesting, if not uncommon, that the groups used conversion and reconversion as ammunition to get the Catholic church to concede their demands for more privileges in the local honour system centred around the parish feasts (Bayly 1989).

The nineteenth century shows many such tactical moves. For instance, in 1807, a number of Vellalars shifted allegiance to the Protestant London Missionary Society to protest against the rights given by the Catholic Jesuit priest to Shanars in the Holy Family church celebrations. They built a new chapel which had a canopy that just managed to block the route normally taken by the procession during the August Assumption, Holy Family's main annual celebration. Once their demands were conceded, they moved back to their own church. Such disputes went on for so long that the Jesuits stopped the celebration of feasts, and taking advantage of the dilapidated condition of the church, closed it. The Christians protested the move and in fact, wanted a barrier built in the church to segregate Shanars from Vellalars. The Jesuits were horrified at the idea and fought it for 20 years. This is not withstanding the fact that they had allowed themselves to be drawn into caste struggles in the first place by designating (as they had done in so many other places) the rights of various groups in the celebration of the feasts of the church. Clearly, the missionaries could be ambivalent about the extent to which they were prepared to go in acceding to the maintenance of local status systems.

Finally, the Jesuits were able to force through the demolition of the church. When the new church was built, however, they were unable to prevent the construction of a barrier separating the different groups. The new church had a massive and infamous 20-foot high brick barrier running the full length of the nave from the main door to the communion rail. It even contained an inner tunnel allowing the priest to reach the altar without setting foot on the space occupied by the contending parishioners. The Shanars, however, continued their protest because they were denied rights in the celebration of the church's main feast. Among other things, and evidently believing that two could play at the same game, they threatened to withdraw their affiliation from the church and convert to Anglicanism (Bayly 1989: 442). The missionaries here were obviously being pulled every which way by their parishioners, who had agendas of social mobility all their own. Parishioners wanted to perpetuate caste and they fought missionary opposition in this regard in order to get their demands authorised.

The kind of spatial segregation described here is no longer formally sanctioned in any church, but it often continues in muted and less explicit ways. The south Arcot Malaiman Udaiyan Christian males and children occupy the middle rows of seats in the church, while Udaiyan women sit in the rows on the right and the Dalit Christians in the rows on the left (Wiebe and John-Peter 1977). In some south Goan villages, the benches closest to the altar are often tacitly reserved for the high-caste celebrants on the occasion of church feasts. Low-caste Kerala Christians usually occupy the back benches in churches where they worship together with the Syrians. In fact, though there is no formal ban on Pulayas attending services in Syrian Christian churches, few of them do so (Alexander 1972). The notorious Vadakkankulam brick caste barrier was long torn down, but Vellalars and Shanars, when they were not persisting in or carrying out their threats to affiliate themselves elsewhere, continued to occupy different sections of the church.

It is true that low-caste converts sometimes suffered in terms of receipt of pastoral care (Alexander 1972) and they are still less visibly represented in positions of authority and power in the ecclesiastical hierarchy. This may be less due to active discrimination than due to the configuration of circumstances that leads to the deprived and less educated getting left out of the race for position and prestige. However, the unspoken preference that prevailed for a long time for admitting only high castes into the priesthood cannot be denied. This was, no doubt, partly based on the apprehension of alienating the high castes and the recognition that a low-caste priest might face opposition from his high-caste parishioners (see Reddy 1987; Wiebe and John-Peter

1977). Whatever the reasons, under the circumstances they were not unfounded. Wiebe and John-Peter (1977) record for the Kovilanoor parish of rural Tamil Nadu, dominated by the powerful Malaiman Udaiyans, that no Dalit priest had ever been appointed there or was likely at all to be. The Malaiman Udaiyans would hardly permit it.

Caste conflicts may be quite intense at higher levels in the church administrative hierarchy. The politics of caste is quite rampant in south India in the Diocesan Councils, main bodies which make decisions affecting the clergy and the people in particular areas. In the Madras diocese, conflicts frequently arise between the Vellalars, upwardly mobile Nadars and higher groups and the Dalits (Caplan 1987: 161–62). In a session held to select a new Bishop in 1974, three names were proposed. The first was that of the Assistant Bishop, widely respected and supported by many for the post. He was of Dalit origin. Two other names were proposed, one of them of a Vellalar minister married to a Nadar woman. Though the Assistant Bishop had a lot of support in the council, the person finally selected for the post by the selection sub-committee which reviewed the recommendations was the Vellalar. Almost all agreed that caste had played a very important role in deciding the issue. The bitterness generated by this controversial decision led to another decision, taken a few months later, to bifurcate the diocese. A new diocese was created in the North Arcot Dalit dominated area, which allowed them to largely escape from the hegemony of the non-Dalits in diocesan affairs.

CASTE OUTSIDE THE CHURCH: ENDOGAMY

Most Christian communities tend to be caste endogamous. Catholic Reddys in Andhra Pradesh or Christian Nadars in Tamil Nadu might prefer to marry among Hindus of their own caste than form an alliance with a low-caste Christian (Hardgrave 1969; Reddy 1987). In Goa, Bamons, Chardos and Sudras do not intermarry. Syrian Christians in Kerala will not even contemplate connubial relations with Pulaya Christian converts. Where marriage outside caste boundaries has begun to take place, it is usually confined to groups which are closer together in the hierarchy.

Thus, Goan Bamons and Chardos may now occasionally inter-marry, but rarely Bamons and Sudras. This is, of course, true for regions where group conversions took place.

Where individual conversions were recorded, the possibility of maintaining caste endogamy receded. In cases of a few individuals or families converting, marriage across the boundaries of caste becomes almost inevitable. High-caste conversion in the Madras Presidency never reached the kind of levels necessary to maintain generation after generation of caste-specific marriages. Endogamy had, more or less, to be abandoned in the face of demographic actuality. Missionary orphanages, whose charges had vague if any caste affiliation, often provided educated girls considered suitable for matrimony with high-caste converts. In contemporary times, marriages are arranged between suitable Protestant families and caste credentials are not always mentioned. Nevertheless, marriage cycles tend to form quickly and the respectability, wealth and lifestyle of families are crucial considerations marking status almost as efficiently as caste background (see Caplan 1980: 221).

Even where it cannot be demonstrated, the ideology of maintaining caste purity or the 'purity of blood' remains. There are Madras Christians, obvious products of non-endogamous unions, who lay claim to caste status, possibly Brahman but more usually Vellalar. The claim is voiced by showing a genealogical link with a well-known and distinguished Christian of the particular caste. Such links are easily traceable because they rarely go back very far into the past. The person claimed as an apical ancestor is usually the original convert to Protestantism, and one who has gained considerable standing and honour within the family and the community. Most 'respectable' Protestant families if so inclined could probably come up with such a prominent ancestor from their genealogical past. The ability to claim such ancestry defines a 'good family', one held in esteem not only within the relatively narrow confines of kinship but within the community as a whole (Caplan 1980). Caste pedigree, therefore, is part of the definition of the 'good family' and enters, as it were, by the back door.

Economic and class considerations are also seen to play quite crucial roles in the making of marriage. Even where caste endogamy is taken for granted, marriage is more likely to take place between families of similar educational and economic background. In cases of the breach of caste boundaries, one often finds that it is the compatibility of class backgrounds that contributes to making a non-endogamous marriage acceptable to the families concerned. Such marriages are usually self-initiated rather than arranged by others (the popularly labelled 'love' marriage), but the consent of families is rarely wholly ignored. Thus, if wealthy, educated and professionally well-established, an Izhava or Pulaya Christian may find it possible to marry a Syrian Christian without raising a furore. Though not frequent, marriages may acceptably occur across the Bamon-Chardo-Sudra caste divide in Goa, when educational and professional criteria are agreeable.

Nadar or Vellalar Christians in Madras might claim that they make elaborate enquiries into the caste pedigree of potential alliance partners, but the breach of caste is tolerated when the families are prominent enough to be able to minimize the possible negative social consequences. Caplan gives the example of a well-employed son of a respected couple, the one Nadar and the other Vellalar, being made offers of alliance by both Nadars and Vellalars. He quotes the young man as saying: 'They were ready to regard me as either Nadar or Vellalar if I agreed to marry their daughter' (Caplan 1987: 125). The odd Dalit family among the urban Protestant middle classes, with enough influence and means, might also in time, find it possible to shed the stigma of its caste origin and enter into alliance with 'good' families.

COMMENSALITY

The question of inter-dining is equally if not more complex for the rules named by people may not strictly conform to the actual relationships between castes on the ground. In Goa, for instance, the upper-caste Bamons and Chardos may claim that they do not eat with lower-caste people. Yet they do go on the occasion of a wedding or other such celebration, especially one at the house of a close neighbour. In some cases, they may be served and eat at a separate table from other groups. The lower castes are but rarely invited to the house of an upper-caste person. If they come for a wedding, for instance, they will generally sit with others of their own caste. The food served to all is the same and it may well be cooked by lower-caste domestic assistants. On other occasions, someone from a lower caste will usually eat separately in the kitchen, maybe even after others in the house have eaten. But it is no longer unusual to see a long-familiar or well-educated and established Sudra person at table with his or her Chardo hosts.

Thus, class intersects with caste considerably in deciding the extent of commensal relations. This is more so in recent times, but was not unknown even earlier. K.C. Alexander (1972) notes that up until the 1960s the Pulaya Christians of Kerala would not be given food inside the house of a Syrian Christian. Food would be given outside the house in a leaf or broken dish. After eating the food, the Pulaya would have to wash the dish before returning it. Izhava Christians belonged to the toddy-tapping community and were therefore also considered to be below the line of pollution. However, because of their high economic position and movement into different professions, they did not face the discrimination of the Pulayas. Inter-dining and even inter-marriage with the Syrian Christians had been possible as early as the first decades of the twentieth century. Today, educated, well-to-do Pulaya Christians will sit at table with a Syrian Christian and Syrians attend their weddings and do not hesitate to accept food from them (see also Fuller 1976).

In the village of Alapuram in Tamil Nadu where Dalits, Christian and non-Christian worked for high-caste Hindu and Christian patrons, they received from them food on certain occasions (see Mosse 1986). When deaths occurred in their families, the Pallars were required to prostrate themselves before their Utaiyar patrons and received cooked rice and other gifts from them. Non-reciprocal food transactions within such a structure of patronage underlined the subordination of the low-caste groups. Pallars could only receive water from the high-castes by having it poured into their hands or mouth. They could not touch the container. They were refused entry into tea shops and did not have rights of access to common water sources. However, Brahman priests serving Hindu families would accept tea or coffee from their non-vegetarian high-caste clients. They would also drink tea from the local tea-shops, run by non-Brahmans.

OCCUPATION

Occupation defines status as it implicates class. In terms of caste status, particular occupations were considered defiling due to their association with polluting substances, such as organic waste products. In Goa, Mahars and Chamars remained lower in status than Sudras, because they worked with sewage and dead animals. The Mahars also, into the early decades of the twentieth century, performed various funerary services, such as carrying the dead body. There was usually only one or so Mahar family in a village or group of villages, and the services they performed were hereditary. For the other castes, occupational specialization is less easily specified. Conversion appears to have paved the way for many to leave polluting occupations. Agriculture was the occupation of many among the low castes, either as tenants or agricultural workers. They were subordinate to the high land-owning castes, but the ideas of performing ritual and pollution-removing services declined considerably.

Among the Sudras, there are different subgroups, which have names suggesting hereditary occupational specialization: *dorjis* (tailors), *shetkamti* (agricultural workers), *dhobis* (washermen) and *render* (toddy-tappers). There are families among these groups, whose main occupation has, for a generation or more, been agriculture. The groups do not behave like castes: marriage and commensality are not limited by the occupational category but could include any person from the Sudra community. Indeed, occupational specialization has, in any case, all but collapsed over the last several decades, helped along by the migration of many Catholics outside Goa and their employment in a variety of jobs. The high castes, Bamons and Chardos, also take on several kinds of occupations. They were, largely, landowners and cultivators in the past but fanned out into other occupations during the colonial period, helped along by a Portuguese education. Today, they are mostly engaged in professional and clerical non-manual occupations, while Sudras and some poorer Bamons and Chardos may work on ships or serve as cooks, waiters, technicians or peons.

In Alapuram village in Ramnad district of Tamil Nadu studied by Mosse (1986, 1996), the upper caste Christian groups of Utaiyars and Vellalars along with the Hindu Maravars, maintained social and economic dominance based on landownership and control of village resources. Low Christian and Hindu castes worked their land and tended their flocks. Christians of the Acari (carpenters and blacksmiths) caste did the work of agricultural carpentry for all the castes, Hindu and Christian, of the village. They received *cutantaram* (payment at the threshing floor) for this work as for maintenance of agricultural tools. However, for housebuilding, making bullock carts or other private work, they were paid in cash. The Christian Acari also performed the rites of divination to establish the auspiciousness of a proposed building site, for which he received gifts of cloth and raw food items.

The Vannans or the washermen also performed some important ritual roles. They announced the first menstruation of a girl to her family and relatives and until recently, received the polluted cloth on such occasions. At death, they received the cloth from the funeral bier. The washerman also provided clothes for women to wear after childbirth and for the chief mourner to wear during the performance of funeral rites. For these ritual services, he received cash and gifts of oil and cooked food. Apart from shaving and cutting hair, the village barber had the task of decorating the funeral bier of the Christians. Pallars, Paraiyars and other Dalit castes were denied the ritual services of the Brahmans as of the Vannans and the barber.

Alapuram had no resident Brahman family. The high-caste Hindus were served by Brahmans from a neighbouring village on the occasions of birth, marriage or death. The Brahmans were given gifts for their services on these occasions. According to Mosse, whose argument runs counter to that of Dumont (1980), the employment of a Brahman priest was not considered necessary for the maintenance of social status within the system. Many families did not employ Brahman priests on their marriages or at other life-cycle rituals. The village temples were served by non-Brahman priests.

Among the Catholics, priesthood was theoretically caste-neutral. Even a Dalit could join the priesthood. However, Dalits were usually posted away from their region of origin in order that their caste status would not be known among the community they served. In Alapuram, whatever the official view, priesthood was considered a high-caste occupation. In fact, masses conducted by visiting Pallar priests were boycotted by the high-caste

Catholics. Catholic Pallars were denied until recently the services of the Vellalar *kovilpillai* (the village catechist and assistant of the priest), a position instituted by the Jesuit missionaries in the region. The Pallars had their own Dalit *kovilpillai*, who was given a salary by the priest for his services and also received a part of the offerings made to the church on the occasions of major festivals.

It was the Potera Vannan sub-caste that performed the services of washerman and barber for the Pallars and other Dalit groups. They were paid annually and also received food on special occasions. They washed the clothes of the first menstruation and provided the cloth for the bier. They acted as funeral priests for Hindu and Christian Dalits. Hindu and Christian Dalits had to show extreme deference in front of their high-caste Hindu and Christian patrons. They were not allowed to wear the *vesti* at full length and till the first decade of the twentieth century, their women had to expose their breasts in high-caste streets. They could not sit on high-caste verandahs and had to use deferential forms of address for the high castes.

THE DISCUSSION ON CASTE

Most of the discussions take off from Dumont's influential, if not uncontroversial or even somewhat offhand, remarks on the presence of caste among non-Hindu communities. The crux of the Dumontian argument is the issue of the 'ideology' of caste. Caste is not perceived purely as an element of social structure, in the way in which Bailey (1963), for instance, views it. Bailey would argue that even racial distinctions between blacks and whites could be seen as a type of caste system because these also ascribe status by birth and are particularly closed and rigid forms of stratification.

Dumont, on the other hand, is concerned much more centrally with the ideological basis of caste, which he sees as inseparable from Hinduism. Of particular significance in this regard for Dumont is the opposition between purity and impurity. According to him, the central principle underlying the caste system is hierarchy—the necessary and hierarchical opposition between the pure and the impure. Status is determined by one's position in this religious hierarchy. It is unaffected by power or economic wealth. A poor Brahman is superior to a rich Sudra. The pure-impure opposition is a primarily Hindu notion and Dumont has, therefore, to reconcile it with his observation that caste-like divisions are prevalent even among Christians and Muslims.

Dumont attempts to explain this anomaly in the last part of his work. As he says (1980: 201):

> ...we have, after all, linked caste to Hindu beliefs about the pure and the impure. If it was confirmed that elsewhere there existed groups in other respects similar, but lacking this link with religious beliefs, then should not these beliefs be considered purely accidental?

He speaks of the Lingayats who do not recognize impurity but are divided into groups that 'must indeed be called castes' (ibid.: 201). His remarks with regard to Christians are similar. He mentions Kerala where Christians are divided into 'groups strongly resembling castes' (ibid.: 203). A little later he refers to Tamil Nadu where the caste system has operated in a Christian setting with 'strength'. How is this to be explained? According to Dumont, adherence to a monotheistic and egalitarian religion for several generations was not enough to lead to the disappearance of the fundamental attitudes on which the caste system was based. Existing in an environnment that is largely Hindu, Christian groups cannot gain independence from Hindu ideas no matter how hard their own value system presumably veers in a different direction.

In the end Dumont decides that it is 'psychological dispositions' (1980: 211) which must be responsible for the presence of caste among groups which lack the ideological support for the system. This is a very different kind of argument from the one which Dumont is otherwise fond of reiterating: the presence of caste must be accounted for in terms of the ideology that renders it meaningful. Parry (1974) and Caplan (1980a) concern themselves with similar questions. Parry suggests that caste values are not the only values that imprint themselves on non-Hindu groups. Different religious communities also have their own distinct value systems, which must be looked at as well.

Caplan argues that it is important to understand 'how members of non-Hindu groups define themselves in relation to caste' (1980: 215). According to him, Madras Protestants demonstrate a great deal of flexibility in relation to caste identity. They claim one kind of identity in a particular context and a different one elsewhere. For instance:

> [a]n individual may refuse publicly to assert a caste attachment, but at the same time subscribe to and proclaim, utilizing the appropriate euphemisms, the benefits of marriage between households who have similar 'ways', which comes of sharing a common origin, 'tradition', and life-style (Caplan 1987: 156).

There are also several contexts in which the Madras Protestants view themselves and act as Christians, part of a universal body of believers, rather than as members of a particular caste. Caplan (1987: 150–52) does show the evidence of ideas of impurity among the Christians. For instance, mourners bathe and change before returning to the house after a funeral. Ideas about commensal and connubial restrictions remain: while high-caste Protestants may accept the cup at the Eucharist from a Harijan minister, they would rarely dine or intermarry with Harijans. However, Caplan appears to think that these ideas are not sufficient to establish the presence of a 'caste system' among the Christians. He argues that the presence of ideas of impurity should not be viewed 'as part of a system of ritual exchanges which express or establish differential caste ranking' (ibid.: 151). In some sense, he ends up agreeing with the Dumontian perspective that caste among Christians is essentially a residue of their immersion in overwhelmingly Hindu environments.

Fuller's analysis of caste among Christians in Kerala develops a more complex argument. He (1976, 1977) distinguishes three levels of ideas and their actualization: theology, ideology and behaviour. According to him, at the level of theology, Hinduism may make a radical distinction between status and power and Christianity may stress egalitarianism. However, theology is the domain of priests and affects ordinary people very little. Ordinary Hindus and Christians share a common ideology of caste, which does not radically separate status from politico-economic realities. They also share an orthopraxy of caste, a common set of caste practices.

Fuller initiates the critique of Dumont, by redefining the terrain of ideology. Dumont's concepts are now relegated to the realm of theology, which is ineffective in influencing people's behaviour to any significant degree. Ideology is what people act on and, at the ideological level, Christians and Hindus make no radical distinction between ideas of status and power. Though Fuller does not explicate his argument sufficiently, this means that ordinary people of either community do not think of status only in terms of ideas of ritual purity and impurity. Other factors intervene, those of wealth and power, the ability to dominate and extract submission and obedience from others.

To say this, as Mosse (1996) argues, is not to concede that caste is only about power and not religion. Rather, politics is itself ritualized and the legitimation of power is in religious terms (see also Robinson 1997, 1998). Thus, among Christians, the legitimation of power centred around the church itself. Church festivals and honours in church ritual became an important mode of signifying and constituting relations of dominance and prestige. In south India, caste power, rank and title were summed up in rights in the worship of the temple deity and in the receipt of temple honours and privileges. Catholic churches in the region provided the location for the articulation of rank, power and status in an almost identical manner (Mosse 1996: 472). Rights to church honours as well as the command over the services of subordinate castes were central to the cultural construction of caste position.

Caste does not persist among Christians merely as a residue of their Hindu environment, 'weakened and incomplete' (Dumont 1980: 210) in the absence of the ritual justification provided by the ideology of purity and impurity (Mosse 1996: 472). It does not exist only because of 'psychological dispositions'. Rather, there is a cultural and ideological context within which caste exists, which has allowed it to flourish among some Christian communities over several centuries. In order to be able to perceive this, we have to reject the Dumontian argument that caste is all about ritual purity and impurity and not at all about ideas regarding power or relative wealth. Fuller embarks on that course, but he does not provide us with any understanding of the means by which the ritual context of caste among the Christians is constituted.

Mosse's analysis of caste ideology and practice among Christians is more elaborate. It depends on the assertion that Christianity is not always unable to accommodate ideas of hierarchy (see Robinson 1998: 88–89). Dumont and Caplan seem to be working within the framework of the question: when Christianity implanted itself in a caste society, why did that society not give way to an egalitarian one? The idea that egalitarianism is an intrinsic aspect of Christianity, is assumed. However, the church could come to terms with certain elements of inequality. In Tamil Nadu, the Jesuit missionaries in the Ramnad region appear to have viewed caste inequalities as social phenomena, with no relation to religion. Hence, they permitted their expression and articulation through the distribution of honours at church festivals.

As I have discussed earlier, like missionaries in Goa, Ramnad's Jesuits would themselves have come from a hierarchically conceived social order. European Christian society of the time was divided into those who prayed, those who fought and those who laboured. All were indispensable to the social whole. However, though labour was dignified, labourers were not. Priests and knights were considered respectable, plowmen and herders were inferior. Against this background, it is not surprising that the missionaries tolerated, if not encouraged, the perpetuation of caste distinctions in church festivities. The churches took on the role of local temples, configuring and expressing the distinctions of rank and power within the community.

However, we still have to deal with the question of the extent to which, if any, ideas of purity and pollution are relevant to Christians and in what contexts these ideas are activated. It is here that Mosse (1996: 474–76) assumes greater interest for us. He argues that there is an explanation for the fact that, as the material from different regions shows, Christians appear to maintain pollution prohibitions in some domains, while ignoring them in others. Domestic purificatory rites are but rarely maintained any longer in relation to birth or menstruation. The 'impure' clothes are washed and kept on such occasions; when they are removed by the washerman, one is not sure if this is because they are associated with negative elements or polluting ones.

The negative and dangerous aspects of transitional moments are recognized; care is taken to keep away the evil spirits that might be lurking around to take advantage of one's vulnerability on such occasions. The ideas of keeping away danger, 'heat' and impurity are often merged. Rites seek to re-establish 'coolness' and auspiciousness (see next chapter). Catholic rituals at birth, puberty or death distinguish between positive and negative forces and sequences and involve processes that separate the negative elements and transfer them to persons defined as appropriate recipients on the basis of their social status. The idea of removing 'pollution' is less relevant.

Christians are conscious of ideas of purity and impurity in relation to certain aspects of the Hindu sacred. States of bodily pollution make a woman vulnerable to attack by demons, *pey* and certain Hindu deities. Menstruating women will not approach Hindu deities or even walk by a temple. However, they will enter a church and receive the Eucharist. A dead body can be brought into the church, and the rites marking life-cycle rituals such as death mirror Hindu ideas more in terms of shared notions of danger or inauspiciousness, than in terms of notions of impurity.

What we need to ask, according to Mosse, is; in relation to what or whom are pollution prohibitions maintained? And we find that it is largely towards inferior Hindu divinities, whom Christians come into interaction with as a result of activity geared towards the management of misfortune, that the rules of purity and impurity are applied. The Christian sacred is offended by sin and sexuality, rather than impurity.

As Mosse (1996: 475) argues, Mary, Christ and the saints are not angered or insulted by a worshipper's impurity. Saintly power is not related to ritual purity. Mary derives her power from sexual purity; the saints derive theirs from their triumph over suffering and, ultimately, death. It is not impurity but sexuality and sin that are inappropriate states for Christian worship. Following sexual intercourse, people are hesitant to enter Church or receive the sacrament of the Eucharist. It is, moreover, priestly celibacy that is more frequently mentioned as the source of sacerdotal power.

MISSIONARIES AGAINST CASTE

The story of caste and Christianity is not complete until something has been said about the missionary opposition to caste. Till now, I have suggested that the missionaries sometimes came to terms with caste inequalities. However, they also fought the grave disabilities imposed by the caste system on those at the lowest levels of the hierarchy. They often took up cudgels on behalf of their lower-caste converts, though they were not always successful (see Azariah and Whitehead 1930; Oddie 1979, 1991). Their support often encouraged converts to strengthen their own

efforts at finding release from the degrading social practices imposed on them. In south India, the missionaries were active in
fighting for the rights of pariahs and converts to use public paths
and to withdraw from providing inferior and degrading services
for the high castes. Mosse (1996: 469) refers to a petition made
by the Catholic Pallars of Alapuram in 1938 to withdraw from the
funeral prostrations they had to make before their Utaiyar landlords. The parish priest referred the matter to the sub-magistrate
of the area, but the ruling at the time was in favour of maintaining the practice. It was some years before the Pallars were able
to extricate themselves from the degrading custom.

The Pallars of Alapuram, in fact, had been fighting the oppressive system since the late nineteenth century (Mosse 1994a: 83).
In the 1890s, the Catholic missionaries supported the Pallars
and other low castes in their withdrawal from inferior temple
service roles such as drumming and providing palm leaves for
festivals. In 1904, the missionaries fought with the Pallars for
the right of Pallar women to cover their breasts in high-caste
streets. Missionaries fought for the right of Nadar women to
cover the upper part of their bodies (see Hardgrave 1968; Hospital 1979; Yesudas 1975) and, both in the north and south of India,
they struggled to establish the rights of Christian converts to
use public wells. In the Telugu-speaking regions of the Madras
Presidency, converts from the leather-working caste got the
encouragement to refuse to work on the Christian Sabbath and
well as to give up eating carrion and playing the drums at village
religious festivals (see Clough 1914).

It was not always the case that the missionaries supported
the low castes purely out of compassion for their inferior social
position. Sometimes, support was given because certain practices (such as providing temple services) were perceived to be
unChristian and to compromise membership of the church. Nevertheless, the missionaries were aware of the fact that the low
castes often came to them because they hoped to alleviate their
oppressive circumstances to some degree. They saw the missionaries as their mediators in the struggle to obtain civil rights
and improve their position. Reverend Kabis, a Lutheran missionary in Tamil Nadu wrote in 1897 that one of the principal reasons
that led the 'Pariahs' to Christianity was their need of a defender.

> There can be no doubt that, very often, one of the chief reasons which leads them [the Depressed Classes] to move towards Christianity is their need of a protector, who shall help them to claim and gain the rights which they are beginning to understand are theirs, and that they hope by becoming Christians to better their miserable condition and to find in the missionary a friend in need and a champion in their oppressed situation...Any missionary who wants to work successfully among these people must be prepared to become to them not only a teacher, but also a pleader and almoner (quoted in Oddie 1991: 158).

Most missionaries did consider themselves responsible for their converts and were concerned about their welfare and protection. This does not mean that they necessarily held out their support as a carrot for speeding up evangelical efforts. Rather, they often found themselves faced with situations requiring their intervention after conversion, that they may not have visualized before.

In 1851, a Jesuit in Tanjore (Oddie 1991: 160) reported that almost all Christians were low caste cultivators serving 'pagan' landowners. The missionaries had been trying to extricate them from such servile conditions through a search for uncultivated land at a low price in order to provide the Christians occupational security and protection.

The missionaries were involved in the efforts that brought into operation the Caste Disabilities Removal Act (Act XXI of 1850). Interestingly, the kind of missionary activity that I have been describing here stimulated Hindu movements for the reform of the caste system. Further, to counter the spread of Christianity, Hindus often found that they had to change their attitude towards those who had been expelled from caste due to conversion and to reframe the rules for their re-entry. It was acknowledged that the traditional modes of expiation needed to be modified in order to make them simpler and less painful, thus facilitating more and more reconversions (see Jordens 1977; Oddie 1969, 1979).

CLASS DISTINCTIONS

I have already had occasion to draw attention to the fact that caste often intertwines with considerations of economic position and lifestyle when decisions are made regarding appropriate commensal and connubial relations. Not many authors deal closely with questions of class distinctions, perhaps because caste tends to occupy the focal point of discussions on patterns of differentiation within communities. Caplan's ethnography (1987) appears to have the most extended analysis of class differences within a Christian community.

Most Protestant Christians in Madras may be divided into two classes: the middle class and the lower class. Few Christians are represented among the very rich industrial magnates or the big bourgeoisie. The middle class is effectively the community élite and is constituted by Protestants with 'top jobs and good salaries, advanced education, plenty of jewellery and dowry for their daughters' weddings and bungalows with many rooms...' (Caplan 1987: 12). The lower class can at best afford a humble lifestyle, simple rented accommodation, education in vernacular schools, modest weddings and a decent set of clothes for church. Below these are the poor, those who have no jobs, no regular meals and no homes.

Caste and class often overlap. Most of the lower class Protestants are of Dalit origin, while Nadars and Vellalars figure more among the middle class. The rules of marriage work to ensure that one weds within one's own caste or at least among those who are economically, educationally and professionally closest. Caste and economic or professional position may not always coalesce but they are more often than not in agreement. For instance, one is more likely to find higher and middle castes among the middle class, and marriages across caste here would not face too much opposition. One is not crossing the Dalit/non-Dalit divide and there is a good deal of economic and educational compatibility.

TRIBAL HIERARCHIES AND MISSIONARY OPPOSITION TO CONTESTS OF PRESTIGE

The missionaries often compared caste society very unfavourably with tribal society. They, by and large, held to the view that tribal society was not inflicted with the elaborate and invidious distinctions of status and purity that characterized caste society. In fact, they believed that this made it easier to spread the Christian message among tribal groups than among caste-stratified communities. It was no doubt assumed that the simple and animistic *adivasis* would respond more favourably to the superior Christian message than would the being mired in the intricacies of caste.

Nevertheless, it is not the case that tribal societies were completely free from distinctions of prestige. In the Dangs district of Gujarat for instance, where Christianity came in the nineteenth century, various social distinctions prevailed. There were ruling Bhil chiefs, ordinary Bhils and subordinate peasants or *gavits*. The *gavits* belonged to different communities such as the Konkanas, the Varlis, the Chodris, the Dhodiyas and the Gamits (Hardiman 1996: 94). The ruling Bhils were considered superior to other Dangi *adivasis*, but the Dangi Konkanas looked down upon them as ritually inferior because they ate beef, monkeys, rats and other 'unclean' foods (Hardiman 1996: 104). Konkanas and Varlis could intermarry, but a Konkana or a Varli who had a sexual relationship with a Bhil would be thrown out of the community (ibid.: 104–5).

The Gamits were considered one of the most inferior groups. It was from among them that the greatest number of conversions was initially recorded in south Gujarat. An already socially disadvantaged people, they had less to fear from social opprobrium due to conversion. Chodris and Dhodiyas yielded a few converts, but the other groups remained largely impervious to the Christian message. Clearly, among Dangi groups of higher status, the possibility of social ostracism and expulsion from the community were much more potent threats that may have acted as a serious barrier to conversions (Hardiman n.d.: 10).

Where the missionaries recognized the existence of social distinctions within tribal groups, these distinctions, like the differences of caste, became the object of their censure. For instance, the missionaries prohibited the celebration of Feasts of Merit among the Ao Nagas. Furer-Haimendorf (1976: 47) records:

> To rise in the social scale an Ao had to give a series of feasts, defined by custom in every detail and necessitating the expenditure of large quantities of food stuff...The ambition to out do their neighbours in the giving of Feasts of Merit stimulated the rich to produce rice beyond the requirements of their household and to rear...buffaloes and pigs for slaughter. Social prestige was not their only reward. With every feast they acquired the right to increased shares of meat whenever another villager gave a Feast of Merit. This system of

> reciprocal gifts made for the smooth distribution of perishable food...The wealth of the ambitious was employed to provide food and enjoyment for the less prosperous members of the community, for at a Feast of Merit there was meat, rice and rice-beer for every man, woman and child in the village.

The probable reason for the prohibition was that animals consumed during the feasts were first sacrificed with the proper invocation being made to the spirits. The result was that in Christian villages the rich, freed from traditional obligations to their neighbours and forbidden from hosting the feasts, often tended to hoard rice or sell it to the highest bidder (Furer-Haimendorf 1976: 48).

GENDER AND CHRISTIANITY

There is a great deal of complexity to the ways in which indigenous modes of gender differentiation were altered or affected by conversion to Christianity. In another chapter (Chapter Five), I deal with the ways in which kinship and inheritance patterns, patrilineal and matrilineal, changed under the influence of Christianity. Here, I would like to discuss Christian ideas about female roles, behaviour and sexuality and look at how these negotiated with discourses they encountered. There appears to be, for instance, a great deal of correspondence between Hindu and Christian notions of feminine identity. This might suggest reasons why Christianity often accents instead of easing patriarchal tendencies in the cultures it engages with.

Ethnographic accounts have shown that ideas regarding the 'good' and the 'bad' woman are common among Hindus in India. The good woman is pure and unselfish. As a wife and mother, she is dutiful, constant and loving. Qualities of tenderness and compassion abound in her. The bad woman, the whore, belongs nowhere and to no one. She usually repudiates family ties or is rejected by her family for her immoral ways and is, therefore, not secure in the legitimate protection of a male authority figure: father, brother or husband.

These notions—about earthly females' behaviour and character—are underscored by the rupture in the conceptualization of the feminine divine in Sanskritic and non-Sanskritic religious traditions.

Sanskritic or Brahmanic Hinduism incorporates the goddess as consort of a male deity. In this position, the goddess is inferior in power and status to the male divine being, her spouse. Marriage binds her into meekness and obedience and robs her of her anger and destructive powers, which emerge powerfully in the goddess-centred *shakti* cults (see O'Flaherty 1980; Ram 1991).

Catholic thought also contains within itself the paradigmatic opposition of Mary and Eve. Mary, the virgin mother of God, is a benign, benevolent presence in Christian discourse. Christian women are typically exhorted to emulate Marian virtues. Iconographically depicted as crushing the serpent beneath her foot, Immaculate Mary (who was conceived without original sin) triumphs over Satan, who in the form of the serpent had lured Eve into the web of temptation. Associated with shame and the loss of primal innocence, Eve remains a disturbing, unsettling figure in Catholic thought.

It is not that the notion of the feminine divine in popular Christianity is without rupture or ambivalence. Warner (1976) explores, using European materials, the troubled relationship between the ideas of Mary's independent power (her power to answer prayers and her powers of intercession with her son), her virginity and her fertility. Medieval beliefs not only celebrated the notion of fecundity associated with Mary and attributed to her the capacity to quicken the womb, but viewed her as having absolute powers, not resting on the mediation of her son, to grant all kinds of boons. The theological resolve to these contradictions was the suppression of the motif of sexuality and the concomitant stress on motherhood through the dogma of the 'immaculate conception'. By locking Mary in motherhood, the discourse allowed the church to emphasize that she had no independent powers, her power flowed from and originated from her son, Christ. Mary must therefore be beseeched to mediate with Christ.

Indeed, in the south Asian context, as Bayly has demonstrated, quite often virgin cults manifest a 'rich mixture of Hindu and Christian motifs' (1989: 368). In the case of the Velankanni virgin, for instance, there are oral traditions linking her to the surrounding Hindu sacred landscape and she is portrayed not as benign protectoress, a divine being deficient in independent power, but as warrior and conqueror. In fact, the cults use the term *shakti* to refer to her supernatural powers. In the next chapter we will witness in greater detail Kalpana Ram's (1991) analysis of popular Catholicism among Mukkuvar fisherfolk in Tamil Nadu. Ram argues that there is a split in the conception of the feminine divine in Mukkuvar popular Catholicism, which partakes significantly of non-Sanskritic Hinduism. Good and evil are symbolized and incarnated by the figures of Mary and the non-Sanskritic Hindu goddess Eseki, respectively. While Mary is seen as completely benevolent and confined to her maternal and nurturing role (good femininity), all the unruly aspects of the feminine—desire, power and the capacity for unpredictability and evil—are projected onto the figure of Eseki. The presence of the figure of Eseki within popular religion testifies to the need to contend with and represent the disorderly aspects of the feminine, which are denied by the figure of the eternally placid Mary of official Catholic discourses.

In Goa, the relationship between Mary as benevolent mother of God and as powerful female divine embodying *shakti* is often articulated through the story told of the seven sisters, who once represented seven temples in Goa. Though no one can identify all seven, the story goes that some of the sisters converted to Catholicism, such as the Church of Our Lady of Cures at Cansaulim and Our Lady of Miracles at Mapusa. Some remained Hindu, including the powerful Shantadurga of Fatorpa in south Goa. Shantadurga, whose cult is popular in Goa among Hindus and Catholics, is viewed as a potent divine figure with the capacity to grant favours, but also to turn her anger on devotees who forget to keep the vows they make to her.

The language of kinship binds the benign Mary and her powerful, *shakti* externalizing 'other' in sororal conjunction. However, in Goa as in the Tamil case described by Ram, the forceful hegemony of the church definitions in the realm of popular religion ultimately ensures an asymmetry in the relationship in that the cult of the Hindu goddess among Catholics remains a subterranean, subdominant presence. While there is an appropriation of *shakti* embodying Hindu goddesses into popular Catholicism, the domination of the chaste image over that of the unruly ultimately mirrors the relationship of these goddesses to the higher female divinities within Brahmanic Hinduism.

Further, this hierarchical representation of the feminine divine is reproduced in discourses aimed at earthly women. Particular strands within Christian and Hindu discourses converge in urging women towards and indeed, obliging them to accept the values of obedience and submission to the husband. As with other cultural patterns, Goan Catholic kinship morality and gender values share much in common with Hindu concepts. Differences with regional Hindu culture are visible in the greater egalitarianism between husbands and wives. For instance, a Catholic wife calls her husband by his first name, something a Hindu woman would never do. However, even Catholic women refer to their husbands as *bhatkar* (landlord), *ghorkar* (head of the house) or, more simply, *tou* (He).

The message of particular Christian texts corresponds with Hindu ideas regarding the status of a husband (as *patidev*, husband-god) or the conduct of a devoted wife (*pativrata stri*). The following text from Saint Paul to the Ephesians (5: 22–25), for instance, is often used for the wedding mass in Goa.

> Wives, submit yourselves unto your own husbands, as unto the Lord. For the husband is the head of the wife, even as Christ is the head of the church; and he is the saviour of the body. Therefore, as the church is subject unto Christ, so let the wives be to their own husbands in everything. Husbands, love your wives, even as Christ also loved the church, and gave himself for it (*New American Bible*).

There are certain elements of patriarchy in the Catholic marriage ceremony. The principle of patrilocality is assumed. The marriage itself takes place in the husband's parish church. A bride attends services at her husband's parish church, though she may continue to visit her natal village or town on the occasion of church feasts there. In the Catholic ceremony, the bride enters the church on the arm of her father and is handed over to her husband at the altar. The notion of the virgin bride entering from the care of her father into that of her husband seems to be similar, in some respects, to the idea of *kanyadan*.

It is from this complex interweaving of cultures that the notion of the good Goan Catholic girl/woman is derived. She dresses modestly and decently and embodies virtue and morality. A girl 'is another's wealth'. She belongs to another family. This idea influences deeply the socialization of daughters. No blemish should attach to their character or else it will be difficult to find them husbands. Girls learn to be modest and demure in their deportment. A careful watch is kept over them after they attain sexual maturity. They are taught to show great restraint in their demeanour. Posture should be reserved and proper. A girl should sit with her legs together, feet carefully out of sight. Aimless roaming is not for young girls. They are taught to be careful about when, where and with whom they go on trips outside the home.

Notions of circumspection and modesty feed into the prevailing ideas about the appropriate conduct for a bride. Shyness and demureness are qualities valued in a bride. The mimosa plant is referred to in Konkani as *loji hokol* (shy bride), for it closes its leaves when touched. Other ideas and practices underline a woman's subordination. Women who raise their voices in front of their affines or fight and quarrel with their husbands are considered bad (*vaitt*). A woman is expected to submit to her husband's will. She must not be pushy and argumentative. It is not unknown for a woman in Goa, particularly in the early years of marriage, to be told by her husband to return to her natal home because of disobedience and intransigence or until she has learnt certain household skills.

Thus, within Goan Catholic culture, there is scarcely any equivocation about the notions regarding a woman's place in her marital home either in terms of her relations with her husband's kin or the service and sacrifice associated with marriage. As we shall see in the blessings given to a young bride in a later chapter, a woman is expected to put her husband's interests and those of his family first, not her own happiness or that of her natal kin. A bride is supposed to show herself willing to accept the duties assigned to her in her husband's house and be pliant before him and his senior relatives. She is also expected to influence her husband to the good. Popular culture reverberates with such ideas. In the field one comes across notions such as this: 'A good woman makes the home. She guides the children and keeps the husband (*ghov*) straight'. Or, 'If a man does not think too much, it is all right. But a woman must think deeply about her actions for the future'. Even more bluntly, one might hear that 'a man thinks with his loins, a woman with her mind and heart'.

Notions of inauspiciousness are associated with widowhood among both Goan Catholics and Hindus. For instance, widows are not permitted or expected to play a prominent role in marriage celebrations. Ideas about inheritance further underline the inferior position of women. These shall be explored more closely later, but a little may be said here. A woman is entitled to maintenance and shelter in her natal home or her brother's until she marries, and in her husband's home after marriage. Entitlement, however, simultaneously implicates disinheritance, transient membership and conditional rights (see Palriwala 1996; Robinson 1999; Visvanathan 1989). Concepts of patriliny and patrilocal residence are deeply embedded in the culture. A woman has residual rights—to support, to residential space in the marital/natal home and to gifts at her marriage and other occasions—but not to a share in property. A man's ancestral property is divided between his sons.

A woman's rights are, moreover, contingent on her brother's goodwill and/or on her keeping her husband and his family happy. Her dependence on her husband and his senior kin is explicitly underlined thereby. In her husband's home, good behaviour as a *sun* (daughter-in-law) is expected of her. In the absence of her husband or of support from him and his family, a woman's position in the marital home can become very vulnerable. We have already seen that a bride can be asked to return to her natal home until she learns to work and to conduct herself in accordance with the expectations of her husband and his family.

I have shown in Chapter Five how Christianity tends to initiate patrifocal tendencies within matrilineal cultures. Visvanathan (1993a) records that the Syrian Christian wedding rite draws an association between Christ and the bridegroom. The reading from the Ephesians quoted above is employed, further underlining the homology between Christ and the husband. Accordingly, 'the love of wives must be submissive and dependent' (ibid.: 108). A woman is said to 'be married' (*ketichu*), she does not 'marry'. Her role is rendered passive, her husband 'marries' her (*ketti*). His is the active role. Hence, the bridegroom enters the church first and takes his place at the altar. Unless he is present at the altar, the bride cannot enter.

The relationship of husband to wife is articulated even more clearly in verses that follow at the end of the wedding rite. They stress that a bride must leave her family for her husband who in turn must love her and treat her with kindness.

If naked, he must clothe her; if hungry, he must feed her, if thirsty, he must give her to drink. As she loves her own life, she must love

> him and, adhering to the commandments, she must live with him
> in love and tenderness (Visvanathan 1993a: 108).

At the end of the wedding rite, the bride must change into the *sari* that has been given to her by the groom. She now belongs to him and his family.

Christianity also introduced a contradictory strain. The Catholic church regards marriage as bringing together by mutual consent two consenting adults. While parental consent is required, the husband-wife relation is made central and their separate and willing consent to the marriage is a must. Husband and wife, man and woman, are equal in this notion of marriage. At the altar, both are asked if they have come to marry 'freely and of [their] own consent'. Widow remarriage is not disallowed within Christianity and Christianity also brings along other role possibilities for women. There is the introduction of the idea of becoming a nun and devoting one's life to Christ in sacred celibacy. Women were also often significant in spreading the faith, particularly within Protestantism.

It must be acknowledged that most communities are but reluctant recipients of the novel trends. In Goa or among Syrian Christians, marriage is still considered a transaction between families, not just between individuals and their parents. It is the parents and other elders who decide on marriage partners. Though the couple concerned may be consulted, this is often a formality. Girls, in particular, are supposed to go along with what their families decide for them. Marriage implicates for a woman the entire set of expectations about her behaviour in her marital home and towards the members of her husband's family that I have already described above.

Indeed, marriage is considered the destiny of a woman and spinsterhood is not an ideal. While it is acceptable for a woman to become a nun and 'offer her life to God', the cultural norm is still that it is within marriage that a woman has her proper role. Socialization patterns train girls for marriage. They are taught the skills they will require as married women: needlework, culinary skills and the like. A nun's role is often described as a spiritual marriage. The nun is the 'bride' of Christ and when she goes to join the order she is sent with her dowry, just as if she was marrying. The dowry usually consists of things she might need such as linen and even money and jewellery, though these will be kept by the order she joins.

CONCLUSION

This chapter has traversed considerable terrain, exploring the whole caste question as well as bringing up issues related to other forms of stratification and differentiation within Christian communities. The theme of gender differences in socialization and ideas about sexuality and behaviour raises interesting queries. Certain denominations of Christianity introduced the idea of sacred male celibacy embodied by the priest. However, the idea of male celibacy rarely ran into great difficulty. Was this because a priest's sacred power was believed to derive from his celibacy? Great ascetic powers are closely associated with celibacy in Hindu discourses, for instance.

Differences in economic position have been accentuated across many communities over the last few decades. Migration, the breakdown of caste-specific trades and the opening up of the urban economic sector have contributed to making available, many more opportunities for employment. Caplan (1987) speaks of the constitution of urban Christian classes. However, the kinds of formations he speaks of, might be more appropriately viewed as status groups. They are not castes, but they do not ignore caste altogether. Caste position along with access to economic resources, education and a particular 'style of life' are important in their construction. Even where the formation of such 'classes' is not clearly discernible, differences in wealth stratify families and lead to enormous jostling for improvement in social and economic position (see Robinson 1998; Ram 1991).

Upward mobility is consolidated and sometimes achieved through marriage, and dowry, particularly the cash component of it, is the critical axis around which the efforts and struggles revolve. Dowry 'rates' have spiralled in the process of families vying with each other to secure the groom with the greatest economic prospects within the appropriate caste category. The details of this entire process are charted more thoroughly in Chapter Five. This chapter has looked more specifically at status as caste, and its implications for social relationships. The Dumontian

perspective proved inadequate for an understanding of caste con-
figurations in Christian communities and was critically reviewed.

There are many strands that emerge that might be worth
pursuit: the modes of political and social differentiation among
'casteless' Christian groups, the shifts in the caste structure of
communities with the changes brought about by modernization,
patterns of gender differentiation and their implications for the
organization of space, the allotment of resources and the negotiation of kinship relations and responsibilities. What has the
modern economy and migration meant for gender roles and
regulations? Are gender differences standard across the economic
and social orders? What are the ways in which caste and economic
position work to organize gender distinctions in a community?

Despite some contradictory trends, the Christian and, in particular, the Catholic perception of gender roles and responsibilities is not unambiguously liberating for women. It would be fascinating to study sermons preached in different local contexts
to understand the ways in which these ideas have been communicated and interpreted. The work that men and women do for
and in the church needs deeper analysis, the levels of their involvement and the kinds of tasks they are usually assigned. It
would be of considerable interest to explore gender differences in
participation in cults and church activities across the boundaries of class and status.

4

NEGOTIATING TRADITIONS:
CONSONANCE AND CONFLICT

INTRODUCTION

A narrative of Indian Christianity takes us almost imperceptibly
into the realm of cultural convergence and communication, dialogue and dispute. While the concept of 'syncretism' or the notion
of 'composite culture' have framed many discussions regarding this
interaction (Diehl 1965; D'Souza 1975; Godwin 1972; Gomes
1987), a much greater degree of sophistication has begun to make
itself present in the literature. Syncretism is, indeed, an extremely
alluring concept, not least perhaps because it seems particularly apt for the south Asian context. Isn't everything in India
(and south Asia in general) so fluid and easily transmissible
(Daniel 1984; Dumont 1980; Trawick 1990)? The fluidity of cultures should not, however, blind us to the modes of signifying
difference. Differences sometimes become manifest in the very
mediation of them.

If syncretism implies the harmonious interaction of different
religious traditions untouched by any foul implications of contestation and struggle, power and politics, then its value in the
Indian context is even more dubious. And we should enquire
further when viewing patterns of interaction. Christianity may
take from Hinduism, but this is not always the case. Hinduism
is not everywhere the base environment, somehow already there,
established and constant. Sometimes, both Christianity and
Hinduism *simultaneously* impact on a different religious and cultural environment. This is what happened among some tribal
communities in the north-east of India. Christianity might take

from these other cultural environments, from Islam for instance or from a particular tribal worldview. Or it might get 'Hindu' ideas through the grid of Islam, or vice versa. Perhaps processes are more complicated than they appear at first sight and some amount of historicization would be essential when understanding the ways in which they work.

The notion of 'composite culture' leaves unaddressed, the question of the negotiation of boundaries. Taking their existence for granted, it rarely enquires into the mechanisms of framing difference. The dichotomy of the 'great' and the 'little' traditions otherwise constructed as the 'doctrinal' and the 'folk'.or the 'text' and the 'context' dominated a great deal of anthropological writing on religion. Most such writing tends to view the 'great' tradition as a static body of essential doctrine, belief and practice. The idea of the 'great' tradition as a systematized set of scripture or doctrine that is standard across times and cultures, abstracts it so entirely from the domain of history that it is unable to perceive the particularity often sculpted in the shape of that tradition. We saw in the last chapter that particular notions of hierarchy were quite compatible with European Christianity during a certain period. And this in contradiction of the received notion that Christianity is doctrinally an egalitarian faith.

Another difficulty with this construction emerges when religio-cultural ingredients traceable to local or indigenous influences are assumed to be only remnants, which will soon fade and give way to the universal great tradition. This allows the dichotomy to be permeated with an implicit hierarchy, permitting covert entry of the idea that one set of traditions is authentic and enduring, the other somehow erroneous and fleeting. The dwindling away of the presumed remnants is not evidenced by contemporary ethnographies. Changes in the relation between Christianity and local traditions is not arbitrary, but may be linked to shifting social and political contexts. More recent writing on Christianity in India (Bayly 1989; Dube 1992, 1995; Mosse 1986; Ram 1991; Robinson 1997, 1998) has configured the terms of the debate rather differently and we shall pursue the themes in greater depth presently. All the literature is rich in materials though, for us to employ in defining issues of relevance or raising worthwhile questions for future study.

CONSTRUCTING BOUNDARIES, MEDIATING TRADITIONS

Among Christian Mukkuvars and Paravas, *jati* boundaries operated as the limits of the community. In other cases, as in Goa, the Christian community was forged out of the conversion of different castes. One is, therefore, interested both in intercaste relations within particular communities and in the construction and mediation of boundaries between Christians and their neighbours in different regions. While the issue of caste has been discussed in the earlier chapter, we have yet to address the question of how Christian groups communicate and mediate differences with their surrounding society.

One of the most remarkable cases is that of Kerala's Syrian Christians. It is of immense interest to try and understand how this fish, pork and beef-eating group of Christians managed to negotiate their status in Kerala society in such a way that they were, and continue to be, held in high regard and indeed, for a long period, acted as pollution neutralizers for their Hindu neighbours in certain contexts. This participation by the Syrian Christians in the moral codes of high-caste Hindu society, however, never completely erased the differences between the groups.

The history of the Syrians shows that they resembled elite south Indian Muslim trading communities in that they were separate from the 'Hindus' but integrated in terms of regional cultural attributes and had a strong sense of their geographical and vocational mobility. They came to own large tracts of land probably as rewards for their service to the Hindu rulers of the Malabar region. They were also granted titles and various kinds of honours and these defined them as a high ranking group within the local hierarchy (Bayly 1989; Neill 1984). As a high caste group, Kerala's Syrians maintained themselves distinct from other (later) Christian converts in the region. They had their own churches and the separate Syriac rites.

It appears that like the Nayars, the Syrian Christians too had a long past of cultivating warrior skills and serving the various ruling chiefs. The local rulers treated the Syrians with the honour due to such client warrior groups. The patronage of the rulers extended to making benefactions to Syrian churches. The Syrians adhered to the rules of ritual purity held by the high caste Nayars and in the region's social hierarchy, were accorded the same position. In fact, they were even granted the right of access to Hindu temples and sacred territory. Syrians of prominent families were patrons and sponsors at Hindu temple festivals. As mentioned earlier, they also often acted as pollution neutralizers. For example, provisions purchased for a Hindu temple could be purified before use by the touch of a Syrian Christian (Fuller 1976).

Ethnographic accounts of contemporary Syrian Christians also shows the extent of their participation in regional social and moral codes. Visvanathan (1993a) describes how at points, the boundaries between the Syrians and the Hindus is extremely blurred, as in the rituals of house-building or in ideas relating to astrology. The ceremonies of birth and marriage also manifest many similarities with Hindu custom, particularly in the use of ritual substances such as sandalwood paste, milk, flowers, areca nut and rice. Hindu symbolic codes, ideas about ceremonial foods and prestations, therefore, inform the domestic ceremonies in all life-affirming rituals.

However, the boundaries between Hindu groups and the Christians do not entirely disappear. Each group maintains its individuality within Kerala society, aware of and accepting similarities as well as differences. Though their cultic traditions have absorbed much from regional cultures, the inner life of the Kerala Syrian community is significantly ordered by liturgical obligations and by its specifically Christian ethic and world view. Death rituals express Christian canonical themes very distinctly, especially in the ideas concerning life-after-death and the anticipation of the final judgement (Visvanathan 1993a). It is suggested that the particular location of the Syrian Christians within Kerala's social structure permitted them to shield their uniqueness while participating, with great honour, in the region's cultural traditions. Their incorporation as a *jati*, on a par with the Nayars, ensured that their internal *jati* culture and traditions could remain distinct and respected as such by other groups, while they maintained their status by following the prevailing norms for inter-*jati* interaction.

If the Kerala instance marks out a group that integrated itself harmoniously with the traditions and codes of high caste Hindu society, it also shows, I would suggest, how much such a group might assimilate from Islamic culture. Kerala's population is approximately one quarter each Muslim and Christian, and one-half Hindu. These fractions may have been somewhat different earlier, but Kerala has long had substantial Muslim and Christian populations. Hence, it is not surprising that Islamic traditions should interweave with Christian ones, as much as Hindu traditions do. Bayly (1989: 263–65) gives a rich description showing that the Syrian Christian cult centred around the Mylapore shrine of Saint Thomas had considerable overlap not only with the south Indian cult of Murukan-Subrahmanya but also with the cults of Muslim *pirs* in the nearby regions. The tradition of Saint Thomas attributes his death to the wound of an arrow or lance which, aimed at a peacock, hit him by mistake.

The motif of the peacock is tantalizingly rich in symbolic possibilities. Early Christian iconography depicts the peacock as a symbol of the resurrection and in one south Indian version of the martrydom, the saint is said to have been shot by a hunter aiming at the most beautiful of a pride of peacocks. The bird dies and is transformed into a human being, revealed as Thomas. As the wounded bird rises into the air, it leaves behind a human footprint on a slab of stone. Certainly, the glorious entry of the saint in heaven following upon his death is prefigured in such a depiction (Bayly 1989: 264).

The motif also binds in with prevailing south Indian traditions. The peacock is the preferred *vahana* of Murukan, the Shaivite deity, just as the lance is one of his typical markers. Other forms of the merging of traditions are perceived. South Indian cults, both Hindu and Muslim, often revere what are said to be the foot impressions of divine and saintly beings. Like some of the forest *pirs* of the Kerala Muslim tradition, the saint was also said to be a creature of the wilds, retreating to a jungle cave and ultimately, falling victim to a forest hunter (Bayly 1989: 264).

Clearly, I would like to argue, the modes of assimilation are not confined to what Christianity adopts from 'Hinduism'. Certain strands within Hinduism assume greater relevance. In the case of the Syrians, it is said to be the warrior traditions: the traditions of the Nayars or the cult of the warrior divinity Murukan. Moreover, the sharing of traditions extends here to regional Islam as well. South Indian Sufi traditions and the Shaivite one had in common the theme of the wounding of the divine being and his subsequent resurrection (Bayly 1989). Syrian Christianity may have absorbed something of Hindu warrior traditions filtered through Muslim cults or perhaps something of Muslim *pir* traditions captured within the Murukan complex.

Patterns of interaction and assimilation may not always be quite so harmonious. There are contexts in which a Christian group's relationship with Hinduism for instance, may assume a particularly antagonistic form. In contrast to our narrative of the Syrian Christians, the ethnography on Mukkuvar popular Christianity shows that its relationship with Hinduism is much more problematically defined. This is a fact that is no doubt linked to the Mukkuvar's very lowly position within the south Indian social hierarchy.

Mukkuvar popular Christianity goes far beyond the doctrinal limits set by the Catholic church. It takes particular strands from Tamil Hinduism, in turn re-configuring and subverting these. But it is not the Brahmanic Hinduism of the high-castes that the Mukkuvars draw on. Rather, Mukkuvar popular religion takes from Tamil non-Sanskritic traditions, though even here the relationship is somewhat uneasy. The tension is most clearly elaborated in the Mukkuvar conceptualization of the feminine divine: the disjunction between her benign and evil forms (Ram 1991: 62). While the image of Mary is dominant in Mukkuvar popular Christianity, all reference to her virginity, a motif so critical in Catholic theological discourse, is suppressed and she is revered simply and unequivocally in her maternal aspect as Maataa. No longer fettered to her role as Mediatrix between those who implore her and her divine Son, she is worshipped as a divine being in her own right.

The Mukkuvar Christian Maataa has, moreover, some qualities akin to the Tamil village goddess, particularly in her power to heal through possession. There is, in fact, a certain ambiguity here because it appears that sometimes the Maataa is viewed as both causing and curing disease. Mukkuvar religion also has a place for Hindu female divinities, such as the non-Sanskritic female village deity Eseki and her companions SuDalai MaaDan and Vannara MaaDan. Within Tamil Hinduism, Eseki has both harmful and redemptive powers in her capacity as a village goddess, and she is worshipped more prominently by the castes who are low in the social order. In this form and in her power to inflict wrath and destruction, the goddess inverts the Sanskritic image of the female divine as the submissive consort of a male deity. By opening its boundaries to the entry of Eseki and her companions, Mukkuvar popular Christianity both sets itself as a distance from Sanskritic imaginings and establishes a close but contentious relationship with Tamil lower Hinduism (ibid: 61–75).

In the popular Catholicism of the Mukkuvar, the goddess Eseki is stripped of her redemptive capacities. It is the Maataa who retains the benign powers of healing. Eseki and her two companions are viewed as purely evil and destructive beings. Ram's ethnography (1991) elucidates how the battles are fought on the terrain of faith healing. The healer's body may be possessed by the Maataa or one of several saints, usually Saint Anthony or Saint Michael. In the course of the healing process, Hindu gods and goddesses are often held responsible for the misfortune faced by the Christians. Eseki and her companions are turned from deities to demons and rage, through the victims they possess, against the divine Maataa and the saints (ibid.: 102–3).

> [Possessed] Girls: *Ei paaTi* (old woman)—can you tell everyone what kind of a demon I am?
> Healer: I know how tormented you are already. I will send you even greater torment until you leave.
> [Possessed] Girls: Do you expect us to believe that you are Mikheel (Saint Michael)? If everyone could turn into a Michael, what is the point of coming into a shrine? People may as well stay at home! In fact, it is not Michael at all—only Cholla (SuDalai) MaaDan pretending to be Michael...

The Mukkuvar fisherfolk are despised by the culturally ascendant upper-caste Hindus but, as they make their living outside the framework of agrarian society, they are not dependent on the latter for their material sustenance. The contests between the Hindu and Christian divinities, waged on the battleground of sickness and healing, may be viewed as encapsulating the antagonism of the fisherfolk to agrarian Hindu caste society. Hindu gods and goddesses are the principal targets of the healers' rebukes. They are said to be the cause of Christian illness and adversity. The relationship of antagonism is condensed in the representation of Eseki as Mary's destructive, demonic Other. This relationship captures the ambivalent, indeed even hostile, stance of the Mukkuvars to caste Hindu society (see Ram 1991).

It is therefore an expression of the autonomy of the Mukkuvar's religious identity that they are able to incorporate Hindu divinities while defining them, in opposition to the benevolent Maataa, as unrelentingly evil. This autonomy can be achieved, it has been suggested, in part because of the separation of these fisherfolk from the social and economic world of the agrarian caste system. What the ethnography illustrates, therefore, is that even while sacred boundaries may be fluid and permit divinities across the divide, if one might so put it, to converse with each other, the relationship with Hindu deities may be contested rather than simply syncretic. The working of the goddess tradition into Mukkuvar popular Christianity, and the redefining it receives on this terrain, simultaneously enables engagement with particular strands of Tamil culture as well as representation, by the Christians, of their separate religious affiliation.

The Paravas of the Coromandel coast were converted to Christianity by the Portuguese about the same time as the Mukkuvar in the sixteenth century. Their position in the regional social structure was akin to that of the Mukkuvar, in that they too were a low-caste coastal community outside the domain of agriculture. However, the Paravas appear to have negotiated their position rather differently from the Mukkuvar and their ability and motivation to do so must have arisen in part because of their access to wealth from the revenues of maritime trade and a certain amount of prestige from their participation in that trade. As pearl fishers, the Paravas benefitted from pre-colonial maritime business and considered themselves the guardians of the coastline. Parava histories draw on these images of the past to construct the community as a regal one (see Roche 1984).

Kshatriya identity is assumed and the mythical lineage of the Paravas perceives them as the direct descendants of the gods. They are sometimes said to be the progeny of Shiva and Parvati, their profession being a result of divine ordinance. Paravas used to good effect, the symbols of Christian identity to shore up their claims to royal origins. Shunned by the high castes, like the Mukkuvar, their resistance was not confined to projecting their battles onto divine mediators in the realms of thaumaturgy.

Far more prosperous than the Mukkuvar, their access to wealth and then to education after conversion, ensured that they could attempt to spread out, urbanize, acquire new skills and enter different professions. All these aided in the process of upward social mobility.

It has been noted earlier how conversion consolidated *jati* identity among the Paravas. The Paravas appear to have adopted, with considerable enthusiasm, the insignia and marks of Christian and Portuguese nobility and high rank. The caste head or *jathithalaivan* wore a gold cross and chain and assumed the title of 'Senhor dos Senhores'. It clearly served the purpose of the Portuguese to patronize this group and its leader the *jathithalaivan*, for they could then recruit the skilled labour of the Paravas to keep the activities on this 'fishery coast' running smoothly. Moreover, by offering the Paravas protection from sea-faring Muslim groups in the region, the Portuguese were able to bind them in clientele and to extract some of the profits of the trade in pearls (Bayly 1989; Roche 1984).

For the Paravas too, the relationship was very beneficial. Their appropriation of Christian customs and practices served to render their caste identity much more cohesive and to lend legitimacy to their claims for Kshatriya status. For the Paravas, as Bayly suggests, elements of a Christian lifestyle combined with their existing codes of moral behaviour to create a unique caste *dharma* (1989: 332). The Paravas retained a series of specialist service castes including barbers and washermen in clientage. Corporate identity was maintained by the strict rule of endogamy and the orthodox marriage was one performed as a sacramental act between caste individuals in the presence of the priest at church. The assumption of Christian names and patronymics by the Paravas underlines their separate religious identity and this is combined with the fact that most Paravas retain no recollection of their pre-conversion family names. It is also a mechanism employed to undergird their bid for upward mobility. Parava historians, for instance, contended that the Portuguese gave only them the right to use these patronymics in recognition of their status. Such a privilege did not extend to other maritime castes along the coast (Roche 1984).

Undoubtedly, for the Paravas, tightening the boundaries of caste around the symbols of Christian identity became crucial for their social aspirations. Their position differs both from that of the Syrian Christians and the Mukkuvars. For the Syrians, maintaining their status was critical; the Mukkuvars lacked the wherewithal to back a claim for higher rank. They distanced themselves and assumed a posture of antagonism towards caste society. The Paravas wanted to be recognized and to move up as an élite group in the caste hierarchy. Their economic success and movement into new trades and occupations was an enormously enabling factor. The traditions of *jati* endogamy and of retaining the services of client castes were basic to maintaining the cohesion of the group. These combined with critical inputs from their Christian patrons. For instance, pushing from memory their low origins, the Paravas took on Christian names and patronymics, associated with the Portuguese nobility. Together, such mechanisms reinforced the corporate identity of the *jati* and set it on its upward climb.

PANTHEONS AND PROCESSIONS

As a function both of their location within milieu often steeped in Hindu ethos, and their separation from it through their distinct religious identity, many groups developed ideas about a complex pantheon of Christian divine beings and the ritual modes by which their power could be accessed parallel to those existing about deities within Hinduism. Throughout western and southern India these ideas developed more fully, given the complex practices associated with temple festivals that they could draw on. Catholicism, with its panoply of saints and the different advocations of the Virgin, was much more likely to partake of such traditions. The divine benches of particular Protestant traditions, were much barer, offering less scope perhaps for more flamboyant devotionalism.

In any case, Catholicism in these regions typically had its feast days, processions and cults and its forms of worship incorporated many aspects of regional devotional traditions. Mosse (1994c: 305–6) gives a detailed account of the Catholic cult of saints in a village in Tamil Nadu's Ramnad district. Christianity in this region did not come with colonial rule. Rather, it trickled into these hinterland regions through trade and pilgrimage networks, following on conversions by the Portuguese along the coast in the sixteenth and seventeenth centuries. It was the Jesuits of the Madurai mission who gradually extended their control over the Christian traditions of this region.

Christians are a tiny minority in Tamil Nadu's population, living effectively in a Hindu social and cultural environment. Mosse's picture helps us to situate another comparative example of the construction and mediation of identity of a Christian group and to relate it to the instances already analyzed. The Jesuits in charge of the Ramnad mission encouraged devotion to the saints, even while they rejected outright anything they associated with the Hindu religion. This encouragement led to the development of complex ideas about a Catholic pantheon that was parallel to the Hindu divine universe. Christian villages evolved forms of worship for their rich calendar of saints' feasts that included processions and the making of offerings and vows. All these were available within the sacred traditions of local Hinduism.

One can argue that there are at least three levels in the divine hierarchy. At the highest levels, the cultic traditions are distinct and separate. The deities of the great tradition of Brahmanical Hinduism are seen to belong to a different universe from the Trinity of Christian divinity. The rites conducted within the churches by ordained priests belong to one domain, the rites performed by the Brahman priest to another (Mosse 1994c: 306). The interpenetration of cults is rare at this level. At the next level, though, the level of Mary and the saints and of the different Hindu village gods and goddesses, the intermesh increases. Catholic saints are included in the pantheon of the Hindus. Christians participate to greater or lesser extents in the worship of Hindu deities, particularly at annual temple festivals. At the final stage, much lower down in the hierarchy of the gods, at the level of ghosts and sundry divine agents of adversity, the interaction in cultic activity is at its greatest (see also Caplan 1987; Robinson 1998). This area of cultic ritual will be examined in greater detail below.

As in some other regions of India, Mary is worshipped as a divine being in her own right and is not confined to her role as Mother of Christ. In fact, it appears that she and Christ together delegate power to the saints, whose power is seen as derivative. She is viewed as entirely benevolent, a representation that calls to mind the image of her held by the south Indian Mukkuvar. In fact, in western India too, Mary is the embodiment of all that constitutes the good sacred; ghosts (*bhut*) have a more ambiguous, potentially harmful quality (Godwin 1972). Saint James is the patron of the village described by Mosse, who guards its territory. The Hindu deities of the village are subordinate to the authority of Saint James. The god Muniaiyar is represented as guarding the south door of Saint James' church and punishing those who make false oaths in the church. Muniaiyar is in fact, here, only playing a role he already plays for the Hindu village god Aiyanar: that of subordinate or guardian deity (Mosse 1994c: 313).

Thus, while Saint James is said to violently punish those who offend him, the actual punitive role is assigned to his 'guardian deity', the Hindu god Muniaiyar. Christian divinities retain the pure and holy powers; the more violent ones are projected onto their Hindu divine subordinates. Nevertheless, the demonization of the Hindu gods and goddesses that we saw among the Mukkuvar does not take place. What really occurs is a split between benevolent and violent powers of the Christian deities. Saint James derives his power from Christ and the Virgin, yet his power is more violent and more circumscribed than theirs. They are benign. Their power is universal. He is more vengeful; his power is limited to the confines of the village. Muniaiyar is said to enact the punishment; but he is acting only on behalf of Saint James and in his name.

Here lies the crux of the difference I perceive with the Mukkuvar representation of the divine. The Mukkuvars demonize Hindu gods and goddesses, holding them responsible for a range of ills and misfortune that the Catholics have to face. This was attributed partly to the antagonistic social relations that the Catholic fisherfolk have with caste Hindu society. With the Ramnad Christians, divine punishment is meted out through subordinate Hindu deities but they are acting out the will of the Christian saint. The reality of the world of Alapuram Catholics is one of shared social interaction with the village Hindus. They are bound together by social and economic ties, by relationships of patronage and clientship, perhaps even kinship. Catholic images of their deities appear to acknowledge the continued relevance of shared interaction with Hindus and their social and divine worlds.

The relationship is hierarchical, however. The supremacy of the Christian divinities is admitted, even while they work out some of their powers through Hindu divine assistants. The hierarchy turns into an absolute divide when viewed outside the social and ritual context of the village. Saint James is perceived not only as a village deity, but also a deity of the 'forest', the world of chaos and disorder outside the realm of structured social life. The 'forest' both really and notionally, as it is mostly employed, is opposed to the village as confusion is to order. However, it is also a world in which the relational understanding of the divine that prevails in the context of the village gives way to absolute values. In the realm of the 'forest', the world of the 'exterior' outside the village, Christian divinities are simply pure and good. Evil is taken on by ghosts, spirits of the dead and Hindu divinities of the lower end of the pantheon. Vannatu Cinnapar or 'Forest Saint Paul', 'Forest Saint Anthony' or Saint Anthony the Hermit (Vannatu Antoniyar) or Saint James in his form as 'saint of the forest' exorcise these demons (Mosse 1994c: 321).

Outside the world of the village, Hindu gods do become demons, purely evil and destructive. The close interaction of Hindus and Christians in everyday social life finds its spiritual parallel in the incorporation of Hindu gods in *village* Christianity. The Hindu divine beings are, however, encompassed by the superordinate power of Christianity and this hierarchical relationship is sharpened into a complete separation when one moves outside the realm of the village, into the 'forest', the more universal world of the non-relational divine. Here all Christian divine forms begin to partake of the untarnished purity that Christ and the Virgin alone claimed in village religion. There is a disjuncture, hence, between Christianity entangled in the social world of village relationships and ritual hierarchy and Christianity as a more universal faith, released from these concerns. In other words, this Christian group like others we have discussed, retains a space for the expression of its separateness from its social and religio-cultural milieu. And, in doing so, participates in the absolute division between 'good' and 'evil', Christian values and pagan ones that its Christian affiliation lends credence to.

I would like to return though, to the world of village religion to bring out much more fully the complex interweaving of traditions that one finds when looking at the celebration of church feasts (see also Robinson 1995, 1998). At the beginning of the festival, usually a 10-day affair, the flag is raised. The raising of the flag symbolizes, for both Hindu and Christian festivals, the movement of the deity from within the sacred precincts to the village as a whole. The flag-pole is not just symbol but embodiment of the divine in the midst of his/her people. The protective role of the deity over the people is captured by reimagining the boundary of the shrine as the boundary of the village as a whole. From the moment the flag is raised up until the end of the festival, residents are not supposed to leave the village for overnight stay and are required to maintain greater moral and sexual purity (Mosse 1994c: 319; Waghorne 1999).

Festivals are marked by ritual processions in which the deity is taken around his/her domains in a distinctive chariot (*ter* in Tamil). He/she receives the offerings of her devotees and returns them in the form of *prasadam*. The Parava festival for Our Lady of Snows at Tuticorin is a lavish affair in which the image of the Virgin is wheeled around the streets surrounding the church on an immense *ter*. The Virgin is considered to be goddess and ruler of the domains she surveys. Her accoutrements and apparel signify her royal status. The deity is shielded by a regal silk umbrella and her *prasadam* in the form of consecrated petals from the garlands that adorn the image and the chariot are distributed among the devotees. The ceremonial exchanges affirm the sovereignty of the Virgin and the loyalty of her subjects (Bayly 1989: 344).

There is no confusion of sacred images though, even while the continuity with Hindu ritual traditions is maintained. At Avur in Pudukkottai district of Tamil Nadu, described by Waghorne (1999), the style of the *ter* closely resembles that used by Hindu temples in the region but there are significant differences. The chariot has three layers of wood rather than six or seven as in Hindu chariots. Each layer is supposed to signify one realm of the Hindu gods. The author, therefore, surmises that the three layers of the Christian chariot signify the Trinity. The carved images on the chariot reference particular events from the life of Christ or that of the saints. The image of the Risen Christ is draped in the auspicious (and pure) attire of the Brahman: silk *dhoti* and upper cloth of white silk with a gold border draped over the shoulders. The devotees hold up their inverted umbrellas to receive the *prasadam* of blessed flowers that adorned the chariot.

The intricate weaving of signs establishes and mediates differences. It is critical that the chariot procession records the rule of the Christian divine over his or her subjects. It is not a Hindu divinity being worshipped, under the 'garb' of Christian images. Neither can we argue that the continued presence of Hindu symbols and ritual elements at these celebrations denotes falseness of faith among the Christian believers. We need to examine more carefully, as I have tried to show above, the different ways in which and the varying levels at which boundaries are drawn and signified. Also, we might wish to remember that these are historical processes and thus, there could well be changes over time. When the religious landscape, as Bayly shows in her work, was one which centred around kings, renunciants and goddesses, the 'declaration' as it were of a much more exclusive religious identity was less crucial. It came in a later period, perhaps hastened in part by the disruptive processes and impact of colonial rule.

One of the best examples has been documented by Bayly, who shows that in the case of the Syrian Christians (1989: 290–94), the colonial period saw a dramatic deterioration in the relations between Syrians and Hindus of the higher castes. The policies of the colonial authorities led to a disruption in the elaborate systems of exchange and joint mechanisms of celebrating temple and church festivals which had existed earlier between the Syrian Christians and the higher Hindu castes. The colonial authorities seemed to think that the Syrians had been forced to contribute to temple festivals and, in fact, ordered a cut in what they conceived of as wasteful expenditure on such festivals. Grants were now made to Syrian churches and this, among other things, exacerbated the tension between the groups. The Syrians had also begun to experience social and economic pressure due to the diminished position of their patrons, the rajas, who entered into tributary alliances with the British. Missionaries in the region added to the general turbulence by equating low-caste Christian converts with the Syrians and campaigning for rights and honours for them at par with the latter.

All this led to greater distinctions being drawn between the Syrians and upper-caste Hindus. By the end of the nineteenth century, Syrians were regularly kept out of Hindu festivals. There were often violent conflicts between the groups. The missionary drive to 'reform' the heathen-influenced rites and practices of the Syrians led to tensions and splinter groups within the community itself. It became a matter of greater importance to fight one's rivals within the community—in court battles for church treasury control or the like—than to regain lost ground with the high-caste Hindus. Tactical conversions of the low castes by the various confessional divisions were initiated on the understanding that greater legitimacy would be accorded legal claims that were based on such progressive action to uplift disadvantaged groups. Syrian social relations with the high-caste Hindus were quite radically transformed. In other words, the relations of a Christian group with particular sections of Hindu society is not something that remains static for all time but might be altered by changing social, political and economic circumstances.

Does Hinduism itself never assimilate from Christianity? Is it always already there, lending and never receiving? Perhaps we need more detailed studies, but Mosse's (1986: 452–53) account of a Hindu goddess in a local area where Christianity has been around for some three centuries or so, gives a fascinating glimpse of the kind of intricate interweaving of traditions that could be revealed. The representation of the Virgin as having only 'cool', benign powers has already been referred to. Sexuality and death are banished from her immaculate presence, crushed in the form of the serpent beneath her feet. Desire, power and the capacity for unpredictability and evil are projected onto various Hindu goddesses. Catholics visit Hindu goddesses when they are infected with *amma noy* (mother diseases).

Catholics implicitly view the Hindu goddess as manifesting the complementary opposite of the Virgin's benign powers. However, Hindus also appear to attribute to the ordinarily violent local virgin goddesses, some of the features associated with Mary, apart from the fact that they worship Mary herself at her major shrines. At Aranmanakaria, there is a shrine to a Hindu virgin goddess. The shrine lies outside the village and the deity is carried into the settlement during village festivals. The virgin goddess has her own festival at which people gather in huge numbers. The goddess is known as 'child birth chaste'. Myths about the foundation of the shrine link the goddess to milk, a substance that is associated with coolness, *and* childbirth.

A shepherdess in the advanced stages of pregnancy came past the spot. Suddenly she fell into labour. Her husband went to the village to call the midwife, and while he was gone an (old) woman in white...came to the woman, told her not to worry and delivered the child. Realising that the Goddess was in that place they built a shrine to her (Mosse 1986: 453).

The Virgin Mary is unaffected by pollution, related to menstruation or birth. Her female devotees may approach her images and worship when they are menstruating or during the period of pollution following birth. Virgin goddesses within the Hindu tradition are known to be angered if approached by women in states of pollution. Unlike other virgin goddesses though, the one here is like the Virgin Mary apparently unaffected by and tolerant towards birth pollution. In fact, in another version of the myth, the shepherdess actually gives birth within the shrine's *sanctum sanctorum*.

The goddess's power is conceived of as benevolent, indulgent and cool. At her festival, her devotees walk over burning coals spread out in front of her shrine in fulfilment of their various vows. The goddess is said to cool the ignited coals, turning them to flower petals. It is difficult, as Mosse (1986: 453) says, 'to decide in which direction the cultural borrowing has gone, but we cannot rule out the possibility of an influence of over 300 years of popular Catholicism on local Hindu cults'.

THE AGRO-RITUAL ROUND

One of the major areas of the interaction of cultures arises particularly in the case of rural, agricultural communities. Where Hindus and Christians live together within the same agro-ecological niche and where they order their lives by the local agricultural round, they very often maintain similar celebrations and rituals (see D'Souza 1993). The extent to which this might happen will vary extensively from context to context and will depend a lot on several factors including the particular pattern of the conversion (individual or group, for instance), the degree of institutionalization of the religious activity in the area (the availability of priests and pastors) and the relationship that missionaries had with the local people and their indigenous traditions. This last is structured, in turn, by the moment and motive of the activity of mission itself.

In Goa, conversion was backed by the Inquisition and the regime was ordered by a strict repugnance of all indigenous 'substance'. Moreover, conversion was largely confined to the districts touching the coast, where whole villages were converted to the new faith.[1] Converts lived surrounded by the inland Hindu districts, but had fewer day-to-day interactions with Hindus for most of the period of colonial rule. Social separateness was achieved, though cultural traditions remained alive. In this region, the pattern of agricultural rituals remains in place with a difference. In terms of their substance, the signs and symbols of the Hindu and Christian religious calendars differ, but they are mapped out in structurally similar ways. What has altered is the religious content or matter carried by the symbols; their relational composition stays the same. The missionaries seem to have permitted Christian rituals to retain indigenous form and function as long as the object of worship was a Christian divinity and the means of worship, such as prayers, were Christian in content. One finds, therefore, that the annual church calendar is moulded in significant ways to accommodate to the rhythms of the indigenous socio-ritual and agricultural world.

An instance may be elaborated, that of the harvest. In the regional Hindu religio-agricultural calendar, the festive year begins with the celebration of the harvest centred around the festival of the birth of Lord Ganesh, which falls around August or early September. The worship of Ganesh is usually performed by the head of the family. An earthen image of the deity is installed on a dais under an arch decorated with flowers, leaves, fruits and vegetables. The principal offering is 21 *modaks* served on a banana leaf (the *modak* is a sweet prepared from lentils and unrefined sugar). On the following day, the new paddy is offered to the deity. In most houses, the deity is immersed on this day, being carried to a nearby river in procession, to the accompaniment of prayers and songs.

The celebration of the harvest feast among Catholics shows traces of continuity with indigenous traditions. As we had recorded earlier (Chapter 2), it is in fact possible that the missionaries themselves realized the importance of the harvest for the converts and instituted its celebration within the church calendar. However that may be, the celebrations are usually centred around the feast of a particular saint, which falls during the harvest season. These might be different for different villages. For instance, in the village studied by the author, the feast is instituted in the name of Saint Bartholomew. However, other villages celebrate it in the name of Saint Lawrence (10 August), Saint Ignatius of Loyola (3 August) or on the day commemorating the Assumption of Our Lady (15 August).

The feast usually commences with a procession to the paddy fields, accompanied by the sounds of beating drums and the playing of music. The parish priest ritually cuts a few ears of grain and these are carried back to the church. As the ears of grain may be placed before the image of Ganesh, so some ears of grain are placed in the arms of the statue of Saint Bartholomew, in whose name the feast is celebrated. Other items such as the flowers and vegetables of the season are also placed at the altar in offering. Interestingly, Catholics refer to the feast as *amchi Gonsha*, *our* Ganesh (Robinson 1995, 1998).

From a different area, the Tanjore, Salem and Ramnad districts of Tamil Nadu, we get another picture of harvest celebrations (see Diehl 1965; Mosse 1986) and rituals marking the different phases of the agricultural cycle. This is an area where Christians are still in small numbers and a majority of them belong to the Dalit community. They interact with Hindus in the course of everyday life. They are connected by bonds of marriage and kinship to Dalits who are not Christian converts. They join with other Dalits in the struggle to earn a livelihood and work for Hindu high-caste landowners. They are also entrusted with the traditional duty of their caste—to perform as musicians at festivals when the village deities are being worshipped. They are part of an intricate web of relations that embeds them socially and culturally in the regional Hindu agrarian caste society. Moreover, this is a hinterland region that was for a long time not very securely linked with the institutionalized church, whose presence was felt more strongly in the coastal areas.

Catholics in this region usually work on fields or shepherd cattle belonging to the more wealthy Hindu high-caste landholders. They maintain the rituals accompanying the first ploughing like their Hindu neighbours. Ploughing and sowing take place at the auspicious moments prescribed for them astrologically and are accompanied by a series of rites. The harvest festival is Pongal and it is the day that the rice of the new harvest is cooked for the first time. The next day is Mattup Pongal or the day when cattle are worshipped and feasted. Christians who labour on the farms of Hindu landowners will perform the ceremonies along with Hindu or Dalit labourers. They receive clothes and gifts from the landlord and with the other workers offer Pongal (the new cooked rice) and incense to the cattle in worship (see Diehl 1965).

Santal converts in central India were few in number and the converted were highly dependent on missionaries for mediation with the British law courts in their disputes against landlords and for employment and educational assistance. This suggests that the likelihood of the success of the prohibitions imposed by the missionaries may have been greater. The missionaries tended to isolate the small Christian communities from their non-Christian neighbours and to insist on adherence to a strict set of norms. The drinking of rice-beer and dancing were prohibited and the converts were forbidden from participating in any of the traditional religio-cultural ceremonies. The main seasonal festival was *Sohrae* or the harvest festival, which falls in the month of *Pus* (December–January). At *Sohrae*, the Santals bless their cattle, make offerings of thanksgiving to their village and ancestral spirits and partake in general rejoicing and merrymaking. A lot of rice beer is drunk and the Santal code of sexual conduct is relaxed for the period of the festivities.

The missionaries considered the drinking and sexual licence associated with the festival as sinful and encouraged the Santal converts to celebrate Christmas week, temporally the closest annual Christian celebration to the *Sohrae*, as their harvest festival. Christmas songs are sung to *Sohrae* tunes and tea, puffed and parched rice and sweets are shared. On New Year's day, the new paddy is offered at the Mass and each household receives a basketful of paddy. Games and competitions are organized (see Troisi 1979). While the celebration of Christmas week in this way does incorporate some of the elements of the traditional harvest festival, it still ensures that the Christian Santals remain separate from and outside of the communal celebrations organized by those who have not converted.

LIFE-CYCLE RITUALS

What one would like to examine, of course, is the ways in which traditions interweave in the making of thaumaturgical discourses.

However, that has been retained as subject for another chapter, where it flows into another related discussion, that of the range of modern charismatic and pentecostal movements and their mediation of indigenous notions of health and fortune. Here, I turn to something else: the celebration of life-cycle rituals among different Christian groups. This is the area of individual or family-based ritual and takes us into a realm that is both separate from and interlinked with the kinds of collective church celebrations, rites and cults we have been analyzing above.

Among most Christian communities, the rituals of birth, marriage and death partake of both Christian symbolism and the associations emanating from local cultural contexts. Some communities have also retained rituals relating to a girl's first menstruation. Among Goan Catholics, the rite of baptism is similar to the Hindu naming (*namakarana*) ceremony because in both, the child is seen as becoming a part of the family and a particular lineage group. At baptism, the child 'becomes Christian'. He or she is also named at this time. Before baptism, a child is simply that (*bhurgem*-child). At baptism, the child is given a name. The name of the child will be that by which she/he is known within her/his family, circle of kin and in her/his caste group. If the child is from a high caste, she/he will be addressed by name by members of the lower castes, who will also add the respectful suffix *bab* (for a male) or *bai* (for a female). Giving the child a name makes the child an individual and confers on him/her social identity. The child is formally brought within the fold of society: family, caste group and religious community.

The blessing of the child with holy water and oil in the baptismal ceremony incorporates her/him as a member of the Catholic church. The child's identification with the collective is inscribed, as it were, on his/her body. The child's name is recorded in the baptismal register of the church and she/he achieves, thus, 'juridic personhood' in the eyes of the church. The child assumes membership of the religious community. The rite signifies the removal of sin and the priest prays that the influence of Satan remains far from the child. By the rite of baptism then, the way is opened to salvation as a member of the church. God's grace is viewed as flowing into the child through the mediation of the priest. The channel having been opened, so to speak, sacramental grace will be communicated to the baptized person at different moments of life, including marriage and death.

The celebrations of baptism are carried back into the home of the baptized child. Friends and relatives gather and a litany of prayers is sung. A festive meal is served to all. The priest is also usually invited to the repast and, on the occasions witnessed by the author, he prayed over the meal for the health and welfare of the child and its family. While the church ceremony is couched in the language of incorporation into the religious community of the Catholics, the celebrations at the home are situated in a different idiom. All those who are invited for the feast, congratulate the parents of the child on the 'new addition' to the *ghor* (family and lineage group). In this patrilineal society, the compliments on the 'addition to the line' are even more stressed in the case of the birth of a male child. Thus, baptism simultaneously marks a child's membership of the spiritual community, his or her incorporation into the family and identification in caste terms and, in the case of male children in particular, incorporation into the lineage.

Syrian Christian life-cycle rituals, like Goan ones, fuse two different aspects. They link the individual to the church and its canons of beliefs and rites; but they are also rooted in domestic and kinship spheres and animated by socio-cultural codes that express the continuity between the Christians and the regional traditions of Hinduism within which they are situated. The two aspects cannot be easily mapped onto a distinction between church-centred and domestic rituals. Visvanthan suggests this from her ethnography of Kerala's Christians, but the distinction does not work everywhere. In Goan marriage rituals, for instance, the nuptials (*resper*) in the church themselves mediate the ritual separation of a girl from her natal family and her incorporation into her marital home. Further, the Inquisition too attempted to insinuate itself into domestic rituals. Its regime is long dead, but it has left its impress on these rites. Visvanathan herself admits that the domestic and canonical aspects of ritual are linked in complex ways. Domestic rites often 'prepare the key celebrants for the canonical rituals through the codes of food, prestation and formalized language'. They are 'marked off' and thus prepared for the rite of passage into which they enter within the sacred space of the church (1993a: 102).

Birth rituals, for instance, are initiated much before the rite of baptism and already mark the child as the central subject of ceremonial activity. The child is fed honey and gold in a ritual not long after its birth and prayers are said for its health, joy in life, love of god and service of men. It is prayed that the child will 'run like a deer and sing like a sweet bird'. The first person to feed the child in this ritual, usually the mother's father, mother or brother, is said to pass onto the child his or her character. Visvanathan suggests that the ceremony 'integrates the new-born within the circumference of human existence by the ritual act of the transmission of qualities from adult to infant' (1993a: 121). Word is sent around to the child's father's house and he and his relatives come for a festive meal.

Baptism takes place 56 days after the child's birth, when the mother's birth pollution is said to have ended. The child is washed and anointed with holy oils and is also given bread and wine as at Communion. A name is conferred on the child and he or she is also confirmed into the church as part of the same rite. The water that is used to baptize the child is prayed over by the priest so that it is invested with the following qualities. It should 'be comforting, joyful, a symbol of the death and Resurrection of the Christ'. It 'should purify the soul and body, it should loosen the bonds of evil, forgive sins, give light to body and soul, and symbolize the baptism of rebirth' (Visvanathan 1993a: 127).

Some Christian communities have retained rituals connected with the marking of a girl's entrance into puberty. The first menstruation is marked among Tamil Nadu's rural Christians, for instance, as among the Mukkuvar fisherfolk (see Fuller 1976; Mosse 1996; Ram 1991). The observation of this ritual may not however, have much to do with the maintenance of notions of 'pollution'. Though menstrual blood is polluting, it is the subsequent menstrual periods that are more hedged around by restrictive measures. The first menstruation in many parts of southern India is an auspicious occasion for it celebrates the girl's fertility and marks her readiness for marriage. Ram (1991: 84) makes the intriguing suggestion that the disappearance or suppression of the rites of menarche among certain convert communities may be related to the extent of the influence of an ideology that views women's sexuality in entirely negative and shameful terms. Christianity's deep discomfort with female sexuality, which has its highest expression in the dogma of Mary's eternal virginity, is certainly well-established.

Marriage ceremonies in many communities and marriage customs related to choice of spouse, prohibited or prescripted categories of marriage partners and the like remain distinctly similar to practices of the wider, surrounding society. Here I will speak a little about marriage rituals and the ways in which they mediate Christian and indigenous notions. In a later chapter a more detailed discussion of the ideas of kinship, family and inheritance, marriage payments and the like will be undertaken. Christianity often interfered in marriage customs, prohibiting some because they were considered to be contrary to Christian living and ethics. Among the central Indian tribal Santals, for instance, the practice of *sindradan*, smearing the bride's forehead with vermilion, was prohibited. The converts no longer wore their bridal wear in the tribe's traditional saffron colour. It was the exchange of rings in front of the priest in church that came to be the central matrimonial rite (Troisi 1979).

I have already suggested possible reasons for the success of these kinds of prohibitory dictates among the Santals. The coercive potential of the regime in Goa has also been referred to. The Inquisition prohibited a wide range of customs and rituals associated with marriage including the singing of particular songs and the use of certain ritual substances. Various transformations took place, but one finds that the structure and meaning of celebrations connected with marriage remain the same among Catholics and Hindus.

An interesting instance comes from the ceremony of setting up the stoves for the cooking that will be done during the marriage. Some days prior to the wedding, a *mantov* or tent of bamboo sticks and palm leaves is usually set up behind the house and stoves of mud (*choolhas*) are made. New cooking pots are placed on them. Behind the stoves, a cross made of palm leaves is placed by the Christians and the Lord's Prayer and some other prayers are said thanking God on the happy occasion and invoking His divine blessing that everything goes well. The auspicious time for setting up the *choolhas* among Hindus and Christians of the region is around mid-day. It is an hour of fulfilment and 'completeness', when the sun is high in the sky and people are replete (*bor potache*).

The Inquisition prohibited Catholics from placing betel leaves or areca nuts under the *choolhas* set up at marriages (Priolkar

1961). These substances are used by Hindus to symbolize the auspiciousness of the occasion. They appear to have been replaced by the symbol of the cross, acceptable within Christianity. A Christian prayer is said for God's blessings. Christian symbols dominate but the web of signification reveals (or perhaps conceals?) other associations which are the complement of the Hindu ritual. Certainly, despite their differences, the ceremonial substances are equally identified with notions of the auspicious and celebratory aspect of the moment.

Marriage is a parting of the ways for a girl and her natal family: she moves to her husband's home and her visits back to her own home begin to decrease over time, especially when she lives a distance away. This is a patrilineal, patrilocal society. Inheritance passes down the male line and girls are considered transitory members of their natal home, 'guests' who go away after a while and therefore cannot be given a share in paternal landed property. Instead, the rights of girls are limited to receiving 'dowry', consisting of jewellery, clothes and items that might be useful in their new homes. The stress on the male line combined with minimal rights accorded to daughters remains among most caste-based agrarian Christian communities, where land is the main inheritable property.

Interestingly, in cases where conversion takes place against a background of matrilineal and matrilocal structures, as in some north-eastern tribal communities, it has the effect of creating and strengthening a patrifocal tendency (see Natarajan 1977; Nongbri 1980). While I shall be discussing these issues more elaborately in another chapter, I might mention that one of the possible reasons for this is the patriarchal inclination of many denominations of Christianity, such as Catholicism, for instance. When Christian communities emerge out of patrifocal Hinduism, as in Goa or among Kerala's Syrian Christians, I have suggested that the convergence of various social, material and cultural elements tends towards the continuation, and perhaps reinforcement, of this structure.

In the light of this, it is interesting to view the ceremony of the bride's send-off among Goan Catholics and some other western Indian Christian groups (see D'Souza 1993; Godwin 1972). Marriages take place in the groom's village or hamlet and after the celebrations and feasting, the bride's family and friends have to return. They are usually escorted to the borders of the village, where the ceremony of the boundary or *shim* is performed. This ceremony underlines the separation of the bride from her natal home; she has been transferred to another family, which now assumes rights over her fertility and labour, her productive and reproductive capacities. A line is drawn along the path, usually using *feni*, a local liquor. The bride's family step across it, she remains on the other side. She cannot cross the line; her place is now her husband's home and his village. The bride's parents will usually bless their daughter that she may bear children and will enjoin her to perform her duties obediently as wife and daughter-in-law in her marital home.

Ceremonies of marriage among Syrian Christians involve intricate negotiations concerning the *stridhanam* (dowry). *Stridhanam* actually changes hands at the *virunnu*, an occasion of formal feasting. The acceptance of the *stridhanam* becomes a symbol of the future incorporation of the daughter-in-law into her marital family. At the *virunnu*, the male elder (*karnavan*) of the girl's family stands on a mat in the centre of the room with his elbows crossed horizontally, as the details of the marriage are all announced clearly and the amount of the dowry is specified. After the dowry has changed hands, the *karnavans* of both families embrace formally and a prayer is said by the parish priest asking for blessings on the match. The marriage can only take place after the girl's family gifts four per cent of the dowry to the church. She is then given a letter called a *desakuri*, which effectively permits her to affiliate herself to her husband's church. On this occasion, a certain amount of the dowry is gifted to the bridegroom's church. These ceremonies, like the domestic rituals I will describe now, formally mark out the families and persons entering into alliance and prepare them for the marriage solemnities.

Each step in the preparation for the marriage is a ritual step and is accompanied by a number of celebratory songs: songs for the bride's ceremonial bath the day before her marriage, songs for the moment she dons her clothes, songs for the journey from her natal home. On the day of the marriage, the ritual of *guru dakshina* is performed. The groom in his house and the bride in hers makes an offering of money wrapped in a betel leaf to his or her first teacher. This is a moment in the ritual of separation, the *yatra choikuga* (taking leave to go on a journey). The teacher blesses the bride or groom. After this, senior relatives will come forward to give their blessings. This completes the series of rituals which set apart the bride and the groom for the ceremonies that will centre around them and their union in the church.

The wedding rite implicitly follows Pauline understandings of Christian marriage as holy and sacred, meant not for erotic love but for the achievement of a greater spirituality. The male symbolism of Christianity assumes dominance when the relationship between groom and bride is compared to that between Christ and his church (Visvanathan 1993a). If the husband is Christ himself, the wife, as his church, is under holy obligation to submit to his (divine) will. The central symbol of the sacred union of bride and groom is the tying of the *thali*, referred to as a cross in the church ceremony, by the groom around the neck of the bride. Then the *mantrakodi* (the *sari* gifted to the bride by the groom) is placed over the head and shoulders of the bride. The couple's hands are joined by the priest and the blessings of the saints, Mary and Christ are called upon them.

The stress on the transfer of the bride to the house of the groom is brought out by the verse which emphasizes that the bride must leave her family to live with her husband and he must, in turn, treat her with love and kindness. At the end of the wedding service, the couple goes to the groom's house for the wedding feast. At this time, the bride is required to change into the *mantrakodi*, symbolizing that she now belongs to the groom and his family. It is not without significance that this ceremonial garment must be worn new and unwashed (Visvanathan 1993a: 108).

At the groom's house, the groom takes his wife's right hand and they enter together with the right foot forward. The groom takes the bride to his mother and places her in her care (*ammae epichu*). The groom's sister or father's sister takes a small *kindi* (bronze vessel with a spout) containing water along with a *kinni* (shallow container) with a betel leaf, some water and a fine muslin cloth containing some powdered rice and some grains of unhusked rice. A hole is made in the cloth. The woman dips the muslin cloth in the water and touches the brow of the bride and the groom thrice. Visvanathan (1993a: 109) suggests that the rite signifies fertility and auspiciousness. Its elements certainly constitute symbols of sexuality and procreation. The *kindi* stands for the masculine principle, the *kinni* for the feminine. Unhusked rice is said to symbolize reproduction and powdered rice, consummation.

The *stridhanam* is not the only material wealth that is part of the exchanges of marriage. After the wedding feast, more gift-giving occurs. One notices that the element of reciprocity is small; most of the gift-giving is unidirectional. And in terms of the monetary value of the gifts, that which the bride's side gives far exceeds what is given by the groom's side. The bride's mother's brother is the first to receive a gift of cloth from the groom's side. He gifts the groom a gold ring in exchange. The bride's mother and paternal and maternal grandmothers are also given gifts of cloth, which they reciprocate with gold rings. After the marriage, prestations flow at regular intervals from the bride's house. The bride brings linen, vessels and other household items at the time of marriage. The gift-giving continues on certain festive occasions and on the occasions of the birth of her children.

Death rituals are framed by the Christian discourses regarding life in Christ after death, but in many communities they also partake of Hindu symbols and notions. These notions often appear when one looks at the organization of household rituals. Christian death in Goa, for instance, is informed by ideas regarding widowhood, the concept of inauspiciousness and the honour due to ancestors, which bring it into accord with regional Hindu traditions. Sometimes, such ideas are concealed behind or enmeshed with Christian beliefs to a very great extent. Among Goan Catholics, death is regarded as the moment of release of the Christian soul from the ties and struggles of life. The body might be reduced to dust but the soul awaits communion with the Maker. Bells toll to announce the death of someone in the village. Neighbours and relations start arriving at the house where a death has taken place. The body is washed and dressed and laid in the front room, the head towards the family altar. The bereaved sit close to the body to receive condolences.

The ornamentation of the body follows certain socio-cultural codes. It is the female body in particular, that is marked in death by the presence or absence of jewellery, symbolizing different social states. A married woman, whose husband is alive, is dressed as a bride in all her wedding finery. Her body is adorned with gold jewellery and she wears the glass bangles that symbolize the married state among all communities in the region. A widow's body is unadorned by jewellery and is buried in black. A widower too is usually dressed in black or sober shades, while a man whose wife is alive is dressed like a bridegroom. The body is identified as Christian by the cross which is placed between the hands as they are joined together on the chest. A rosary may also be entwined between the fingers.

At the time of the funeral, kin, friends and neighbours gather at the house. The priest comes to pray over the body, which is lifted by four close male kin and carried to the church. The mourners walk on either side of the bier. The priest intones the rosary or other prayers, to which the people give appropriate response. The body is taken into the church and laid before the altar. Mass is celebrated. After the Mass, the coffin is carried to the cemetery, where the final prayers are said. The readings, sermon and final prayers express the realization that mourning for the dead person is part of coming to terms with the loss, for relatives and friends. The individual death is also located within a framework that gives it meaning in terms of collective beliefs. Continuity is underlined by the understanding that the dead person enters the mystical body of the church. The last journey is not an end but a prelude to a new beginning: resurrection and union with Christ 'when He comes again in glory'.

The coffin is lowered into the grave and each person shovels a spadeful of earth over it. When a man dies, his widow's glass bangles are broken on the edge of the coffin before it is lowered into the grave. Once home after the funeral, all jewellery other than the wedding ring is removed. A woman who has been widowed does not take a lead role in marriages or other festive celebrations. The room where the person died is kept locked with a lit lamp in it. The liminal period, during which earthly bonds still exercise a pull on the dead person, continues until the requiem service is held a month after the death. At the end of this period, the room is opened.

A few days after the death of her husband, a woman visits her brother's house. She is accompanied by another widow from her affinal village. In her brother's house, she enters the kitchen where food, a dish of oil and a set of black garments are kept for her. The woman accompanying her oils and combs out her hair. The two eat, take the clothes and leave. They are usually not received by anyone during this visit because the sight of a widow, as in regional Hindu ideas, is considered inauspicious. The visit however, marks the end of the period of intense mourning during which the widow would not have moved out of her house. Through the symbol of the garments, it signals her re-entry into the social world in her new station.

A month after the death, a requiem service is held. This is the 'Month's Mind'. Informants say that with this Mass the dead person's soul is 'at peace'. The Mass is an occasion to pray, according to Christian tradition, for the 'peace of the dead person's soul' and that his 'sins may be forgiven'. People also assert that a person's incorporation into the realm of ancestors is completed by this ritual. Before the Month's Mind, the spirit of a dead person is still about. With the ceremony, the spirit is assimilated with the ancestral shades; the deceased becomes a *purvoz* (ancestor), is entitled to respect and honour and must be remembered on appropriate occasions. On occasions of marriage, for instance, among both Christians and Hindus, a meal is served in honour of the ancestors of the bride and the groom.

While the holding of meals in honour of ancestors was prohibited among the converts by the Inquisition, it persisted and this is perhaps because it was reframed by particular Christian notions. The Hindu feast is known as *mellianche jevan* and certain categories of relatives, usually affinal, are feasted in the name of the ancestors. Among Catholics, the meal is termed the *bhikran jevan* and poor persons (*bhikarin*) from the village are invited for it. It is conceivable to argue that the Inquisition forced this transformation. The shift may have become a means whereby the meal for ancestors could be preserved by merging it with notions acceptable within the Christian tradition—a simple act of kindness to the poor and deprived.

Thus, the Month's Mind not only preserves its Christian purpose of praying for the peace of the soul of the Christian dead but also, very interestingly, appears to function as a parallel to the Hindu ceremony of *sapindikarana*, which is held at the end of the mourning period for a dead person. This is the occasion on which the dead person is united with the ancestral spirits of the house. At this ceremony, four pots are filled with water, camphor and sesame seed. Three are offered to the *pitras* or *purvoz* and the fourth to the *preta* (the ghost of the person who has just died). The contents of the fourth pot are then poured into the other three. With this, the *preta* joins the ranks of the *pitras* (ancestors).

Death rituals among the Syrian Christians bring out the clarity of Christian ideas regarding eternal life after death, though they also show, in part, the impress of regional traditions. The dying person is turned facing east (the direction associated with the Second Coming of Christ). Hands are folded across the chest in an attitude of prayer. The priest comes to the house and recites the creed of faith. Eyes, nose, ears, mouth, hands, legs, feet and stomach are anointed with holy oil. Holy communion may be administered. With the completion of these rites, the person dies a Christian death, a death 'in the faith'. Following death, the eldest son closes the eyes of the dead person. Neighbours and kin arrive at the house, bringing food and beverages. The kitchen fires of the house remain unlit.

The body is bathed and dressed in clean clothes. It is laid in a hearse and taken to the church. Much of the funeral service in the church relates to the idea of Christ's Second Coming. Christ will come again at the Last Judgement and save those who have lived good Christian lives. Holy oil is poured over the body a second time and the priest prays for the peace of the soul of the deceased. The body is lowered into the grave with a veil over the face and prayers are recited referring to the soul's entry into the presence of the Lord. The death marked a period of fasting for all present. On return to the house, vegetarian food is served to all, breaking the fast. The house is in mourning though, and meat, fish, eggs, curds, milk and ghee are not served.

For 40 days, the house remains in mourning, signified by fasting and abstinence. It is believed that the soul of the dead person is still around during this period, not freed yet from attachment to earthly bonds. The third, ninth, 16th and 30th days after the death are marked by mourning feasts with vegetarian food. For 40 days, the lamp in the room where the person died remains lit. The 41st day signifies the end of the mourning period and is marked by the cooking and serving of non-vegetarian food (Visvanathan 1993a: 132–44). The dietary restrictions initiated by death partly assimilate Hindu death taboos and notions regarding the auspicious and inauspicious, while the discourse on the expectation of life after death is explicitly framed by Christian traditions. In earlier centuries, Syrian death rites had paralleled Hindu ceremonies to a greater extent (see Chapter Two). The distinctions instituted themselves much more later, perhaps as a result of the struggles between the communities during the colonial period.

Mosse attempts to explicate more distinctly the relationship between Christian death rituals and concepts and practices of purity and impurity arising out of caste beliefs and ideology (1996: 463–65). Christian funerals resemble those of Hindus, for in the Alapuram village of Tamil Nadu studied, both communities bury their dead. Death is marked by wailing and the tolling of bells. A Paraiyar drummer announces the death to relatives, who bring the customary gifts of rice and cloth. The sons and daughters of the deceased wash themselves in the village tank. The village barber collects water to wash the body and prepares the sacred thread for the chief mourner to wear across his body, from right to left. Agnatic relatives pour oil and cleansing powder on the dead person's body and the orifices are sealed with turmeric and betel leaf. Ankles, toes and wrists are tied together with strips from a new *sari* by the barber, and a coin (later to be given to the washerman) is placed on the forehead. The body is washed and dressed and placed on a wooden bier.

The priest, wearing black vestments, comes from the church to bless the body, accompanied by altar boys carrying a cross and lighted candles. He circumambulates the body in an anti-clockwise direction, sprinkling holy water and dispensing incense. The bier is taken to the church, accompanied by the tolling of church bells and the keening of Paraiyar women. Paraiyar drummers lead the procession and the barber lets off firecrackers. The bier is rotated in the church to face towards the altar, where the priest in white vestments conducts the funeral Mass. The grave is usually dug by Paraiyar or Chakkiliyar service castes. Women do not usually follow the cortège to the grave. The barber cuts the threads on the body and removes the jewellery. Money and betel leaf are placed on it and collected by the Dalit funeral servants. The barber shaves and removes the sacred thread of the chief mourner, who marks a sign of the cross over the body in the grave. Earth is shovelled over the body and candles and incense sticks left burning at the site. Mourners arrange payments for the drummer and other service castes and take a purificatory bath before returning to the house.

High-caste Utaiyar and Vellalar funerals are along these lines. The lower-caste Natar or Pallar Catholics cannot command the services of the village barber, washerman or drummers. They have their own inferior service castes. For instance, the Pallars are served by a Dalit barber-washerman 'funeral priest' and by Chakkiliyar funeral servants, who perform tasks such as the digging of the grave. On the third day after a death, agnatic relatives pour water on the grave and smooth the earth. They light candles and burn incense at the grave and return home for a wash with oil. The final rite usually occurs after 16 days, during which period there are prohibitions on the holding of weddings, the performance of pilgrimage, the completion of new houses, sexual intercourse and the preparation of certain foods. The final rite consists of the installing of a cross on the grave, the removal of a widow's *thali* and the 'tying of the turban' performed by affinal relatives. The widow bathes and is garlanded with a *sari* before her *thali* is removed and dropped into a dish of cow's milk. The chief mourner is greeted with a tray of turmeric water by the women of the house, when he returns from the cemetery after installing the cross. He is presented with *dhotis* and towels, first by his affinal relatives and then his agnatic ones.

Mosse argues that the theological emphasis in Christian funerals is on rites, such as extreme unction, before death, while Hindu rituals stress rites after death. The popular practice, however, brings both together and Christians take over from Hindus the elaborate set of rites concerned with separating the dead from the living even though they do not share their ideas on the rebirth of the soul. Structurally, Christian and Hindu rituals are similar: they effect a separation and transition between living and dead and work to manage the danger and pollution surrounding any death. The body is bathed and participants wash and prepare themselves against any harmful influences. The journey from the house to the cemetery involves the crossing of the boundaries between the living and the dead. The transition is completed on the 16th day, when heat and impurity are removed and the mourners re-enter social life, renewing ties with affines and others.

Hindus and Christians share a repertoire of symbolic substances and procedures that effect these transformations (Mosse

1996: 466). Cooling and purifying substances include turmeric, cow's milk, betel and water. Particular procedures define sacred spaces, such as circumambulation. Certain operations ward off evil spirits: the lighting of lamps, drumming, letting off firecrackers or the tying of threads. Blocking the orifices protects against pollution, while cutting the threads on the body at the grave effects separation. Christians employ the same ritual specialists as the Hindus at their funerals, as at some other life-cycle ceremonies. Nevertheless, in some ways the church stands outside the realm of distinctions between the pure and the impure (ibid.: 469–71). It is not that inferior castes perform servile tasks such as digging the grave because they are impure; the reverse could be equally true. Purity and impurity are less important in themselves than as an idiom to express relationships of patronage and dependence, dominance and inferiority. Funeral service is referred to as *atimai velai* (servile work), rather than as impure.

'Impure' duties such as drumming or performing funeral service become acceptable when the remuneration is increased and when one can use the kind of drum employed by high-caste temple musicians and on auspicious occasions, such as weddings. The implication of servitude eliminated, the roles are more palatable. While caste distinctions do enter the church in terms of the distribution of rights and honours in festive celebrations, critical ideas of purity and pollution are kept outside (Mosse 1996: 475). The black vestments and anti-clockwise circumambulation of the priest signify the sombre aspect or inauspiciousness of death, rather than impurity. No temple would allow the entry of a deceased body; the Catholic dead are taken inside the church. During the funeral rites, the dead person is symbolically identified with Christ. She/he will rise again like Christ who died and rose from the dead. Death is finally understood against the background of Christ's sacrifice. His death redeems the dead and brings them to everlasting life.

CONCLUSION

Several themes and issues have emerged from this chapter and might be briefly recalled. I have argued that syncretism is perhaps too easy a tool to be employed in the study of popular Christianity in India, particularly when what is usually studied is the relationship between Hinduism and Christianity and what the second takes from the first. The comparative perspective I adopt throughout this book enables us to see that while the relationship between Hinduism and Christianity is critical to the narrative of Christian communities in many parts of the country, it is not the whole story. In some places, tribal religions or Islam are equally if not more significant and they have to be woven into our accounts.

Where Christianity is in obvious interaction with Hinduism, the nature of that contact need not be self-evident. There is no guarantee that Christianity or Hinduism are always in agreeable association with each other. Or that Christianity borrows from Hinduism wholesale, rather than from specific strands of it. It has been established very definitely that the fact that assimilation does take place may never be read as an indicator that differences do not persist or go unrecognized. The extent and form of association as well as the nature of differences that persist have been related to a complex configuration of elements. The temper and constitution of the religious and political regimes within which the interaction between missionaries and local people gets established plays a critical role for the kind of popular Christianity that develops in a particular area.

Hinduism may give as well as receive, and the relationship between Christianity and local traditions rarely remains a static one. Shifting social and cultural circumstances are likely to reconfigure it in different ways. We still need more careful enquiry into many issues. Greater ethnographic detail is required with regard to Christian iconography and festive regalia, the symbols and substances different Christian groups employ on different ritual occasions and the meanings they give to them. We need more and deeper accounts of the nature of the relationship between Christian and other divine hierarchies. Do the forms of reverence addressed to each differ? Are they assigned different terrains? Different forms and degrees of sacred power? How are gender and status implicated in the construction of the pantheons and the styles of devotion?

In general, the somewhat richer ethnographic material relates to the south and west of India; central, north and eastern Christian communities are ripe for further analysis. Caste communities have been better served by anthropologists and sociologists than tribal ones. Christian traditions require differentiation: does Catholicism actually encourage greater assimilation than Protestantism? Or why has there been greater ethnographic interest in Catholic communities? In addition to Hinduism, the relationship of Christianity with Islamic and Sufi traditions needs more careful examination in those areas where it is likely to be of some relevance. The aim is not accretion, but a more sophisticated understanding of patterns of interpenetration across traditions and cultures than has often been achieved.

NOTE

1. Goa may be divided into the 'Old Conquests' taken over by the Portuguese in 1510 and the 'New Conquests', which they did not command until the eighteenth century. The 'Old Conquests' consist of the districts now identified as Tiswadi, Mormugao, Salcete and Bardez. It is in this area that the large-scale conversions we have spoken of in Chapter Two took place. The area of the 'New Conquests' consisting of Pernem, Ponda, Bicholim, Canacona, Sanguem, Quepem and Satari came under Portuguese control in the late 1700s. These areas remained largely Hindu and mass conversions were not initiated here, partly due to the new political realities facing the Portuguese at this time given the context of the changing nature of their power relations, both with Indian states and other European countries. Hence, Goan Catholics were surrounded by Hindu areas, but were largely socially distinct. Cultural continuities remained though, indexed in part by songs recording the converts' concern with and consciousness of Hindu ways or the shared ritual traditions that emerge in a variety of contexts.

5

KINSHIP, MARRIAGE AND INHERITANCE: THE SOCIAL AND MATERIAL IMPLICATIONS OF CONVERSION

Several changes in family organization, the categorization of kin and the material arrangements regarding the ownership and distribution of property accompanied conversion in different parts of the country. Communities also devised strategies to ensure that prevailing customs, of kinship or inheritance or gender valuation, did not undergo enormous transformation. The kinds of changes initiated varied with the type of community: tribal or caste, matrilineal or patrilineal. The overwhelming interest in caste often meant that kinship was sidelined in much of the literature (see Mosse 1986: 67).

In some studies, an understanding of the patterns of gift-exchange and alliance and shifts in property relations has been attempted. Less attention, though, has been paid to the analysis of kin categories, terminology or behaviour. Fewer attempts have been made to map out the ways in which Christian understandings of family and kin relations articulate indigenous notions. How do Christian ideas about the *compadrazgo*, for instance, configure kinship relations in different ways in particular areas? How do the church's rules on marriage conflict with indigenous ideas about ideal alliance partners? This chapter will try and draw out from the available literature, some material to elucidate the kinship dimension of religious conversion.

PATRIFOCALITY IN A MATRILINEAL SYSTEM

It was with the kinship structures of tribal communities, and particularly of matrilineal ones, that Christianity clashed with a certain violence. I have argued already that Christianity has a patrifocal tendency and this created tensions within matrilineal communities. Trends towards patrifocality assumed strength. I shall also try and unravel in what ways and why the movement towards the nuclear form of the family is associated with the coming of Christianity. The Khasi are a very interesting case of a matrilineal tribal community having converted to Christianity. As Nongbri notes, 'Christianity being highly normative in its outlook tended to put restrictions on the social behaviour of its converts, which sometimes went against the prevailing norms of the society' (1980: 8).

The Khasi are one of the tribal communities of the north-east that came into contact with Christian missionaries during the British period. I argued earlier that the coming of the British to the hilly regions of the north-east led to enormous social, political and economic disruption in the area. Tribal worldviews were unable to contain or explain the kinds of shifts taking place and the expansion of social and cultural horizons resulting from the integration of these isolated regions with the wider world. The upheaval enabled conversion and was a way of dealing with it. Christianity was the religion of the rulers and brought the material benefits of education and employment. Some of the Ao Nagas, the Khasi and others in the region who converted developed a rapport with and looked for support towards the missionaries in ways that were not always replicated elsewhere. This increased somewhat the chances of changes in their social organization, brought about through missionary influence.

Among the Khasi, traditionally, ancestral property passed down from the mother to the youngest daughter. The youngest daughter was known as the *Khadduh* and she was the heiress and the custodian of the property and the religious cult of the family. She was responsible for the performance of particular rituals. On marriage, the elder daughters were usually allotted plots of land near their mother's house. The most important structure was the Khasi *ing*. The *ing* was constituted by a number of matrilineally related households, which could trace genealogical links with each other. The *ing* worshipped common deities and had a common ancestral cult. Religious occasions were celebrated in the *ing*. Celebrations of birth, marriage and death involved the entire *ing*. The ancestral rituals involving, for instance, the bones of the dead being put into the family cromlech, were also *ing* celebrations (Natarajan 1977; Nongbri 1980).

Conversion slowly began to lead to a decline in the *ing*'s importance, particularly in relation to the performance of its religious functions. The religious fragmentation of the *ing* resulted, due to the loss of the ritual purpose that had held the households together in the *ing*. Consequently, the hold of the mother's brother over the household, critical to the organization of matriliny, also began to decline. In its place, paternal authority increased. The church regarded the father as the head of the family: he played certain key ritual roles such as leading the daughter to the altar at her wedding and giving her in marriage and handing over the child for baptism. With the modification of the *ing*, social and religious customs with which it was centrally associated, began to recede. These included the care of the family cromlechs and memorial stones, funeral ceremonies and ancestor worship. The *ing* also became smaller in size, for families now migrated on a scale not seen before.

Non-matrikin started to assume a greater importance in the changed familial set-up. The *Khadduh*, particularly those residing in urban areas, began to surrender their rights to inheritance, if they had not been divested of them, so that they did not have to fulfil the social and religious obligations expected of them within the traditional system. Some of them did not stay in the ancestral home, but set up new residences with their husbands. They also did not act under as many safeguards from their maternal uncles or brothers as in the old arrangement. Matrilineal inheritance prevailed, but some changes came about. Women depended less on the male relatives in their matriline. They managed independently or came to depend more on their husbands. With the setting up of independent, nuclear residences, importance began to shift from the male matrikin to the husband and father.

The role of the youngest daughter underwent change. She was no longer responsible for the ritual cult. And her mother's brother's supervision of her conduct decreased. Changes in property arrangements meant that the *Khadduh* was deprived of that share in property which accrued to her as the keeper of the family's religion. However, she could and did still inherit other ancestral property, though family members in distress would no longer come to her for assistance. In fact, the *Khadduh* continued to inherit the bulk of property, but now her siblings, male and female, could also be bequeathed a share of the assets. Hence, the *Khadduh* assumed much more centrally, the role of owner of property in place of her earlier significant role as custodian of family wealth and family cult. This really increased her freedom, for she would be able to do with her share in property more or less what she wished, without having to account for her decisions to the male elders in the matriline (Nongbri 1980).

The tendency towards the nuclearization of family arrangements increased, particularly in urban areas. This came about as a consequence of women setting up independent residence with their husbands. Educated Khasi women began to add their husband's surname to their own after marriage. The father's role received greater impetus with the increase in his economic independence and income, that resulted from migration and new forms of employment. He could will his earned income as he pleased. The right to bequeath self-attained property as one wished had existed earlier (Natarajan 1977). It acquired more significance against the background of the easing of earlier inheritance controls, the fact that family arrangements now made wives and children more dependent on the husband/father and on the fact that, with the opening up of economic opportunities, the amount of such property available increased.

THE CLASH OF CHRISTIAN AND TRIBAL MORALITY

Sanctified, monogamous marriage must be said to be the Christian ideal. Divorce is always frowned upon and illegitimacy and sex outside marriage stridently condemned. The missionaries tended to be horrified by what they perceived as tribal permissiveness with regard to matters concerning sex. Tribal traditions could accommodate premarital sex and children born of unmarried mothers. Among the Khasi, courtship was the traditional mode of entering a matrimonial alliance, and the free interaction of the sexes meant that premarital sex and pregnancy were treated with a certain amount of tolerance. Divorce was allowed and illegitimacy was unheard of because a child would belong by birth to its mother's house (Natarajan 1977). The imperative of proving paternity was absent.

Santal norms also permitted divorce and polygyny. A child born out of marriage could be socially reinstated by the following means.

When a child is born to a Santal girl out of wedlock, the girl's father and household are semi-outcasted (*Pante-Begar*) and they can only return to the tribe by arranging a father for the child. This can be done in two ways. First, if a person is proved to be the *genitor*, whether he accepts the paternity or not, he either has to marry the girl or pay for a 'bought husband'. Second, if the village cannot prove who the real father is, then a substitute father is arranged. In both instances, the *Nim Dak Mandi* [naming ceremony] removes all traces of illegitimacy and the child takes the *bongas* [ancestral spirits] of his father (Troisi 1979: 163).

Marriage by purchase of a husband! The missionaries must have recoiled in dismay.

Divorce was also customarily allowed among many tribal groups. Among the Santals, divorce could be granted on the grounds of adultery, sterility or barrenness or the suspicion that the wife practised witchcraft. Either the man or the woman could ask for a divorce. A man could seek divorce on the grounds that his wife was too extravagant and wasted family resources, that she was lazy or constantly ill. A woman could ask for a divorce if her husband could not supply her with all her needs or if he wanted to marry a second wife against her will. The guilty person would have to pay a fine called *chadaodi* or divorce money. If the husband is the one seeking the divorce, he would have to pay the *chadaodi* and could not claim back the bride-price he had paid. If the wife is at fault, her father would have to return the bride-price paid to him at the time of the marriage (Troisi 1979). Divorce was also permitted among the Khasi, for instance, and the remarriage of divorcees raised no problems among most tribal communities (Furer-Haimendorf 1976; Natarajan 1977).

The missionaries opposed the Santal practice of marriage by 'buying' a husband, just as they opposed divorce and premarital sex wherever these were customarily found. Toda polyandrous practices and Santal polygyny were equally appalling in their eyes. Cohabitation, without marriage, that had been permitted among the Khasi was disallowed by the missionaries. The couple was suspended from participation in any Christian rituals until the marriage rite had been performed (Nongbri 1980). Among the Ao and other tribal groups, the missionaries were against the continuation of the dormitory system among their converts. In accordance with this system, older boys and girls did not sleep in their parents' houses, but in separate halls, where they received training in many skills particular to their sex.

Among the Ao Nagas, the boys' dormitories were known as *morung*, and these were central to the organization of social life. The *morung* provided labour teams for village work, trained boys in hunting and other skills and constituted a locus for the organization of many social and cultural activities. The free inter-action of girls and boys was permitted and they often gathered in the evening, after a day's work, for singing and dancing. The missionaries forbade their converts from using the dormitories, for in them they would have to interact with those who had not converted, the 'heathen' (Furer-Haimendorf 1976). They further objected to the unhindered sexual interaction between girls and boys that the system seemed to permit. Among the Christians, families attempted to take over the care and socialization that had been the responsibility of the elders of the *morung*.

THE CHURCH'S LAW OF CONSANGUINITY CONTRADICTS INDIGENOUS RULES OF ALLIANCE

Things become even more interesting and complicated when one realizes that the church also has rules governing marriage and these dictate not only the form of the marriage ceremony or the sacramental character of marriage but also lay down guidelines about who may or may not be married. For instance, the Catho-lic church has elaborate rules regulating matrimonial relations between close kin. For the most part, marriages between cous-ins and other close blood relations is prohibited. The rules of consanguinity prohibit marriage in the direct line of descent between all ancestors and descendants and in the collateral line up to the third degree of relationship. This would include all those related in the direct line such as grandparents, parents and their dependants, and all close relations in the collateral line, such as aunts and uncles, nephews and nieces and cross-cousins and parallel cousins.

Traditional systems of alliance in many parts of India, particu-larly in the south and the west, often permitted cross-cousin mar-riage. Parallel-cousin marriage was not permitted. Sometimes, the cross-cousin was the preferred marriage partner. Bayly (1989) records the fascinating case of Parava Catholic marriages, quoting from a *jati* leader's nineteenth century report. In his report, the Parava leader, Dom Gaspar noted that marriage customs and gift-exchanges among the Catholic Parava remained very similar to those among the wider Tamil Hindu population. Gifts of sandal, rose water, areca nuts, betel nuts, tender coconuts and garlands were presented to the bridegroom by his sisters at the time of the tying of the bride's *thali*. Customary gifts were also made by the bridegroom to the bride's brother.

Dom Gaspar noted further (quoted in Bayly 1989: 336) that:

> in pursuance of the customs of us the bride...ought to be married to her father's sister's sons but it is prevented by our religion and consequently the bridegroom ought to grant tithe [sic] of the dowry obtained by him on such marriage as a gift commonly called waasatpady sucandram to the sister's sons of the bride's father and such donor [sic] should in return of that grant a suit of clothes to the bridegroom and in case of not having granted the above clothes the bridegroom shall deduct a certain sum commonly called anjoo pon and pay the remaining part of the money to them.

Bayly rightly interprets this to mean that the Paravas preserved a 'fictive' marriage system that ran alongside their adherence to Christian rules regarding permissible alliances. Marriages were conducted outside the traditional Tamil alliance system according to which a man's ideal marriage partner (*urimai penn*) is his matrilateral cross-cousin. However, the marriage did not take place until permission, as it were, had been sought by means of the *waasatpady sucandram* of the men who had the first, preferred right to the bride, her father's sister's sons. In other words, the right of the father's sister's sons is acknowledged ritually in the course of the marriage ceremonies when the bridegroom presents them with a part of the dowry he obtains. In turn, perhaps as a sign of the acceptance of the marriage, he is presented with a suit of clothes.

In Goa, the church's rules of consanguinity combined with the institution of the legal right of the daughter to inherit, brought in by the Portuguese, reconfigured kinship and inheritance patterns in complex ways. The prohibition of marriages among close kin prevented a man, in the absence of a natural heir, from marrying his daughter to a close kinsman in order to retain property in the patriline. The Portuguese law giving the daughter rights of inheritance also clashed with the indigenous cultural norm of patriliny. At the time that the Portuguese entered Goa, family property and inheritance in the region were governed by customary laws. In general, property passed down the male line. Widows and unmarried daughters were maintained from the income of a dead man's estate. The daughter's 'share' was the dowry she received when she married (see Derrett 1977).

After conversion in the sixteenth century, the converts were brought under the laws which governed Catholic Portugal at the time. The law on inheritance which governed Portugal and other parts of Catholic Europe had developed out of early Roman law. According to Portuguese inheritance law, a woman could inherit her father's property either exclusively in the absence of a male heir or shared with her brothers (Warner 1976). Widows did not inherit under the law, but got only as much as Hindu law already gave them—the right to maintenance from their husband's estate. The new regulations applied to the converts in Goa, but they consistently appear to have devised strategies to escape from them. Daughters conventionally released their share in ancestral inheritance in favour of their brothers. They rarely took up their share in immovable property. This emerges quite interestingly from what an old woman had to say about her grandmother Maria Ermalinda D'Costa, who was born in 1867.

> Maria's mother was one of two children, the other a boy. Against his parents' wishes, her brother joined the priesthood...Despite the fact that this meant he would have no heirs, half his father's landed property was left to him. This property could be inherited by him...but on his death would, in all likelihood, pass on to the church. Maria's mother took with her, when she married, a dowry consisting of a silver dining set, jewellery and other items that had been bought from the [proceeds of] the sale of the other half of the property...She did receive her share of her father's property but this was in the form of a dowry consisting of movable items (Robinson 1998: 175).

Even today, daughters customarily sign off their rights to ancestral property before they marry. Immovable property is retained in the male line. In the absence of male heirs, the propertied groups devise various means to ensure that property is retained in the patriline. Marriages are sometimes arranged between close patrikin and dispensations are sought from the church to enable such marriages to take place between consanguinous relations. The cases outlined here are from Robinson (1998: 176).

Mathilda D'Mello married her mother's brother's son. Her mother had two brothers. One died at a young age. Since he had no children, his property fell to his brother and sister. It would have to be divided between them and would then be parcelled out amongst their children. To avoid division of the property, the surviving brother and sister agreed to a solution. The property would go to the brother's son and he would marry his father's sister's daughter. Mathilda...married her...matrilateral cousin and their uncle's property came to her husband. Thus, Mathilda was not given a direct share of this immovable property which was retained in the patriline but...she was married to the person who inherited it.

Bernadette Viegas was the last of four children, one boy and three girls. The two...[older] girls were already married when an accident took the life of the only son. The married daughters having been given their dowries, the house and estate would fall to Bernadette... Bernadette was married to her father's brother's son, a boy from the same village.

José Figueiredo, the younger brother of Vincente, had only two daughters and no son. His elder brother had one son and no other children. José's elder daughter, Maria, was married to her father's brother's son. While the younger daughter was married off later with a suitable dowry, the father's land and house devolved upon Maria. Through her marriage, not only was property prevented from going outside the family, but the two branches of the patriline were united.

In all the cases, despite the absence of male heirs, women did not inherit directly. Various strategies were devised to retain property in the patriline. Suitable male blood relations were sought within the close circle of kin. All the marriages that took place contravene the church's rules of consanguinity. To contract such marriages, the Catholics would have needed to procure dispensations from the church. Permission for such marriages was contingent upon the payment of compensation in kind or money. While no dispensation is available for marriages in the direct line of descent, in other cases it is possible to get one *if* a proper case is made for its requirement. The local parish priest had the discretion to dispense with the first, second and third collateral impediments.

In two of the cases, a woman ended up marrying her parallel cousin, her father's brother's son. This kind of marriage is not permitted by indigenous tradition, though matrilateral cross-cousin marriage is customary. Cases of parallel-cousin marriage among Catholics are very rare and one hears of them only in relation to stories such as I have been telling here, stories involving the looming threat of fragmentation of ancestral property or the death of the patriline. I shall speak a little later in this chapter about the daughter's share, which informs in part the set of ideas relating to dowry practices among Catholic Goans and some other Christian communities.

The church's rules on marriage also affected Mosse's Tamil Catholics (1986: 78). The marriage pattern followed by most castes entailed that a man ideally married his father's sister's daughter (FZD). She was his *urimai penn*. When one such marriage had been conducted, the obligation of a man to marry a son to his sister's daughter declined with successive marriages. The alliance is not taken for granted. The girl's qualities and her dowry, the boy's employment and prospects and the pair's horoscopes are factors taken into account. However, there is still a preference for marriage among relatives. FZD marriage and cross-cousin marriage in general do take place among Catholics, though the church's regulations, which may not be dispensed with easily or without cost, appear to have been at least partly responsible for the reduction in their incidence.

THE *COMPADRAZGO* COMPLEX

The complex ways in which kinship may be configured within Christianity emerges from an analysis of ideas surrounding the institution of godparenthood. From a Christian point of view, baptism marks the entry of a new member into the community of the church. Catholic thought views it as superceding the bonds of natural kinship with another bond, the bond of spiritual kinship, kinship between members of the religious community. The *compadrazgo* emerges as an elaboration of this understanding. The *compadrazgo* (see Gudemann 1972) relates to the institution of godparenthood and consists of three sets of relationships.

The first set of relationships is that between parents and child. This is in the realm of 'natural' kinship. It is a blood tie. It is established by birth. The second tie is between the godparents and the parents of the child. The third is the one between godparents and their godchild. The last two ties are 'spiritual' in character. They are established at the moment of baptism. The fact that they are 'spiritual' ties is underlined by the rule that parents cannot act as godparents to their own children and the preference that godparents should not be close relatives of the child or its parents. The accent is on the distinction, in fact the opposition, between the natural ties formed by birth and the bond of spiritual kinship formed with the religious community at baptism.

The church expects godparents to initiate the child into the spiritual community at baptism and to guide and instruct the child in the proper conduct of a Christian life through his or her growing years. It is also expected that godparents will raise or be responsible for their godchild when his or her parents are unable to do so or are deceased. How are godparents looked at by the community? In what relation do they stand to the kinship circle? Among Goan Catholics, there is a definite tendency to select godparents from among the circle of kin, merging rather than separating natural and spiritual kinship. The godparents of the first child and definitely of a male child are chosen from among the father's agnatically-related kin. For girl children and subsequent children, there is sometimes one godparent from the paternal side and one from the maternal side.

Sixteen year-old Savio is an only child. His godfather is his father's younger brother and his godmother, his father's mother.

Michael is the first child of his parents. His father's parents were selected as his godparents.

Antonio and Ana are brother and sister. His godparents are his grandparents on his father's side. Her godparents are her father's elder brother and his wife.

Maria, Joaquim and Filomena are three teenaged siblings. Maria is the oldest. Maria's godparents are her father's sister and her husband. Joaquim is the second child of the family. His godparents are his father's only brother and his wife. Filomena is the last born. Her godmother is her mother's brother and her godmother, her mother's mother.

Christalina's godfather is her father's younger brother and her godmother is her father's mother. Her younger brother Lawrence has
as his godparents his father's elder brother and his wife.

(Examples from Robinson 1998: 154).

Godparents are often a generation older than parents. They are
often close agnates for it is said that children, particularly male
children, belong to the house or *ghor* of their father. Spiritual
relations are not opposed to or distinct from natural ones, they
are superimposed on them. The ties of godparenthood are
mapped upon already existing blood relationships. Baptism is
itself the ritual marker of the birth of a child. It simultaneously
marks a child's membership of the spiritual community and the
family and, in the case of male children in particular, incorporation into the lineage or *ghor*.

Among Goan Catholics, no distinction is made between godparents and blood kin, nor are the responsibilities of godparents defined purely in spiritual terms. They are *soiri* (relatives)
and they give gifts to their godchild at baptism and marriage
and other occasions as other kin would. In fact, in most cases
godparents are relatives and very close ones at that. Catholic
discourse envisages baptism as a kind of giving up. The natural
parents of the child hand over the child to its godparents at
baptism, for initiation into the larger religious community of
the church. Spiritual relationships take precedence over natural
ones in this conception.

Spiritual and natural ties coalesce among Goan Catholics.
Spiritual relationships intensify rather than supercede or oppose natural bonds. We will see a little later that the notion of
joint living is quite strong among Goan Catholics. The eldest
son usually lives with his parents, and brothers often hold property jointly, at least till their father's demise. Even when brothers take up separate residence, they live close to each other and
share in expenses related to the marriage of sisters or maintenance
of aged parents. Children therefore live with or close to their
paternal grandparents and older agnates. Perhaps because these
links are important for the Catholics, they stress them through
compadrazgo ties, adding the weight of religious legitimacy to
bonds already central within kinship discourse and practice.

KINSHIP TERMINOLOGY AND BEHAVIOUR

Few scholars have paid active attention to kinship terms of reference or address among Christian communities. We need to understand Christian kinship terminology for its own sake and for what it might be able to tell us about the modes of negotiation with indigenous patterns of the classification of kin. Kinship terminology has implications for kin behaviour and kin roles and throws some light on ideas about marriage and affinal relations. Mukkuvar kinship terminology conforms with the features of south Indian patterns of kinship in the radical distinction drawn between cross-cousins and parallel cousins. This is in accordance with the south Indian preference for cross-cousin marriage (see Ram 1991: 170).

In Mukkuvar kinship terminology, parallel cousins are assimilated to the status of siblings. Marriage is impossible with them. Male parallel cousins are called *anna* or *thambi* (elder brother and younger brother). Within this group, one's own siblings are each further distinguished by being referred to 'sibling who has been born with oneself'. The main feature of the system is the divide between parallel cousins and cross-cousins. The terms used for the male cross-cousins also describe them as potential bridegrooms. The Mukkuvar, moreover, call the male cross-cousin *more mapillai* or the bridegroom by customary law. After marriage, husband and wife use the same terminology to describe each other's relatives as they employed prior to marriage. This practice can only be understood if one assumes that affines are also consanguineous relatives (Ram 1991: 170).

Mukkuvar kinship terminology shows an equivalence between consanguineal and affinal relatives in terms of classification patterns. Ram (1991: 171) tabulates the list of terms used by a man for his wife's kin. The classification manifests equivalence with consanguineal relatives since the same terms are used for some categories among the latter. A man calls his wife's father and mother *maamaa/maamii*. The same terms are used for mother's brother and mother's brother's wife. A man calls his wife's elder sister *anni/mahini*, using the same terms for his younger brother's wife as well. A wife's younger sister and younger brother are *kolundi* and *machaan* respectively. These terms are also employed for a younger brother's wife and a younger sister's husband respectively. Again, a wife's elder brother and an elder sister's husband are also *machaan*.

We may also look at the terms employed by a wife for her husband's kin (Ram 1991: 171). A woman calls her husband's father and mother *maamaa/maamii*. Her husband's elder sister is called *anni/mahini*, a term also used by the married woman to refer to her elder brother's wife. The same terms are used for the husband's younger sister and a woman's own younger brother's wife. The husband's elder brother is *machaan/ataan*, while his younger brother is called *kolundan*. These terms are also used by a woman for her elder sister's husband and her younger sister's husband respectively.

In consonance with south Indian patterns, Mukkuvar kinship terminology makes no sharp division between wife-givers and wife-takers, a distinction that is critical in other parts of India, particularly in the north. While giving us this wealth of detail, however, Ram is silent on the statistical occurrence of cross-cousin marriages among the Mukkuvar. Most marriages are caste endogamous and take place within the village or, at best, the local district but do they take place predominantly among real or classificatory cross-cousins? The significance of this question, of course, relates to the ban on such marriages by the church. One would like to have more information on whether and under what circumstances such alliances are forged among the Mukkuvar.

Ram's (1991: 168) only help in this direction is a rather oblique reference to the incidence of cross-cousin marriage among castes in the south of India in general. She quotes Beck's tabulation of cross-cousin marriages in Tamil Nadu drawn from different ethnographic accounts, which shows that they vary at between five and 15 per cent of the total number of marriages. Accordingly, she argues that marriage preferences do not necessarily show up in terms of the statistical dominance of the preferred type of alliance among the southern Indian castes. The Dumontian argument of looking at preferential alliance from a structuralist point of view is quoted approvingly by her. She contends therefore that the rules rather than any discernible statistical trends are dominant because the rules serve as a normative model for the society. These models structure kinship behaviour, terminology and the overall ideology of kinship. The model even influences those who do not actually practise it. For instance, hypergamy serves as a 'conscious model' even for north Indian castes for which it is not a custom.

In the absence of other concrete information, presumably this is meant to suggest that the incidence of cross-cousin marriage among the Mukkuvar is low. However, Ram also says that there is an emphasis on *sonda kalyanam* or marriage with one's own relatives. If there are few marriages among cross-cousins in recent times, is this a change from the past? What could be the likely reasons for such a change? Is the incidence of cross-cousin marriage lower than what might be expected (however low that expectation is itself) for the region? Is the Catholic church's prohibition on consanguineous marriages at all relevant for understanding the low incidence of cross-cousin marriages? If the number of marriages among 'one's own relatives' is low, then what does the retention of a terminology which strongly suggests a preference for cross-cousin marriage mean? Is it an attempt to locate non-consanguineous marriages within the regional ideal of *sonda kalyanam*?

From Goa we get another illustration of kinship terms and notions. Catholics and Hindus use very similar kinship terms, though some terms are pronounced differently by them and some Portuguese terms have entered Goan Catholic kinship terminology. The changes probably relate to the influence of the Portuguese language on the local language, Konkani, spoken by converts. Over the long period of Portuguese rule, the Konkani used by Catholics came to contain a number of Romanized or Portuguese words. These were used to express Konkani vocables. Further, Konkani syntax came to reflect that of Portuguese to some extent (Mascarenhas-Keyes 1994). Konkani came to be read and written in the Roman script among the Catholics, a shift which reflected and in turn probably affected the pronunciation of words. Among Hindus, Konkani is usually written in the Devanagari script.

Similarities extend beyond kinship terminology to include ideas about kinship, rules and behaviour. Despite the long reign of European Catholicism, with its particular representation of kinship relations, Goan Catholic kinship resembles regional patterns. In the European Catholic model of kinship, kinship is ego-centred and bilateral. In other words, lines of kinship are viewed as extending bilaterally outwards from any particular 'ego', either male or female. The system is characterized by perfect bilateral symmetry, an equal balance of kin on both sides of ego. This notion of kinship is embedded in Portuguese kin terminology. In Portuguese Catholic kinship an ego, either male or female, refers to all female kin of his or her parent's generation, whether related through the mother or father, as *tia*. Similarly, all male kin of the parent's generation are *tio*. Portuguese terms such as *tio*, *tia* and *primo* and *prima* (male cousin and female cousin) operate in accordance with the European Christian kinship model. This model embraces distant bilateral kin within such inclusive terms as uncle, aunt and cousin. It disallows, as has been noted earlier, marriages among kin who fall within the degrees of prohibition. These include grandparents, parents and their dependents apart from aunts, uncles, nephews, nieces and all manner of cousins.

Goan Catholics view kin very differently. They typically make a distinction between patrikin, their wives and all other wife-takers on the one hand, and matrikin together with wife-givers on the other. The kinship system here, unlike in the south, takes into account the hypergamous patterns of marriage whereby wife-takers are seen as superior to wife-givers (see Vatuk 1969; 1975). An ego is placed in one of the two groups and the kin terms he or she employs would have to be in accord with that placement. Unlike the European system which does not differ for a male or female ego, this system looks different depending on the sex of the ego. A female ego, particularly after marriage, has a very different understanding of the system. She belongs to the group of wife-takers, while her natal family, including her brother, belong to the group of wife-givers.

According to this mode of tracing kinship relations, the group of patrikin including the *kaka* or *titiv* (father's brother), the *baba* or *pai* (father), their wives and other wife-takers, either on the father's side or the mother's are distinguished from wife-givers. These wife-takers would include, for instance, *bhavoji* (father's sister's husband or mother's sister's husband). Wife-givers include the people from the mother's side, particularly the *mama* or *meyno* (mother's brother). The group also includes relatives from the father's side, such as the father's brother's wife's brother, also called *mama*.

The terminological distinction between wife-givers and wife-takers receives expression through particular modes of expected behaviour. A woman must defer to her husband's kin, particularly senior males such as his father and elder brother. She refers to the latter as *der*. Portuguese speaking Catholics might add the honorific *mano* (brother-in-law) to their husband's brother's name while addressing him or referring to him. Wife-takers are treated with much respect when they come to the house and great care must be taken to see that they are well looked after and given no cause for offence. A married woman's natal family usually goes out of its way to ensure that the best is provided in terms of hospitality on such occasions.

It is not surprising that Portuguese terms which have entered the kinship system of Goan Catholics are used in ways that conform with their own ideas of kinship and are not employed in a manner that is cognate with European Catholic usage. Among the Portuguese terms in use are *pai* (father), *mai* (mother) and their cognates *shepai* and *shemai* or *papai* and *mamai* (grandfather and grandmother), *titiv* or *tiv* (uncle), *titin* or *timai* (aunt) and *kunhad* (brother-in-law). These derive from the Portuguese *pai*, *mãe*, *tio*, *tia* and *cunhado* respectively.

Terms such as *pai*, *mai* and *kunhad* are used by the Catholics in a manner that is parallel to the Hindus' use of the terms *baba, avoi* and *bhavoji. Bhavoji* is the term used by a man for his sister's husband and by a woman for her husband's sister's husband. Among Hindus, the term for father's brother (*kaka*), the closest agnate on the father's side, is different from that used for other wife-taking relatives (*bhavoji*). Among Christians, father's brother and father's sister's husband are brought together under the same term (*titiv*). The term *kunyad* is used for wife-taking relatives of ego's generation. There appears to be a generational distinction, but the terms are restricted to wife-taking relatives.

Within Portuguese Catholic kinship, all males of ego's parents generation are called *tio*. The Goan Catholic term *titiv* or *tiv* is derived from *tio*. However, its use is restricted to male *wife-taking* relatives of the parents' generation. As such, it is a cognate of the terms *kaka* (father's brother) and *bhavoji* (father's sister's husband, mother's sister's husband and mother's sister's husband's brother) used by the Hindus. For all *wife-giving*

male relatives of the parents' generation, term *mama* is used by
both Hindus and Catholics.

Another term that is of interest for analysis is *tia*. In the Portuguese system, *tia* is a term that may be employed for all female
persons of the parents' generation. The derived term *timai* among
Goan Catholics is used only for women of the parents' generation who have entered the family through marriage. These are
the wives of agnates such as the father's brother. *Timan* is used
for women who have left the group through marriage. These
include the father's sister, father's sister's husband's sister and
mother's sister's husband's sister. The term used for the wives
of those who have given women to ego's own family is *mami*.
The mother's brother's wife and the father's brother's wife's
brother's wife are thus both *mami*. While the terms for uncle
and aunt (*tio* and *tia*) have been adopted by the Catholics from
the Portuguese, they have been incorporated into the kinship
system in a selective manner and moulded so as to fit indigenous notions of kinship.

THE IDEA OF 'JOINT' LIVING

It has already been suggested that Christianity contains
patrifocal tendencies and that, by laying stress on the husband–
wife relationship, it implicitly invites the nuclearization of families. The Biblical text that is often drawn upon in Christian discourses on the family and marriage is that from the Gospel of
Mark (Chapter 10, Verses 6–7):

> But from the beginning of creation God made them male and female.
> For this reason a man shall leave his father and mother, and be
> joined to his wife.

In the Catholic church, while parental consent is a requirement
for marriage, what is also stressed is the importance of obtaining free and willing consent of the man and woman to be wed.
At the wedding rite, the couple are asked if they have come to
marry of their own consent. Christian discourses lay emphasis
on the good relations that should be maintained between husbands and wives. Not only are husband–wife relations stressed
within Christianity, it appears that the husband-and-wife unit

is perceived to be the basis of a new family group. The growth of nuclear families, each centred around a conjugal unit, is intentionally or unintentionally encouraged.

Hindu kinship lays a much greater emphasis on the relationship between a man and his sons as constituting the basis of the family residential group. Wives enter the group and become one with it. The notion that is of central importance is the unity of patrikin and their wives. If this contrast between Christian and Hindu notions of the family has contributed to actual differences in the household composition of Hindus and Christians, we should be able to perceive a large number of nuclear families among the latter and an equally large number of 'joint' familial arrangements among the former.

The theory will have to contend with another set of realities. For one, it has been agreed now that there is no such thing as persistent 'jointness'. The 'joint' Hindu family existing in perpetuity is a myth. At different stages of their developmental cycles, households may move from being nuclear to being joint and, further, to different degrees of jointness (Kolenda 1968; Shah 1974). The greatest degree of 'jointness' is to be found when married sons continue to stay in the same house with their parents, unmarried brothers and sisters, share property in common, pool their expenses together and eat from the same hearth. This type of jointness does not occur often and may be, in any case, only one stage in the domestic cycle of the group. When there is more than one married brother or when parents die, brothers usually set up separate households. They may continue to share property in common, while eating at separate hearths. Property division does not always follow immediately upon the setting up of separate commensal units. There are different elements to the concept of 'jointness', and they may not all come together in a single household unit.

The second problem is that the hypothesis tentatively suggested here has to come to terms with the fact that regardless of the ideal of joint living among Hindus, actual analyses reveal the presence of large numbers of household units that cannot be described as joint. Let us understand the different types of household categories before moving ahead. Various scholars use different categories, though one of the most systematic efforts at classification has come from Pauline Kolenda's (1968) work.

Twelve different categories are distinguished. These are what we may refer to as the nuclear or conjugal family, the supplemented nuclear family, the subnuclear family and the supplemented subnuclear family. There are several types of joint households including the lineal joint family, the supplemented lineal joint family, the collateral joint family, the supplemented collateral joint family, the lineal–collateral joint family and the supplemented lineal–collateral joint family. The final two categories are the single person household and the amorphous category of 'others', which includes all those types that do not conform to any specific, discernible pattern.

The different types are described by Kolenda (1968). A nuclear or conjugal family refers to a family consisting of a man and a woman and their unmarried children. This basic household unit may be supplemented by other relatives. A supplemented nuclear family therefore consists of one nuclear family and one or more unmarried, separated or widowed relatives of either of the parents. A subnuclear family is constituted by a part of a nuclear household. Thus a fragment of a former nuclear family consisting of a widow or divorcee with unmarried children may constitute such a household. One may also think of the possibility of a supplemented subnuclear family composed, for instance, of members of a former nuclear family and some other unmarried, divorced or widowed relative, who was not part of the original nuclear unit. Such a household may have a widow and her unmarried children and, perhaps, her widowed mother-in-law.

The collateral joint family consists of two or more married couples with a sibling bond between them. A typical example, of course, is of brothers, their wives and their unmarried children. Such a family becomes a supplemented collateral joint family when some other unmarried relative such as the widowed mother or unmarried or widowed sibling of the brothers joins the household. A lineal joint family is constituted by two couples with a lineal link between them. An example may be that of parents and their married son. Such a family will be a supplemented lineal joint family if it is joined by another relative, such as the father's widowed brother or sister or a son's wife's unmarried sibling. A lineal–collateral joint family includes at least three couples who are linked lineally and collaterally. The typical example is of parents and two or more married sons and their unmarried children. Finally, such a household, if joined by another relative such as the father's widowed or divorced brother or sister, becomes a supplemented lineal–collateral joint family.

According to Dube (1961), it is the nuclear family or the small joint family (with two married couples) which is and probably always has been typical of India. Kolenda's analysis (1968) also suggests that it is the small joint family that is the most typical household unit in India. The nuclear family and the supplemented nuclear family are also equally common. Lineal joint families are much more common than collateral joint families or lineal–collateral joint families. Joint families may be found both among the wealthy landed castes and those with less landed property. While joint families can occur across castes, they are found more often among the higher castes. Though the ideal Hindu household unit is the patrilineal joint family consisting of an agnatic descent group of males, three or more generations in depth, their wives and unmarried daughters, actual households rarely manage to match up to it. And among the lower castes, the distance from the 'ideal' is only greater.

Data from Goa indicates that Hindus and Christians share the ideal of the residential unity of the patrilineal, patrilocal joint family. However, due to migration and people working in different towns, a large number of Hindu households are actually nuclear, supplemented nuclear or, at best, lineal joint in composition. The number of joint families among Christians is also low. While the eldest son and his wife usually live with the son's parents, younger brothers and their wives take up separate residence. Often, the house is partitioned to accommodate the brothers. Sometimes, another house is built close to the old one, on land owned by the family. Cooking is done on separate hearths, but brothers may still own property, including agricultural land, in common and share in its income.

Division of property usually follows the death of the father or, sometimes, the death of both parents. Brothers keep and use their salaries for their own nuclear families. Younger brothers may contribute to the maintenance of their parents and brothers will also share in the expenses of marrying off a sister. Separation rarely comes about with the marriage of the first son. It is when there is more than one married brother that the younger will usually seek to set up a separate residence. It will be in rare cases that a wife's relatives—parents, siblings or other kin—form part of her married household. If she is the only child of her parents or has no brothers, a married woman may have her parents living with her.

The tendency towards the lineal–collateral joint family structure is small. One married son often lives with the parents but the joint living of married brothers is rare. This cannot be readily attributed to the influence towards nuclearization contained within Christianity. The pattern of married brothers setting up separate households is common across India. While a large number of Catholics live in nuclear families, they often reside close to their patrikin, who live in other sections of the same house or close by in the village. Brothers continue to hold property together even when they live separately and they pool money to meet certain kinds of expenses. Joint living certainly constitutes an ideal for Catholics. Residence is patrilocal. A woman moves to her husband's house on marriage and, even if the facts don't quite fit the model, Catholics like to assert that 'brothers should live together and share everything together. Their wives should live and cook together'.

The data available shows that while the Catholic high castes have a slightly greater tendency towards 'jointness' than the low castes, there are a significant number of lineal joint and nuclear supplemented households across castes. Most nuclear supplemented households consist of the nuclear family and the widowed father or mother of the man. Lineal joint households are composed by a married son residing with his parents (see Gomes 1987; Robinson 1998). Overall, the pattern of household composition one observes is similar to that available from data relating to Hindu households either in Goa or elsewhere. A greater trend towards nuclearization is not clearly discernible, and the presence of nuclear households notwithstanding, the idea of the 'perfect' family remains that of the joint family.

Close by in suburban Mumbai, by the 1970s, patrilineal, patrilocal Catholic families had started the practice of separate residences for each conjugal couple. In the absence of their parents, married brothers certainly did not share the same hearth and often not even the same residential space, though parents and their married sons sometimes lived together and cooked together. As in Goa, the tendency was towards dividing the ancestral home or setting up separate houses alongside it. Alternatively, another floor would be added to the family house (Godwin 1972).

South Indian kinship and family organization differs from the pattern described above. While some of the upper castes, notably the Brahmans, aspire to the model of the patrilocal, patrilineal joint family, non-Brahman groups often manifest very different family and kinship patterns. The preference for marriage between relatives and the equality between wife-takers and wife-givers have already been dwelt upon. Post-marital residence is more often determined by economic and political considerations; the patrilineal, patrilocal joint household is not the taken-for-granted norm. If conditions are so dictate, uxorilocality is easily adopted and the pattern of localized alliances mentioned earlier ensures that affines tend not to live at any great distance from each other.

Proximity and the significance that the brother–sister bond has in the context of cross-cousin marriage ensure that a married woman has continued access to her natal family and is even regarded as having responsibilities towards them. Further, since the distinction between natal and affinal kin is blurred, marriage does not constitute for a woman, a severe break from her former ties. A woman's natal family remains deeply concerned about her fertility and well-being and the well-being of her children, for they are potential marriage partners (see Ram 1991: 169–70). Decisions regarding post-marital residence are made on the basis of a variety of practical considerations. Economic opportunities and the availability of co-operation from kin are significant concerns. There is a greater opportunity for individual choice.

Among the Mukkuvar, virilocal residence is often the chosen option, but there is also scope for uxorilocal and neolocal residence. Sometimes, a pattern of shifting residence may result. Ram details particular cases, of which two are summarized here (Ram 1991: 171). In the first case, the wife had initially moved to her husband's home after her marriage, and lived there for two years. The marriage had, however, taken place without the consent of the groom's family. So the bride was faced with some amount of hostility in her marital home. It was in accordance with her wishes, therefore, that the couple returned to her natal village, KaDalkarai Uuru. The husband quoted a Tamil proverb to account for the move: 'Thai ki pin thaarum', or 'behind the mother, go the family.' The family resided in the wife's natal village, though the husband returned to his own village for a few months in the year to dive for oysters. In another case, a couple settled in favour of residing in the wife's natal village, after a period of several years during which they moved seasonally between her village and the husband's village. The final decision was attributed to the husband's frequent ill-health and the fact that the wife's mother had made an offer of financial assistance to the couple.

The Mukkuvar, like other low-caste groups across India, live predominantly in nuclear households. Even when more than one nuclear family live under the same roof, the sharing of resources or hearths is very rare. There is a radical disaggregation of the various functions (income sharing, division of labour, collective cooking and the like) attributed to joint households. Under such circumstances, the sharing of residence appears to be related largely to the scarcity of accommodation. Among the Mukkuvar, the wife's relatives may quite commonly be part of her marital household. The 'supplemented nuclear household' thus consists of a nuclear family and, often, the parents or siblings of the wife.

Looking at 288 households in KaDalkarai Uuru, where she did her fieldwork, Ram (1991: 179) gives the reader the figures for different household compositions. The number of conjugal or nuclear households is very large at 163 or 57 per cent of the total number of households. Supplemented conjugal households are 28 in number, around 10 per cent of the total. There are 16 subconjugal households (6 per cent). Nine (3 per cent) of the households are supplemented subconjugal in composition. There may be two kinds of lineal joint households: uxorilocal and virilocal. There are 23 of each type of household (8 per cent) in total, as well as three supplemented lineal joint households.

Collateral joint households again could be fraternal, sororal or cognatic in composition. There are just two of each type in KaDalkarai Uuru. There are three cognatic supplemented collateral joint households and there is one fraternal supplemented collateral joint household. There is also only one supplemented lineal collateral joint household in the total. There are four single person households (1 per cent) and two households composed in ways other than those described above.

Ram's data shows that a married daughter is as likely to be living with parents as a married son. In cases where married siblings share residence, it is as likely that one might find married sisters living together as married brothers or married brothers and sisters. In 46 per cent of 'supplemented conjugal' households, parents were supported by their daughter and her husband. There are several cases of married women taking responsibility for their younger brothers, after the parents' death. Several factors combine to ensure that a woman's ties with her natal family remain close after marriage and the networks of co-operation are dense. The relative equality of wife-givers and wife-takers, marriage near at hand and the possibility of uxorilocality are some of these factors (Ram 1991).

Residential clusters of married siblings are quite common. Other kinds of clustering revolve around siblings living close to their married children, siblings and their parents or even siblings, their married children and affinal kin. Uterine, affinal and consanguineal links are more critical than agnatic ones in the formation of residential clusters. This is not atypical of patterns viewed elsewhere, particularly among the lower castes. The implications of this system of kinship and family organization for women may be quite positive. Marriage does not constitute a radical break in their lives or separate them from their parents and siblings. They often live in the same house with them or very close by. They can extend support to their parents and younger siblings.

By keeping finances and hearths separate and by having the option of establishing a separate residence, brides are able to side step the close supervision of daily work that is typical of the patrilineal joint family. The fact that siblings often live side by side means that they can offer each other financial assistance at times of crisis. As Ram says (1991: 181), the brother-sister bond in this part of the country is not only about the protection offered to sisters in the event that they suffer maltreatment in their marital home, as is the case in the north of India. Rather, sisters are in the position of being able to offer financial and material assistance to their brothers in times of crisis. They may pawn their jewellery in order to finance a trip overseas, for instance, or may offer their homes in the case of a need for accommodation. Married women also keep close contacts with their female siblings and may offer them the same sorts of help if necessary.

The contrast with the norms of patrilineal, patrilocal joint households could not be greater. However, the story gets more complicated. Even though Mukkuvar women seem to have far more autonomy and security than women married into joint, patrilineal households, their families are still called upon to make large marriage payments in the form of dowry. How does the system work? We turn in the next section to an understanding of patterns of gift-giving, inheritance and marriage payments among different Christian communities.

MARRIAGE PAYMENTS

The fact that many Christian communities have a system of marriage payments in the form of dowry has been of interest to a number of scholars (see Caplan 1984; Ifeka 1989; Montemayor 1970; Ram 1991; Robinson 1998; Visvanathan 1993). Perhaps this is because the 'evil' of the dowry system has led to the deaths of many young Hindu brides in recent times and has, consequently, aroused scholarship's curiosity about how such a system functioned within Christian communities. Moreover, caste and dowry are inextricably linked. The attention to one determines interest in the other.

The idea of *kanyadan* is closely tied up with the dowry system. High castes, in particular, have long held the idea of making a settlement on the daughter at marriage. This is the *stridhan* and it is considered to be part of the concept of *kanyadan* (Caplan 1984). The virgin daughter (*kanya*) is given as a gift (*dan*) in marriage. The idea of the purity of the *dan* (the authenticity of the act of giving) is brought out further by adorning the daughter with precious jewellery and sending her accompanied by other material gifts. The bride is perceived as being given as a gift to somebody of superior status. The *dan* par excellence, the *dan* which confers on the giver the highest spiritual merit, is *dan* made to a Brahman. In parallel, the gift of a virgin bride with her dowry to a man of superior status confers prestige on the giver (see Dumont 1980; Parry 1979).

Within this system, the group which receives the bride is obviously superior to the group which gives the bride and this fact is underlined by the unidirectionality of gift-giving patterns. Gifts at and after marriage flow in one direction, from wife-givers to wife-takers. The direction may never be reversed. The system is hypergamous and there is a relationship of inequality between wife-givers and wife-takers. Castes lower down in the hierarchy have not been known to have adhered to such a system traditionally, though many are now following some form of the dowry system. In the past, these groups often followed a system of giving bridewealth.

Scholars have argued over whether the dowry can be seen as a kind of pre-mortem inheritance, connoting a female right to property, or whether it is in fact a disinheritance, a substitute for the woman's lack of rights to property (see Goody and Tambiah 1973 and Madan (1975) on different sides of the debate). It is a fact that in most communities the dowry symbolically severs a woman's economic ties to her natal family and excludes her from any rights to inheritance, which rights are secured by her brothers. Moreover, unlike inheritance, dowry has the specific aim of linking the daughter with a suitable groom and is often the result of a bargain between the parties involved in arranging the match.

It is necessary to point out that the *stridhan* or dowry traditionally endowed on a daughter usually included jewellery, clothes and household goods such as vessels. These were for use in the marital home. There was usually a moral agreement on the appropriate amounts to be given of such movable properties and hard cash was rarely part of the *stridhan*. No daughter went empty-handed and giving her an appropriate dowry only raised the standing and prestige of her family. In recent times, there has been an escalation in dowry payments and a completely new element has been introduced in the transaction. The property transferred at marriage now includes consumer items such as cars, refrigerators or television sets as well as substantial amounts of cash.

The amounts of cash and the consumer items to be given are decided less by what a family wishes to endow their daughter with as a mark of their own prestige than by what the family of a prospective groom demands as the price of the marriage. Such payments, appropriately enough, have now come to be known in the literature by the term 'bridegroom price' (see Srinivas, 1942 for an early use of the term; also Gough, 1956). There is enough evidence to suggest that the bridegroom price rarely remains the property of the bride, but is made over to the groom's family and is often employed to endow his sister/s at marriage or to recoup resources that have already been spent for that purpose (Sharma 1984). It becomes, in other words, a circulating resource in a society where there are few means available to acquire wealth quickly.

The amounts demanded as dowries for grooms are related to their educational qualifications and employment and career prospects. Investment in the son's education is recouped through his dowry. The rationale is that the girl he marries will benefit from his education and career and should, therefore, contribute to it. Doctors, engineers, those with permits to work and settle in the USA ('green card holders') command very high prices. Other factors are involved in setting the rates. A family with a girl of exceptional beauty or one with a girl having good professional qualifications may be able to lower somewhat the price demanded.

How does the dowry system operate among different groups of Christians and what are dowries utilized for? Discussions about *stridhanam* are the first stage in the negotiations of a marriage among Syrian Christians. It is only when these are successfully concluded that the public announcement of the betrothal takes place. The amounts which exchange hands vary according to different circumstances. The *stridhanam* given to each daughter may alter in accordance with the time and the circumstance of her marriage.

Syrian Christian informants speak of a 'rate' for each economic class. The rate goes up annually. The actual amount of money that will be paid is decided according to the prevailing rate, but there is also usually the possibility of bargaining and negotiating over the sum. Several factors are significant in these arrangements, including the economic position of both the families, the educational qualifications of the bride and groom, the kind of employment they may have or even the colour of the woman's complexion (Visvanathan 1993: 111). In the main, it is the economic promise of the groom and his qualifications and training that are of critical importance in setting the rates of dowry. This is certainly true for the Mukkuvar, the Goan Catholics and Madras Protestants (Caplan 1984; Ifeka 1989; Montemayor 1970; Ram 1991; Robinson 1998).

What are the constituent elements of an appropriate dowry? Dowries traditionally included 'jewels, cooking vessels or other household goods, and clothes' among the Madras Protestants

(Caplan 1984: 217). Among Goan Catholics, dowry transactions in the past included similar kinds of items: household goods, jewellery and clothes. Certainly, cash payments were very rare. If ever made, they were made at the discretion of the girl's family. Amounts were not decided on or demanded by the groom's family. The entry of cash payments and demands into the system has taken place over recent decades in most communities.

As Ram records (1991: 190), the earliest two marriages for which she was able to gather data showed no cash payments whatsoever and even the quantities of jewellery that exchanged hands were very moderate when compared to current standards. In one marriage, conducted in 1925, the bride was given jewellery worth 10 *powan* or 100 grams of gold. This would have amounted to about Rs 14,300 worth of jewellery. In the other marriage, which took place in 1933, the jewellery was worth about Rs 5,720 and there was no cash payment.

Godwin writing about suburban Mumbai in the early 1970s, gives a list of items that constituted the 'traditional dowry'. The dowry was agreed upon by both parties prior to their giving final consent to the marriage. It was normally a formal agreement and often took the form of a signed, written document. The items of jewellery and even the number of pieces of clothing to be brought by the bride would be listed. Money, apart from what was considered necessary to cover wedding expenses, was rarely part of the transaction. Despite the possibility of some negotiation, there were clearly some community norms regarding what constituted an appropriate dowry. According to Godwin, the traditional dowry consisted of the following items: money for expenses on the boy's side, jewellery consisting of two gold rings, some gold bangles, at least one pair of gold earrings, two gold bead chains, four to six small gold bangles and a pair of silver anklets. In more recent times, a wristwatch has been added to this list. He notes that the 'amount of dowry has risen considerably today'. An amount of Rs 4,000–5,000 might be given, apart from clothes and jewellery (1972: 79).

It does appear that the poorer low castes often engaged in socially 'unmarked' marriages. These marriages differed from the upper-caste norm in that they entailed no asymmetrical exchange or relationship of hypergamy. The practice was to share the modest expenses of marriage. In most cases,

> ...the groom's family gave the girl a 'plain' (i.e., brass or metal) ring, and a cotton sari or two; the bride's family gave her a cotton sari, perhaps a simple bead rosary or a pair of 9-carat gold earrings, and a wooden box to store her scanty possessions (Ifeka 1989: 275).

Again,

> ...if a dowry was given it was typically very small—a few utensils or clothes or the like. Sometimes gifts were exchanged. The bride's family gave a suit of clothes to the groom and his gave one to the bride (Robinson 1998: 173).

The rates of dowry in present times are decided by the kinds of factors already listed. The lower castes have shifted more clearly to a system of dowry and the desire for upward mobility ensures that families of girls are willing to offer large cash sums to strike alliances with grooms who have good jobs and have moved up on the financial and social scale. The bride's family is actually asked to foot a considerable part of the bill in the project for upward social mobility. We have already seen that one kind of rationale for dowry is that the amount spent on educating sons has to be recouped.

In other cases, brides and their families are being asked to finance new and, sometimes, quite ambitious undertakings. They are contributing capital for entrepreneurial schemes and investing in opportunities for more attractive jobs. Among the Mukkuvar, women are investing in the new fishing technologies or financing their husbands' attempts to emigrate overseas in search of better paying jobs (Ram 1991: 192). What does this imply about control over the woman's dowry? Who exercises this control? Does the woman have a great deal of say in how the money she brings with her on marriage is spent or how her jewellery and other material assets are utilized?

This does not appear to be the case unambiguously, though there are inevitably difficulties in ascertaining information in this regard. Given the legal ban on dowry, Ifeka (1989) stresses that women are unwilling to mention the amounts they receive from their natal families and are reticent about whether the money is controlled by the bride or is deposited in a bank account operated jointly by the couple. More than a decade earlier, Godwin (1972: 80) shows for suburban Mumbai that the dowry may have been given to the bride but it 'was considered more as an acquisition of the boy's family than as the property of the girl'.

Visvanathan (1993: 111) is explicit. Control over *stridhanam* is not exercised by a woman, but by her husband and his family. *Stridhanam* may be employed for marrying off the husband's sisters. It may be invested in land or used for other purposes. Data relating to the Mukkuvar (Ram 1991) shows that the bride has little independent control over her property, which is regularly dipped into by her husband or members of his family. Dowry is a survival fund for families that are unable to cover the costs of living through the proceeds earned from fishing. Women are not always forced into selling their jewellery or using their other assets to help their families. They may willingly accede to using their property to pay for food, medicines, clothes or even household repairs.

The woman's consent may not always be sought while using her property and it may be used even if her willingness to give it up is not forthcoming. Husbands often use the bride's dowry for investment in fishing equipment, which is seen as a benefit for the family as a whole. A bride may not always be enthusiastic about such investments, particularly since the returns are not always assured. However, women perceive themselves as having a stake in raising the productive assets of the household and may not resent the use of their property for such a purpose. Women do resent it if their property is employed for unproductive uses, either to fund a husband's drinking habits or to finance other marriages in the family.

The nature of household formation and kinship relations among the Mukkuvar means that it is not only a bride's marital household that lays claim to her property. Her natal family may also expect to get monetary assistance from her, either to help marry off her siblings or to tide over a financial crisis. These demands are couched in the language of requests for loans, though the loans are rarely repaid. The claims made on the bride by her natal family may cause tension with her in-laws. In order to protect her interests and those of her children, a woman has to negotiate between competing claims. She may not always find the going easy, particularly when the extent of her autonomy is in any case unsure.

CONCLUSION

This chapter set out to explore the 'kinship' dimension of conversion to Christianity and in doing so it has traversed zones of matriliny and patriliny, caste and tribe territory, the interior and the coast. Christian kinship is an enormously neglected terrain and one has to persevere to draw out relevant material and make it speak. Christianity, in its different denominations, incorporates particular ideas about morality relating to the family, to kinship and marriage. These ideas were sometimes in accord with indigenous concepts and practices, more often than not in discord. The norms of matrilineal societies in particular were set at considerable dis-ease due to the presence of Christianity.

The need to protect indigenous norms of kinship is not necessarily conceived as an end in itself, but is also bound up with ideas about status and patrimony, gender valuation and the division and organization of household resources and labour. Christianity itself does not always speak with one voice. Within Catholicism, there is a strong patrifocal tendency, but also a contrary strain towards individualism. Convert communities show remarkable talent, as it were, for appropriating kinship and religious norms and making them comply with indigenous social and cultural requirements. Ideas about appropriate alliance partners or inheritance are not easily given up for they interweave with concerns regarding the material and social continuity of groups. Marriage payments, for instance, both invoke ideas of *kanyadan* as well as revoke any claims on the part of the daughter to inheritance.

The area of kinship and the family is an area that is literally pleading for more reasearch. We know very little of the dynamics of kinship processes among different Christian groups or of how these processes are now changing. It is within the circle of kin and the family that a child is socialized into life-roles and cultural expectations, that resources are garnered and distributed, that religious ideas and morality are taught. It is only when we understand more fully the different types of kinship structures among Christian groups and the expected behaviour and role of different categories of kin that we will be able to throw more light on these themes. Until then, the little material we have tantalizes us. It certainly shows that we may by no means assume that the kinship of convert communities is simply the 'same' as that of those around them. At the very least, the resemblance we perceive is actively negotiated, not passively absorbed.

6

Cults, Cures and Challenges to the Church

Indigenous Cults of Healing

If hierarchy has been a feature of Indian Christian communities, it has not always been accepted by those at the bottom with quiet compliance (see for instance, Alexander 1968; Manor 1971; Mosse 1986; Newman 1990; Rayan 1992; Yesudas 1975). While attempts at social mobility and improvement of status have always been around and have, in fact, been part of the impulse to convert among certain groups, it is in more recent decades that novel modes of protest have developed. The churches have always had an ambivalent attitude towards caste and other forms of hierarchy and inequality but their role in challenging these is also notable. The 'breast cloth' controversy is only the most famous documentation of the role of the missionaries in standing up for the rights of the lowest social groups. In recent decades, churches have come out even more clearly on the side of the unprivileged.

Churches have traditionally though, been sites for the articulation and maintenance of inequalities of caste, class and gender. It has only been in areas outside the church proper that marginalized groups have carved for themselves, arenas of cultural potency. Possession, shamanistic cults and visions are the typical cultural means for the expression of autonomy and power. These tend to be closely interlinked with practices of healing prevalent in different communities. While such practices are uniformly denounced by church authority structures, they often manifest an intriguing combination of interrogation of and submission to Christian theological notions.

These cults have been the 'traditional', as it were, locations of protest for low status groups among Christian communities with hierarchical structures. The cults provide a space outside the confines of the church for the exercise of greater control over ritual activity. Practices and beliefs of healing which are central to the organization of this kind of cultic activity are commonly shared across religious boundaries. Hindus, Muslims, Christians and others of similar economic and social status flock to the indigenous healers for cures and they, in turn, may belong to any religion (see Bayly 1989; Caplan 1987). A Muslim healer in Madras may meditate upon Allah in order to draw the powers of the goddess *Shakti* into himself to confront demonic possession among Christians, Hindus or other Muslims. There is a cultural agreement on the ideas of evil and misfortune that shape such practices.

The human world is seen as being impinged upon by various capricious, hostile and potentially hostile forces which must either be avoided or placated to prevent them from doing harm (Caplan 1987; Godwin 1972; Ram 1991; Robinson 1995, 1998). These forces are viewed as intervening actively in people's lives and often causing physical or mental illness and affliction. Sometimes, these spirits assist human beings in causing harm through sorcery. The usual sites for the concentration of evil spirits across most regions of India are boundary areas and places associated with death or accidents. Cremation grounds and cemeteries, trees, wells and boundary walls or the margins of fields or villages—it is in such places that *bhut*, *pey*, *khetro* and other demonic spirits are thought to congregate. These spirits are often ancestral spirits and they are sources of affliction, particularly if they are displeased with their descendants or restless because they had died violent or 'bad' premature deaths, either through drowning, illness, murder or fatal accident.

The *pey* or *bhut* of a person who died a premature death can enter not only one of his or her descendants but also anyone who is foolish enough to venture into the fringe or wilderness areas that *pey* are said to typically haunt. The spirits of those who committed suicide or were murdered or met with an accident are perceived as being very malevolent. They are typically dissatisfied and since they have no resting place, they await someone whom they can then seize. The world of the village is a social space, well ordered, inhabited and regulated. The world outside the space of the village, the wild, is chaotic, evil and dangerous. *Pey* or *bhut* are typically thought to come from margin areas of the village or from 'outside'. It is believed to be dangerous to venture outside the village boundaries, into areas which separate inhabited places, particularly at liminal moments such as dusk, when day is passing into night (Deliège 1999).

It is the sudden and inexplicable onset of illness or the coming of unexpected misfortune that is usually attributed to the intervention of spirits. Among Goan Catholics, such afflictions are called *variancé* and the ill person is taken to the *gaddhi* (healer) for diagnosis and treatment. The *gaddhi* may be male or female and is usually a member of one of the low castes. There are no Christian *gaddhi*. The *gaddhi* asks the patient and his or her relatives various kinds of questions. For instance, enquiry is made about where the family comes from and what the symptoms of the illness are that the patient is suffering from. The *gaddhi* asks if there has been a recent death in the family of the afflicted person or if he/she had been to the house or funeral of a dead person in the period before the illness struck.

The *gaddhi* usually asks for a detailed account of the places to which the patient had been in the days or weeks prior to his/ her illness. It is on the basis of such questioning that the *gaddhi* eventually makes a diagnosis and prescribes some form of remedy. Remedies vary. The *gaddhi* might recommend the making of an offering, usually of one or two chickens, to the spirit of the dead person who is perceived to be afflicting the patient. Other means, including the wearing of charms, are also sometimes recommended to make the spirit of the dead person depart from the patient whom it has possessed. The families of patients tend to involve themselves a good deal in assisting the *gaddhi* in diagnosis or in taking action themselves to remove the demonic spirit. Beating the patient or dousing him or her with water are among the practices commonly adopted.

The family may also reach certain tentative conclusions regarding the identity of the spirit even before they take resort to the healing specialist. The healer usually takes note of the family's suspicions while determining the spirit's identity. The vitality of ideas and practices of spirit affliction can be observed more among the lower castes and is perhaps related to the fact that they retain a degree of control over the ritual activity involved in these practices. Church-centred ritual is controlled by the upper castes and classes. Males, rather than females, dominate.

Not surprisingly, therefore, wherever elements of patriarchy and caste hierarchy are strongly embedded, the victims and, even more likely, their healers are often women (Deliège 1999). In Mukkuvar Christian villages (Ram 1991: 87), the rigid rules of the surveillance, control and seclusion of women implicitly acknowledge them as a source of dangerous power, though one not recognized by the doctrine of the church. Women take on the attributes of this illicit power through possession and it enables them to breach the expected everyday norms of respectable female behaviour. Indeed, women are viewed as being particularly susceptible to attacks of sorcery or spirit possession. Menstruating women and pregnant women are especially vulnerable to attack.

The practice of seclusion, however, cannot be read simply as a materialization of Hindu ideas regarding pollution. For instance, among the Mukkuvar, the regimen of seclusion is visible only during the first menstruation and after childbirth. And on these occasions, it appears to be related more to ideas of the danger of female power than to ideas regarding pollution. At menarche and childbirth women are polluting to those around them. However, they are more in danger themselves from forces which are attracted to the blood and heat of their bodies. The binding of a woman's stomach after childbirth is linked with the need to keep evil spirits at a distance (Ram 1991: 90). Certain evil spirits are perceived as particularly blood thirsty and drawn, therefore, to menstruating women (Caplan 1987: 202).

The female body is the site for the working out of practices of seclusion and control that are perceived as critical for the maintenance of social honour or patriarchal authority in communities configured centrally around these values. In such communities, when the healer and the demoniacally possessed are typically woman, there is an enormous potential for challenge and resistance to entrenched ideologies. As Ram (1991) and Visvanathan (1993a) show through their ethnographies, the symptoms of agony of the demoniacally possessed are an acknowledgement of the strength of social and religious norms but also offer a site for the victim's violation and interrogation of them. Women roll around in a dance of agony, as the demons within them are tormented by the Christian divine. Their hair unruly, their clothes disordered, they dance with a wildness and strength and freedom of movement not permitted them by the rules of normal female behaviour.

Deliège's data from a south Indian village in Tamil Nadu describes a typical case (1999: 265) of the female possessed.

The trance starts slowly. First the woman slightly turns her head. The movement reaches a crescendo and finally her whole trunk is weaving or drawing circles. Her hair is suddenly untied and at the end the movements are extremely fast. While thus shaking, she may repeat some words; in the shrine of Arockyai Mary, they generally shout more and more loudly: *Mattave! Mattave!* (Mother! Mother!). The crisis then reaches a climax and the woman suddenly collapses, totally exhausted. But the demon is then in her, and it can be interrogated by the people present. Usually it will give its identity and the reason why it possessed the poor woman. It might also insult the people present or blaspheme, threatening both human and supernatural beings.

Among Syrians, Visvanathan (1993a: 223) notes that 'the church expresses a closed space for the enactment of the liturgy; it is holy, closed, an official space. It is also a male bastion in the ecclesiastical sense that the priests and servers who are the controllers of the ceremony are male. However, this situation is challenged by the ...role of women in the paranormal situation of possession. In fact, cases of possession present themselves in the guise of prophetic transformative gestures and statements'. Cases of *bhadam* or possession usually occur in the courtyard, *outside* the church rather than within. It is women, Hindu or Christian and often of low caste and class position, that are the typical victims of possession. A Christian woman screamed and cried out to Mary, shaking off her husband's hand when he attempted to restrain her. She called her husband Satan, crying:

He is Satan. If it were my father or my brothers, they would have let me stand here to pray. For some time here, I was happy calling out to the *Matav*, but see, the devil pulls at my arm (Visvanathan 1993a: 229).

Her husband finally managed to take her away but as she went, she told those who were watching her that Satan had always been so. Just as she achieved a state of happiness, he would take her away. She said that since Satan was her husband, she had to go with him, but her father or brothers would have let her stay. (Visvanathan 1993a: 230)

The mode of possession not only allows women to scream, dance or move in ways they could not imagine under normal conditions, it also permits them to express rebellion against the persons and structures they are forced to obey by the rules of social and religious conduct. Here the woman loudly rebukes her husband as her tormentor and oppressor, even as she laments the absence of her natal kin, who would apparently have understood her better. Church and society give the husband authority over the wife; it is only in *bhadam* that a woman can give vent against them. The church is hierarchical and the priests are male. Priests are often considered corrupt and essentially interested in their own material gain rather than the spiritual welfare of the community. In *bhadam* women can rage against the priests themselves.

Visvanathan (1993a: 231) heard one woman screaming out to God to plead with Him to tell the priests not to step on the child. There was no child nearby and onlookers took her words to refer to priestly suppression of the innocence of the infant Jesus. People remarked to each other that she spoke the truth.

CHARISMATIC AND PENTECOSTAL CULTS

Demonic possession, visions and the shamanistic cults of healing feed into the Charismatic and Pentecostal movements that have become a familiar part of Christian life in many parts of the country. The growth of sects offering fundamentalist and millennial versions of Christianity is not a trend that is limited to India or even the Third World, but has been seen in many regions of the world. Such sects remain outside the fold of mainline churches and differ from these theologically in that they stress the significance of the Holy Spirit within the Christian Trinity and emphasize particularly the 'gifts' of the Spirit (Caplan 1987; Robinson 1998).

Charismatic and Pentecostal cults are part of movements within Christian groups of all denominations that originated in the late nineteenth and early twentieth centuries. These movements seem to have welled up more or less simultaneously and independently in different parts of the world. They were very prominent in the United States and have since spread to many parts of the globe. These cults rely on the biblical teachings in the New Testament that speak about the power and the gifts of the Holy Spirit. Charismatics and Pentecostal Christians believe that they can obtain these spiritual gifts or powers through prayer and can use them in a variety of ways, particularly to heal people of physical ailments or remove afflictions caused by evil spirits.

It is not clear how the Charismatic movement came to India or became widespread here. It appears that the movement was already in existence by the middle of this century among Christians in major cities and other urban areas. From there it seems to have spread slowly to other places. In Goa, the movement grew out of its initial restriction to small groups of Catholics. These were probably influenced by the teachings of Charismatic groups who came from outside Goa, possibly from nearby cities such as Mumbai and Pune (Robinson 1998). In south India, it appears that sectarian Pentecostal groups have been in action for many years. A significant presence of Pentecostals was reported from south India in the 1920s and 1930s. The movement grew after the Second World War and by the 1980s there seem to have been a large number of congregations of Pentecostals (Caplan 1987).

There is a fragility to such associations for some of them are just tiny prayer groups or cells and some are actual, independently existing sectarian congregations. The beliefs and rites of such different groups may be identical. There is also a tendency towards rapid schism among such groups, which leads to their multiplication. Groups have varying degrees of stability. Some survive barely a few years for lack of resources or the capacity for expansion. Others contrive to have longer lifespans if they manage to raise money among their adherents or obtain help from a sponsor. It is interesting to quote from Caplan a conversation which brings out aptly the problems of survival of such groups.

A young man entered the office of the Bible society and the following conversation took place.

Official: Who do you represent?
Visitor: I am from the Universal Church of Christ.
Official: I have never heard about your assembly.
Visitor: We are new. We started only a few months ago.
Official: Where were you (affiliated) before?
Visitor: Most of us were with the Church of God [*another Pentecostal group*], but we came away from there.

Official: How many are you?
Visitor: We are about 25 families in all.
Official: Who is your pastor?
Visitor: You would not know him, sir, he is not ordained.
Official: How do you support yourselves?
Visitor: We give tithes of 10 per cent. But we pray daily for God's help to find an organization to help us (Caplan 1987: 215).

Mainline churches have usually had very uneasy relationships with these movements. In theory, the Charismatic movement, which is prominent among Catholics, has been approved of by the church at Rome. However, in most places some priests will be associated with the movement, while others oppose it because they see it as disruptive of church order and as having a tendency to promote conflict within the church. Pentecostal movements among various denominations of Protestantism have had an equally tense relationship with the principal churches. Caplan mentions that orthodox churches more often than not, refused to allow their pulpits and premises to be given over to Pentecostal preachers and regarded them with some disdain. As he says: 'Prophets were frequently ridiculed—"Johnies jumping for Jesus" is one epithet I heard—stigmatized, and denied any official hearing in CSI [Church of South India] parishes' (1987: 240).

The features of Charismatic and Pentecostal meetings go a long way towards clarifying what it is about them that attracts a particular category of clientele. For it must be noted that in most areas it is the groups lower down in the social and economic scales that are attracted to these cults. Indeed, they bring into such movements, some of their ideas and practices with respect to spirit affliction and healing that I have described above. In Goa, meetings of Charismatics usually take place in small groups. The group will meet in the house of one of the members. Larger groups form when Charismatics from two or three villages get together. Meetings are usually held once or twice a week, during the evenings when people are free from work. Most Charismatics are lay persons, but there are some nuns and priests associated with the movement. Two priests are well known to be very powerful Charismatics. These are Fr Savio and Fr Rufus. There are some others as well. Most of the priests associated with the movement tend not to be linked with any particular parish but go from place to place organizing meetings and working with various local groups.

The priests deny that there is any class or caste dimension to the movement. As one told me:

> It may be true that many of those who join us are from the lower social groups. But we do not preach caste or any such thing. Nor do we tell them to fight the other castes or start conflicts in their local churches. We only talk about God and the power of the Holy Spirit to transform people's lives...(Robinson 1998: 202).

There is nothing intrinsic to Charismatic teachings or beliefs that links them unequivocally with a particular social group. It is therefore necessary to examine the particular contexts within which these beliefs function and to understand how the movements offer to those lower down in the social and economic structure, a means whereby they can challenge the hierarchical social order and the presence of élitism and inequality within the church.

What is the nature of worship at Charismatic and Pentecostal meetings? One of the meetings attended by the author in Goa was led by Fr Savio and two lay persons, a man and a woman. The meeting began with the Charismatics standing up and singing aloud spontaneous praises to Christ and the Holy Spirit. They clapped as they sang. There were a few moments of spontaneous prayer by different members. Then came the moment for people who had been cured to give their testimonies. After each testimony of faith there was another period of singing, clapping and spontaneous prayer. Later, there was the praying over the sick and the healing of afflictions. This brought the meeting to an end. This was the essential pattern of most Charismatic meetings.

This is a pattern vastly different from the church centred Mass. At Mass, specific prayers are said and these are led by the priest. The church is a male bastion and in the organization of space and ritual it, more often than not, privileges the high caste over the low caste, the male over the female, the rich over the poor and the doctrinal or clerical over the lay. At Mass, people have to follow a particular postural pattern: at certain times everyone has to sit or kneel, at other times, everyone has to stand. An emphasis is placed on passivity, on listening and responding to the priest rather than on taking a more active part in the service.

Charismatic meetings encourage spontaneity. While there are leaders who open the meetings and often say the first prayer, they are not always (or only) priests and clergymen but include lay persons as well. After the initial introduction, anyone from the group can take up the prayers 'as they might be moved by the Holy Spirit'. People are encouraged to bring up their own concerns in their prayers. They might pray aloud for their families, their financial needs or their illnesses. No control is exercised over the order of the prayers. Both men and women participate and there are no caste or status distinctions to be seen. Most of the members are, in any case, from the lower social and economic groups. After each prayer, there is a pause during which someone else may speak. If the pause is long enough to assume that no-one else wishes to make an individual prayer, the leader (or someone else) may start up a hymn of praise and the meeting proceeds. In Charismatic meetings, there is clapping, singing and sometimes even dancing. All these are seen as accepted forms of worship. No regular order is imposed: people may stand, sit or kneel as they feel motivated to do.

Those who join the movement are typically attracted by the spontaneous character of worship enabled by it. As one Goan Sudra male said: 'In the church it is all very rigid—sit, stand, kneel and all that. When I joined the Charismatics, it was so different—spontaneous prayer, clapping, singing. I liked it' (Robinson 1998: 204). The higher social groups keep away from the Charismatic movement. Perhaps they perceive in it a challenge to the position they have traditionally enjoyed in the church. Certainly, the rigid hierarchy of the church benefits more those at the top. The privileges of those on high are maintained by the ordered, hierarchical form of worship generally seen at Mass or other church celebrations (Robinson 1998).

Visvanathan (1993a) talks of the restraint which most Syrians see as central to the form that worship should take. Caplan (1987) also suggests that the Christian middle class keeps itself aloof from fundamentalist Christian movements. The attraction of Pentecostal movements is explained by the gullibility of the uneducated who chase after miracles and are easily exploited by the evangelists. The middle class considers itself too sophisticated and educated to be drawn into such movements. The controlled and dignified forms of religious expression of the orthodox church are preferable for them. Those who follow the Pentecostal cults speak of the failure of the orthodox church to meet the spiritual needs of its people. What is highlighted is the 'excessive formalism' and 'coldness of worship', the absence of strong, evangelistic sermons and the dearth of pastoral care. By contrast,

Pentecostal rites are perceived as 'warm' because they permit individual spontaneity and emotionalism. The messages of these assemblies provide genuine spiritual food for they are fairly didactic and hard-hitting and the groups nurture their members, rendering emotional support in times of adversity (Caplan 1987: 224).

What is interesting is that Pentecostal and Charismatic doctrines and beliefs tend to be consistent with popular notions about the aetiology of affliction (see Mosse 1986). Ideas about spirit affliction and healing get taken seriously within these evangelical cults, which recognize that misfortune may be brought about by several kinds of evil agents, who are perceived as being in the employ of Satan.

The themes of possession and healing emerge repeatedly in what people say about their reasons for joining these cults. At one meeting in Goa, a lower-caste man said:

I had heard about the Charismatics but had not thought of joining them. But about eight months ago, I fell very ill. Even the doctors could not tell exactly what was wrong, though they thought it was some viral infection and were giving me treatment for that. But I kept getting worse and very weak. My wife suspected that there was some evil spirit at work. She said that we should go to the *gaddhi* or do something to find out. We were wondering what to do when a friend of mine came to see me. He had joined the Charismatics. He told me they drive out spirits and cure illnesses and all and perhaps I should try it. He said he would call Fr Savio to see me. I agreed to try it. The next day, the Father came and he prayed over me. At once, I felt I was getting better. Since that day, believe it or not, I started responding to the doctor's treatment and got well soon. I then decided to join the Charismatics (Robinson 1998: 204).

Narratives from south India reveal similar patterns. One evangelical leader spoke of her conversion. Some time after the incident she describes below, she was converted, and received the Holy Spirit.

After my marriage and the birth of my two sons bad things stormed into my life. My husband and his sister wanted to kill me so that he could marry her daughter. They paid a sorcerer and he sent...[sorcery] so I was unable to move my limbs or speak. I was in bed for six months. With the help of some Christian friends who prayed for me I regained the use of my hands and my speech. Still, I was not happy. I wanted to die and I bought some poisonous fruits. I thought my husband would try to prevent me from taking them, but instead he encouraged me. So I ate them, and became unconscious. My friends rushed me to the Government Hospital. After a few hours the doctors said I was dead. They covered me with a white cloth. My friends prayed at my side all night, and the next morning when the staff came to take me to a post-mortem my limbs began to move and they rushed to call the doctors. I realized then that God did not want me to die (Caplan 1987: 236).

As Caplan (1987) notes though, Charismatic and Pentecostal beliefs, like those of orthodox Christianity, are sharply dualistic. They regard spirit possession as the work of the Devil and those who join these movements are urged to stop all practices of spirit propitiation, even those relating to deceased ancestors. While Christians can merge their ideas about spirit possession with the movement, they must also give up their beliefs regarding ancestral shades. Charismatics in Goa often give up all practices with regard to spirit propitiation or at least claim to have done so. Alternatively, they continue such practices by visiting the *gaddhi* when they believe that harm has been caused by ancestral spirits but go to the evangelists with other cases of spirit affliction.

The confrontations between the victim possessed and the charismatic figure are dramatic and offer a site for the conquest of evil by Christ and the Holy Spirit, the victory of Christianity over the pagan faiths. No appeasement of the spirits is permitted. When a particular spirit requested a small blood sacrifice on the lines of Hindu exorcist techniques, the response was to abuse it and confront it with the power of Christ, manifest in his name, his words as contained in the bible and elements such as holy oil and water blessed in his name. The charismatic healer often speaks in tongues, further evidence of the presence and power of the Holy Spirit. It is argued that the spirits driven out by Hindu exorcist methods are free to return to attack a victim again. Spirits exorcised by the evangelists are driven below into the abyss, from where they can never return (Caplan 1987; see also Stirrat 1992).

Heterodoxy, Conflict and Challenge

Shamanistic cults and evangelical movements both offer to those at the lower end of the social scale, an arena of autonomy and power, which they are effectively denied within the confines of orthodox churches. Shamans are usually from the lower castes and can often be women. The cults take different forms. There may be possession by Hindu divinities or Christian ones. The evangelical healing sessions draw a much sharper divide between the possessed and the charismatic prophet. Non-Christian beings possess a person; the Holy Spirit does not. He cures by the fullness of his presence, not through possession. Even the evangelical cults fall in the realm of the heterodox. The church is wary of them. They are considered a threat to orthodox Christianity and their prophets and leaders a threat to the clerical orders.

The Christ Ashram in Nuvem, Goa, is a cultic centre set up by a low caste labourer Miguel Colaço. There are different legends relating to how Miguel came to set up the *ashram*. In one, a small boy gave him a cross that he had found in the vicinity of Nuvem and Miguel took this as a sign that he had a mission to cure people. In another, he found a cross in the mines where he worked and started performing miracles of healing. Hindus and Christians come to the *ashram* to be cured of a variety of mental and physical ailments. Miguel is known as a healer and exorcist. He is said to lift spells and deflect evil from those who come to him. Miguel cures using Catholic symbols and texts: holy water, the rosary, hymns and the litany (Newman 2001). His power comes from the realm of popular Christianity but is unacceptable to the orthodox church. He practises outside the confines of the church.

Most shamanistic cults flourish outside the church proper, and those who take recourse to them often do so against priestly injunction. Since it is to Mary rather than Christ that women turn when possessed, priests among the Syrian Christians caution against honouring Mary while forgetting Christ himself. They constantly stress divine hierarchy of Christ over Mary, of the male over the female and the canonical over the unofficial and popular. As one priest said:

...If you put Mary before Christ, if you pray to Mary while forgetting Christ, it is a grave error. Remember that Mary is nothing without the grace of God, that she is nothing without Christ...(Visvanathan 1993a: 228).

Conflict with the church and with those who command the spaces of the church go hand in hand. In Goa, the Charismatic movement has offered to those who are involved with it, a means that they can employ to challenge the high castes on their own ground, within the church. In the Goan village studied by the author, a group of Charismatics, mainly Sudras, approached the parish priest and asked him if they could conduct a small prayer service in the church after the afternoon Mass on Good Friday. The priest agreed, not knowing the nature of the service they wished to conduct. In the evening, a group of Charismatics came to the church to pray. They began to praise the Holy Spirit and sing and clap in the manner of evangelical worship.

One of the Chardo *gauncars* of the village came to know what was happening and he gathered together other Chardos and came to the church. The Charismatics were ordered out, but they refused saying that they had the parish priest's permission. The Chardos went in anger to the parish house to demand an explanation from him for allowing the low castes in to start their 'singing' in the church. The priest denied he knew the nature of the celebration, even saying that had he known he would have refused permission. The Chardo *gauncars* demanded that the church be closed. There was a scuffle between the groups and several people received minor injuries. The Chardos ensured that the church doors were closed and locked before they returned home (Robinson 1998).

Clearly, the low caste Charismatics were challenging the hierarchical organization of their church. It is the major confraternity, consisting of Chardo *gauncars*, which has the right to organize celebrations on Good Friday, to conduct the afternoon Mass and to occupy the main spaces of the church. The other social groups may only participate in the Mass or pray quietly in the church at other times. They do not have the right to conduct their own service on different lines. Their struggle appears to have been to extract precisely such a right. One Charismatic said: 'We wanted to have our own service. These people organize everything. We also want a role in the celebrations' (Robinson 1998).

The Chardos perceive the Charismatics as a threat to their position in the church. They view the spontaneous prayer and worship, the singing and clapping of the Charismatic form of devotion as a challenge to the sedate and ordered organization of reverence to the divine, which is characteristic of liturgical celebrations. They also clearly comprehended that their right to oversee the Good Friday celebrations was being defied by the Sudra Charismatics. Alternate modes of worship offered by the evangelical cults have opened the way for resistance to entrenched hierarchies in the church. Traditional shamanistic cults of possession and healing gave the lower social groups a space outside the church for the exercise of ritual control. They occupy an ambiguous position within popular religion though, and have no doctrinal backing to enable them to enter the church itself or act as a legitimate alternative to it.

Some churches have attempted to minimize the threat of the cults by bestowing nominal approval on them. The Catholic church for instance, has approved of the Charismatic movement, on condition that it does not attempt to draw its members away from participation in the rites of the church. The evangelical cults, moreover, have a firm biblical basis to their teachings. They also attract some priests and clergymen into their fold. Their effectiveness as an alternative to orthodoxy is thereby strengthened. Catholic Pallars in Tamil Nadu have begun to turn increasingly to the heterodox, more strongly egalitarian Christian cults in a movement of resistance to the persistence of caste discrimination within their church (Mosse 1994a: 97). Not all those who are members of evangelical cults will leave their mainline church completely. Some continue to attend worship in their church and also participate in evangelical meetings. For others, ties to the established church may just be formal. They receive baptism into a sect and pay tithes to it and are committed members of the cult (Caplan 1987).

The availability of new sectarian identities changes the rules of the game entirely. Now, dissent is not against one's position within the system. Conflict is not to improve upon one's place in the hierarchy. The struggle is against the system itself. Opting out is a real possibility and an immensely more radical one. A strengthening of the Charismatic and Pentecostal movements could bring about a critical shift: the complete and lasting transfer of religious affiliation from the established churches to these cults.

DALIT LIBERATION: ANOTHER MODE OF RESISTANCE

Not all resistance to upper-caste hegemony within the church stems out of indigenous cults of healing or the Charismatic and

Pentecostal movements. Not all is extrinsic to the church: some is encouraged and articulated by priests and theologians themselves. I had already spoken earlier of the missionaries' involvement in the battle for Dalit rights, particularly during the colonial period. Here I want to look at the struggle for the rights of Dalits in the post-colonial period and the formulation of the notion of a Dalit Theology. These movements have taken shape particularly, though not only, within the Catholic church.

The Christian Dalit Liberation Movement, formed in the 1980s, became the forum for the promotion and co-ordination of Dalit struggles against caste discrimination within and outside the churches on an all India basis. Christian Dalits are, according to the members of the Movement, 'twice alienated'. As Saral Chatterji (1988: 16) notes, 'they are regarded..in the same way as are the Dalits and tribals and they suffer from the same economic, social and educational disparities as the other Dalits. In addition, the hope of the Dalit converts for a better life, free from stigma and humiliation, appears not to have been fulfilled for the bulk of them within the churches'.

The most significant demand that has been taken up by the Dalit Christians and, in turn, endorsed by the mainstream church is that Dalit Christians should be accorded the same reservation and welfare benefits that are granted to Scheduled Castes professing the Hindu, Sikh, and Neo-Buddhist religions under the Constitution (Scheduled Castes) Order 1950 (and as amended in 1956 and 1990). The Dalit Christians should be given Scheduled Caste status and privileges so that they can enjoy the same political rights and socioeconomic benefits as all other Scheduled Castes.

Scheduled Caste Christians are not recognized as such under the law and they are not, therefore, eligible for the benefits of positive discrimination sanctioned by the Constitution. Dalit Christians are fighting for just such recognition and for the extension to them of the benefits accorded to Scheduled Castes. It is argued that most Dalit Christians are poor, educationally backward, politically powerless and social outcastes. The demand is that the Indian Government restore to them their legitimate rights and cease to discriminate against them on the grounds of religion.

The Constitutional order of 1950, known as the Constitution (Scheduled Castes) Order, 1950 listed Scheduled Castes and Tribes using the list employed by the Government of India

(Scheduled Castes) Order of 1936. Consequently, the third para-
graph of the 1950 Order specifies that no person professing a
religion other than Hinduism may be deemed a member of a
Scheduled Caste. This was amended in 1956 to include Sikh
Dalits and again in 1990 in favour of Buddhist Dalits. Christians
argue that the exclusion of Dalit Christians from these benefits
amounts to religion-based discrimination and contravenes Constitutional principles prohibiting discrimination on the grounds
of religion, race, caste, sex or place of birth.

On 18 November 1995, a *dharna* was staged at New Delhi
outside the Sacred Heart Cathedral. A prayer meeting took place
attended by Mother Teresa and Bishops and priests along with
Christians of all denominations in support of the Dalits' demand
to be included in the list of Scheduled Castes. As a sign of the
wholehearted solidarity of the Christian community, all Christian schools throughout the country remained closed for a day.
Despite this overt support extended to them, Christian Dalits
believe that the leadership of the church is ambivalent about
their demands and problems and they continue to protest against
various forms of discrimination that persist within the church.

The rumbling within the Catholic church has been particularly acute, perhaps because caste was tolerated to a greater
extent here. In a recent memorandum presented to the Catholic
Bishops' Conference of India (CBCI) in Chennai on the 21 January 2000, the Dalit Christian Liberation Movement asserted that
while the CBCI had in recent times expressed a lot of concern
about the question of discrimination against Dalit Christians,
precious little positive action had resulted. The changes brought
about had been 'meagre' and a host of problems still remained.
Marginalization in admissions and appointments to Christian
institutions, marginalization in vocations, and in the sharing of
power and authority in the church were specifically raised as
important concerns.

The document states (http://www.dalitchristians.com/Html/
DCLMtocbci.htm) that:

> The marginalization of Dalit Christians in our Christian minority
> institutions (in admissions and appointment) all along the several
> decades has very severely affected their social and economic mobility
> and progress. The degree of marginalization is alarming and appall-
> ing since Dalits are a majority in the Catholic Church, but they are
> only about 6% as students and employees in most institutions.

The document asserts that this exclusion has caused the community decades of poverty and economic loss. It is necessary, according to the memorandum, to institute a vigorous policy of reservation for Dalits within Christian institutions and to follow it strictly. A specific attempt is made to dissociate the responsibilities of the government from those of the church itself. It is argued that the church cannot leave it up to the government to solve all the problems of the Dalit Christians. Whether or not the government acts in favour of the Dalit Christians, the church is obliged to do what it can through a policy of reservation in its own institutions. If this does not happen, a small percentage of caste Christians will continue to enjoy the power and opportunities available through these institutions, while the majority of Dalits remain excluded.

The church is castigated for speaking of justice without implementing the concrete rules of distributive justice itself. In fact, it is explicitly stated that the church cannot put the burden of justice on the government. The church has to recognize that it has access to resources in the secular world. It owns property, institutions and financial and material resources, which it can employ to help the Dalit Christians. As the document categorically argues, the responsibility of the government does not absolve the church of the need for action. All the following summaries are from (http://www.dalitchristians.com/Html/DCLMtocbci.htm).

> The reservation we ask from the government is a case of constitutional equality irrespective of religion. But reservation for Dalit Catholics in the Church is necessary as there is a clear case of inequality within. Our elegant preaching for equality and liberation to the oppressed only goes to strengthen the plea for reservation to the oppressed. We cannot set right inequality without some norms of distributive justice. We may call it reservation 'option', 'preference' or priority. But the thing is it must be done and done without further delay.

A long set of appeals is part of the document. Some of the important ones are outlined here. They are listed because they reveal the extent of deprivation and discrimination in various areas of religious and social life still perceived by the Dalits.

> Appeal to the Bishops to see that priests, nuns and authorities stop supporting caste Christians against Dalit Christians and instead openly oppose discrimination and close down the churches and services in places where discrimination on the basis of caste is practised.

Appeal for increase in the number of Dalit Bishops. The number of Dalit Bishops is stated to be alarmingly negligible and is seen as a grave injustice. It is declared to be a matter of conscience for the church to look at the woeful representation of Dalits at higher levels of the clerical hierarchy. Of 140 CBCI Bishops, perhaps less than 6 per cent are Dalits, even though the majority of Catholics are Dalits. A strong appeal is made for a special drive to appoint about 85 Dalit Bishops over the next five or ten years in order to ensure equitable representation. Voluntary retirement for incumbent Bishops with a social conscience is recommended to enable the release of posts. In vacancies that already exist, it is requested that Dalit priests be appointed. The request for Dalit Bishops it is said is made not with a sense of narrow possessiveness, but in order to ensure the dignity and credibility of the church as an institution which truly upholds equality in a caste-ridden society. The need for the appointment of a Dalit Cardinal is also stated.

There should be an equitable number of superiors, provincials and heads of institutions from among Dalit priests and nuns. The CBCI is requested to take steps to constantly follow up and see that Dalits are given priority in admissions and appointments. About 60 per cent of the Catholics admitted to courses or appointed to various posts in institutions should be Dalits. There is an insistence that policies be formulated along these lines. It is expected of the CBCI to come up with its own policy statements that are appropriate and adequate so that others can follow the model.

It is requested that a considerable number of seats be reserved for Dalit Catholics in St. John's Medical College, Bangalore and any other Catholic Medical Colleges. A large number of Doctors (even a second generation of doctors) have come up among the other Dalits, thanks to the reservation for them by the government. The number of Dalit Christian doctors is stated to be negligible.

It is requested that primary or basic education is made free for Dalit Catholics in Catholic institutions just as the government ensures free primary education for Scheduled Castes. Educational Scholarships and fee concessions for rural Dalit Catholics are urged. It is requested that hostels offer a 50 per cent concession to poor Dalits. It is recommended that more technical rather than strictly academic programmes be started, keeping in view the needs of Dalits today.

Power sharing is a crucial issue and the extent of deprivation perceived by Dalits in this area is highlighted. Empowerment is considered of immense importance and this means sharing power at all levels. The marginalization of Dalits in vocations to priesthood and among the religious, is put forward as a matter of serious concern. Their underrepresentation at the level of Bishops, diocesan officials and administrators is pointed out. The fact that Dalit heads of institutions are minuscule in number and that they are also poorly represented in national organizations, is articulated. The general complaint is that resources have not reached the Dalits proportionately. Power sharing with Dalits is declared to be a vital step for initiating long-term changes and for sustaining the process of transformation.

> The CBCI is requested to constitute an apex body, which can take up the issues of Dalit Christians, follow them up and resolve them. There could be regional bodies to deal with representation of local issues. These bodies should have mandatory power to take action or impose some sanctions wherever needed. These actions of these bodies and the enforcement of decisions by them need to have a certain transparency. A major difficulty is perceived in the autonomy exercised by separate dioceses, congregations and institutions. This leads to major problems in streamlining the ways in which Dalit concerns should be dealt with.

> There is an appeal for more concerted effort by the CBCI and the whole church to get the Constitutional reservation for Dalit Christians. The CBCI is also exhorted to take steps to demand from state governments that they include Dalit Christians among the Backward Classes until the demand for inclusion in the Scheduled Caste list is addressed.

The language of the document remains respectful throughout, but the demands are voiced with clarity and forthrightness. It is obvious that Dalits no longer fear to speak out and have indeed, received international recognition and support for their struggles. The World Council of Churches (WCC), as part of its Ecumenical Action of Racism announced a Dalit Solidarity Programme. The programme's intent is to focus the attention of the WCC member churches on the situation and struggles for justice of Dalits in India. The Seventh Assembly of the WCC held in Canberra in 1991 had recognized the Dalits as the poorest of the poor and among the world's most exploited people. The Dalit Solidarity Programme was conceived out of that recognition, to concentrate on projects, consultations and exchanges that give a direct impetus to the realization of the struggle for emancipation of Dalits, both Christian and non-Christian in Indian society.

The WCC is made up of 334 member churches and associate bodies throughout the world, described sometimes as a fellowship of over 500 million Christians. Some of the member churches are in India. It is difficult for such a diverse fellowship to engage in concrete action without preparation and consultation. The problems of Dalits had been mentioned in WCC assemblies by Indian delegates in 1980 and then again in 1983 and had been heard with sympathy. Little action resulted, however. It was only in 1989 that the WCC commission on the combating of racism met in south India and some of the delegates visited Dalit communities. This led to the recognition of Dalit concerns.

Material on Dalit issues was put together to share with WCC member churches at the Canberra Assembly of 1991. At this assembly, it was resolved that the WCC would continue to work with indigenous peoples everywhere and ensure that issues identified by them are acted upon and their communities and organizations receive a hearing in the international community. In this significant development, the WCC placed the Dalits of India among the category of indigenous peoples. The WCC has now resolved to uphold the struggle for liberation and identity of the Dalit people and to establish co-operative ventures with Dalit groups across the religious divide with a view to spreading consciousness of their situation through exchange visits and publications. It has urged member churches in India to include Dalits in WCC meetings and delegations.

The Dalit Christian Liberation Movement is not the only representative group of Dalits in India. There are said to be over 5,000 Dalit groups, not all of them solely Christian, across the country. Some are political groups, such as the Dalit Sena, or the Republican Party of India. There are educational groups, such as the Dalit Education Facilitation Centre in Madras. In south India, there are also the Dalit Christian Liberation Movement and the Dalit Open University in Andhra Pradesh. There are several groups of Dalit writers and poets in different parts of the country and there are also Dalit student groups. The movement to create a Dalit theology has led to the Tamil Nadu Theological Seminary establishing its own Integrative Dalit Liberation

Movement. The history of Dalit struggles and the elements of a Dalit theology are now part of courses taught at several different seminaries.

Competition is inevitable, but the most critical challenge to the Dalit Christian struggle in recent times seems to be coming from associations aligned with India's Hindu right-wing organizations. Among these is an association calling itself the Poor Christian Liberation Movement. The Poor Christian Liberation Movement, that might well be an organization floated by the Hindu Right itself, tends to express views in concurrence with those of the BJP-led political regime. Its President, R.L. Francis, speaks out in RSS publications, such as the *Organizer*. The Poor Christian Liberation Movement has claimed from time to time that Dalit Christians have not suffered in BJP-run states and it voices concern that Christian missionaries tend to exploit the religious sentiments of the poor people.

The organization is opposed to the Dalit Christians receiving recognition as Scheduled Castes and it chastizes the church for allegedly misleading poor people by converting them with the promise of social and economic uplift. The Poor Christian Liberation Movement asserts that the church should give equality to Dalits in its own organizations, instead of looking to the government for benefits. The organization is also opposed to the recourse had by Dalits to international associations such as the WCC in its struggles. In line with Hindu right-wing views, it argues that it is necessary to build a 'Swadeshi church' and to cease looking towards the Vatican or the WCC for assistance and support.

OUTLINES OF A DALIT THEOLOGY

Turning from political battles, we need to ask ourselves what exactly is Dalit theology, in which so much interest has been expressed over the last decade or so. We know that in the late 1880s Phule used the Marathi word 'Dalit' to describe the outcastes and Untouchables as the oppressed and broken victims of Hindu society. It was in the 1970s that the young intellectuals of the Dalit Panther Movement of Maharashtra began to use the term as a reminder of their oppression. In their definition they included Scheduled Castes and Tribes, neo-Buddhists, workers, labourers, small farmers, women and others who were exploited politically, economically and on the basis of religion. Since then, the term has become a rallying point for the oppressed people of India. Terms imposed on the Dalits from outside such as Scheduled Castes, Untouchables and even Harijans have been rejected (see Webster 1990; Zelliot 1972). 'Dalit' has become for the Dalits, a term which they perceive as describing their situation as oppressed people and also as a positive affirmation of their identity.

The term, as we have seen, has been adopted by Christian Dalits as well. Among them, the idea of a distinct Dalit Christian theology that expressed their own lived experiences took shape under the influence of ideas received about the Black theology movement in the United States and the People's theology movement in Korea. Why was the need for a Dalit theology felt? As Prabhakar argues, the insensitivity of

> Indian Christian theology to dalit concerns and the deeper dimensions of their struggle and aspirations for fuller humanity, despite the majority of Christians being of Dalit origin, makes imperative the formulation of a Christian dalit theology, with a universal appeal (1988a: 1).

Thus, Dalit theology seeks to express the lives, the struggles and the oppression of the Dalits in their own words. However, it is not a theology that seeks to isolate the community. It is a theology that wants to come to terms with the specific contextual experience of oppression and discrimination of the Dalits, with the suppression of their history, their culture and their religious traditions. It does not in the process neglect more universal concerns for it is infused with a commitment to the idea of a single human community, to the idea of justice and equality for all humanity.

Much of the available scholarship has shown that conventional or classical Indian theology has remained largely conservative (see Boyd 1969; Clarke 1997b; Forrester 1980; Massey 1988). It grew out of, and was largely limited to, the experiences of some nineteenth century high-caste converts, mainly Brahmins, who sought to initiate a dialogue between Christian traditions and the high philosophical traditions of Brahmanic Hinduism. It is beyond the scope of this book to discuss the theological and philosophical writings of these thinkers, particularly since their work was barely known outside a fairly narrow circle of educated elites. A little, however, may be said so that the concerns of contemporary Dalits regarding the making of an indigenous Dalit theology may be understood.

Some of the names associated with Indian Christian theology are Krishna Mohan Banerjee (1813–1885), Brahmabandhav Upadhyaya (1861–1907), Nehemiah Gore (1825–1895), Narayan Vaman Tilak (1862–1919), Pandita Ramabai (1858–1922), Kali Charan Chatterjee (1839–1916), H.A. Krishna Pillai (1827–1900), A.J. Appasamy, P. Chenchiah, V. Chakkarai and A.S. Appasamy Pillai (1848–1926). Krishna Mohan Banerjee for instance, propounded a theology in which Vedic religion was seen to achieve its fulfilment in Christianity (Forrester 1980: 128). Like Ramabai, Upadhyaya came to believe that he was Hindu in everything save religious belief. He called himself a Hindu Christian and his theology identified the principle of catholicity and the kind of synthesis between philosophy and religion characteristic of Thomism as keys to the creation of a distinctively Indian theology (Forrester 1980: 131). Gore had a particularly orthodox understanding of Christianity, though he also believed that Christianity fulfilled many of the promises of Hinduism. He identified Hindu concepts such as *vairagya*, *namrata* and *kshama* as preparations for the Christian faith (Boyd 1973: 83).

Christian theology of this variety clearly wrestled with the problem of loosening the faith from its perceived 'western' origins and integrating it with Indian religious traditions. Even so, this kind of theology remained an adaptation of the elite. If it is only ever read about and rarely seen in practice, it is because it did not become a part of the lived experience of different Christian communities, which interacted with various strands of Hinduism and other religious traditions completely on their own terms and in a variety of different ways. Indian Christian theology remained a philosophical not an anthropological adjustment. It was a text-centred theology and based itself on written traditions. It is worth noting here that the texts that Indian Christian theology dialogues with, such as the Vedas, would not have been accessible to Dalits as a rule. The idea of cultural contextuality in Indian Christian theology expressed itself as an adjustment to Brahmanical religious and philosophical traditions. Some Indian Christian clerics and theologians were highly suspicious of interpretations produced by more lowly converts, seeing them as lacking in theological soundness.

Arvind. P. Nirmal (1988: 65), a pioneer in the exploration for a Dalit Christian theology, noted the drift of Indian Christian theology.

> Most of the contributions to Indian Christian theology in the past came from high caste converts to Christianity. The result has been that Indian Christian theology has perpetuated within itself what I prefer to call 'Brahmanic' tradition.

Consequently, the experiences and lived reality of the majority of Christians, who come from the lowest rungs of society, are overlooked in the workings of this theology. Indian Christian theology made no attempt to come to terms with the experiences of the lowliest. It was largely limited to the philosophical contemplation of Brahmins and other upper-caste Christians and failed to engage in dialogue with non-Brahmanical Indian traditions. Other interpretations were available. Indian Christians, even some non-Brahmins and others of more lowly backgrounds, had made attempts to merge Christianity with sets of ideas and beliefs other than those which emanated strictly from high Hinduism.

The *Kabirmat Darshak Granth* (Sources of the Kabir Religion) written by a merchant convert in Saurashtra in 1881 detailed many features of the Kabir sect, pointing out how its hidden meaning was fulfilled by Christianity. Kabir and Christ were both viewed as assuming human form and suffering every kind of pain (Boyd 1973: 85–86). In more recent times too, Ghura Master, a converted Chamar near Varanasi, sang Bhojpuri songs attributed to Kabir. In these songs, he likened the *nirgun* tradition of north India, of which Kabir was an exponent, to the sacramental vision of Catholicism. The *nirgun* tradition is a countertradition to caste Hinduism and focuses its devotion on a formless God without attributes. Kabir's *bhajans* captured the voice of protest against caste society as well as devalued radically the significance of the phenomenal world. Kabir likened the whole body to thinly woven cloth. Relating his body to the symbol of the cloth, Ghura Master re-imagined, in his songs, his whole body as cleansed of sin and untouchability by the water of his Christian baptism (Schmalz 1999: 188).

Bhajans among Bhils and the outcaste Dheds of lowland Gujarat spoke of the coming of the *Nakalanka Avatara* or Spotless Incarnation born of a virgin. These songs accommodated many elements from Islam and tribal beliefs, apart from their references to Sanskritic Hinduism (Boyd 1973: 87). An attempt was made to merge such elements with beliefs from within Christianity. In the Punjab, the baptized wandering *faqir* Golah Shah, preached a kind of pantheism in which he held Christ to be the ideal *faqir*, for he taught the way towards emancipation (Webster 1976: 124–25). Such indigenous interpretations no doubt existed in every Indian region and in many different languages, which would render them impossible to detail here.

These interpretations, however, by and large remained outside the margins of formal theological discourse and practice (see Tiwari 1988). Missionaries and elite Indian Christian theologians and clerics often tended to be unenthusiastic about the interpretations and oral traditions of the lowest social groups. For instance, Kali Charan Chatterjee baptized Golah Shah and visited him several times, but had serious reservations about his tendency towards pantheism and about the practices of wandering *faqirs* in general. He argued that 'the habit of begging and going about the country without control or supervision..opens a wide door to looseness of life and doctrine, that should on no account be encouraged in the infant Church of India' (Webster 1976: 125).

No serious attempt was made until recent times to understand the interpretations and experiences of the lowliest social groups or to incorporate them into theological discourses. Only the political and social changes of the post-colonial period paved the way for a shift of perspective. The most dramatic articulation of this shift came about in the 1970s. Under the influence of Liberation theology, a creative amalgam of Christianity and Marxism, emanating from South America, a concern with questions of social and economic justice began to receive expression in theological discourses. The idea of a Third World theology came into being. However, the injection of the concept of material poverty and class relations alone could not do justice to the experiences of Indian Dalits (see, for instance, Abraham 1997; Chatterji 1988; Clarke 1973, 1988; Devasahayam 1992; Elwood 1980; Fabella and Torres 1993; Massey 1988, 1990, 1994, 1995).

As Saral Chatterji (1988: 9) argued, a theology of the poor is insufficient. The idea of the 'poor' does not convey much about 'who the poor are, or the genesis of these sections and reasons for their persistence'. Poverty is subjectively constituted and one needs to pay attention to other forms of oppression that constitute the experience of poverty including caste, race, gender, culture and religion. Chatterji therefore rejects class as the sole foundation for the constitution of an alternative theology and argues that caste, its ideology and morphology and the nature of oppression and inherited inequalities perpetuated by it must become the basis for the formation of an Indian Christian Dalit theology.

Dalit theology is visualized as a counter-culture to the theology of the Brahmanical elite. As Oommen (2000: 26) notes, Dalits felt that the theological task in India could not be the preserve of the 'Brahmanic Tradition' within the Indian church.

> Dalit theologians were of the opinion that the theological and cultural domination of Brahmanic traditions within Indian Christianity, ignoring the rich cultural and religious experience of the Dalits had to be ignored, if not rejected completely (ibid.: 26).

Dalit theology must be a reflection by Dalits for Dalits, of themselves as Christians and members of a single human community. An authentic Dalit theology must be an expression of the sufferings and aspirations of the Dalits. It is the story of their pathos, their protest and their hopes. It narrates their subjugation through history but also becomes the means and expression of their liberation (Amaladoss 1997; Amritham and Pobee 1992; Ayrookuzhiel 1986, 1988, 1990; Clarke 1997a and b; Irudayaraj 1990; Massey 1994; Nirmal 1989, 1991, 1992, 1994; Prabhakar 1988a, 1988b, 1997). Dalit theology necessarily has a historical and sociological dimension. Oppression and subjugation are viewed as human creations, not part of a God-given destiny. These can and must therefore be changed. Transformation is not only possible, it is imperative. It is necessary to the fulfilment of the promise of this theology and its commitment to difference from conventional, alienating theologies.

Dalit theology requires a commitment to listening, because Dalit history and culture are contained in oral traditions, in legends and folk stories, in music and in religious symbols and practices. Dalit theology is Christ-centred. Christ is perceived as a Dalit, a carpenter's son, reviled and rejected by the priestly elite of his times. Non-Dalit theologians have also attempted to explore the concept of the solidarity of Christ with the poor and the outcast. For George Soares Prabhu (1994), the best expression

of Christ's relatedness to the struggles and privations of the
faithful poor is the Christological symbol of the incarnation. For
the deprived, then, the idea that 'The Word became flesh and dwelt
among us' (*New American Bible*) can have a powerful impact. Flesh
symbolizes unity and kinship. It encapsulates the idea of organic
wholeness, the idea that what happens to one, happens to all.

Christ identified himself totally with the poor. He was the
one who was hungry, the one who was the thirsty, the naked,
the imprisoned. He was rejected, outcast, spat upon and reviled.
He was, in a word, Dalit. Christ's dalitness is best symbolized
on the cross. Christ crucified is Christ broken, crushed, mangled. Rayan (1992) argues that Jesus suffered outside the camp
in order to affirm the inborn dignity and native purity of all
human beings, of all castes. Christ's cleansing of temple is also
of importance for Indian Dalits, who interpret the incident in
terms of its implications for the Gentiles. Dalits in India have a
long history of having to fight for rights of entry to temples.
Christ emptied the temple of those who had colonized it and
restored it to the Gentiles, returning to them the rights of entry
and worship. The act endorses Dalit struggles for temple entry.

The theology clearly works towards an understanding of divine
power not as dominance but as frailty and humility. The obligations of the theology are towards sacrifice and love on behalf of
the weak and the deprived. There is little anthropological material yet to enable us to show the workings of such a theology.
What would Dalit Christian community worship look like? How
would Dalit Christian ritual life be constituted? Some elements
are available in songs, stories and prayers. Prabhakar (1997: 419)
has rewritten the Christian Creed for Dalit theology.

> We believe in God, our Mother and Father;
> Sustainer, Protector and Helper of Dalits.
> Our ancestors were an original people of India
> Enslaved in our own country by evil forces
> And Broken, oppressed and segregated as
> Outcastes and Untouchables through the ages.
> Our cries for liberation from harsh caste-bondage
> Were heard by God, who came to us in Jesus Christ
> To live with us and save all people from their sins.
> We believe in Jesus Christ, born to virgin Mary
> And anointed by God's Spirit as the Son of God
> To unseat the proud and unjust rulers
> To bring down the rich and mighty

And to exalt the poor and oppressed
He will bring justice to all humanity.
Suffering as the Human One and Servant of God
He took our oppression and pain upon him
And laid down his life on the cross to redeem us
He was dead and buried but rose again to live forever.
He created a new humanity and a new future under God
To realise our full humanity and image of God in us
Jesus Christ is our Lord, Saviour and Liberator.
We believe in the Holy Spirit, our comforter
Who enlivens and unites and empowers us
To obtain the glorious freedom of the children of God.
We believe in the Church, the Body of Christ
And His fellowship to create equality and justice on earth.
We believe that Christ will come again
To judge all nations, according to their deeds to justice
And to establish God's rule of righteousness,
Forever and ever, Amen.

The Exodus liberation paradigm had tremendous implications for Liberation theologians in Latin America. It has also influenced the articulation of Dalit theology in India. The account from the Biblical text of Deuteronomy recounting the toil, affliction and oppression of the ancestors of the Israelites is used to construct the movement of the Dalits from a 'no people' to 'God's people' (Oommen 2000: 32). According to A.P. Nirmal (1994: 33):

> The historical Dalit consciousness depicts even greater and deeper pathos than is found in the Deuteronomic Creed. My Dalit ancestors did not enjoy the nomadic freedom of the wandering Aramean. As outcasts, they were also cast out of their villages...

Dalit theology needs to listen to the ways of protest and resistance worked into Dalit renderings of their early history. It also needs to widen the definition of 'text', incorporating the oral traditions of the Dalits, their folktales and songs. The rich communitarian values expressed through Dalit celebratory forms are worth recollecting (Oommen 2000: 36). Indeed, one may find that the kinds of dialogue popular Christianity fosters with non-Brahmanical Hinduism and other traditions, which this book has recorded, will require recognition by a Dalit theology. As we have seen throughout, meaningful systems of interaction and shared practices and symbols have been moulded by people and communities in everyday life-situations (ibid.: 36–37). Their re-collection and recovery by theologians may be vital to the process of theological renewal.

Working from within the discipline of theological studies, Clarke (1997b) offers one of the first systematic attempts at giving an anthropological grounding to Dalit theology by exploring the world of the south Indian Paraiyar. Listening to Paraiyar Christian accounts, he culls out two biblical narratives that are of central significance to them. The first is the story of the meeting of Nicodemus and Christ. Nicodemus, the rich man, came to meet Christ, the Dalit, at night. He needed his help, but he did not want to be seen conversing with him. The second story is that of Christ's encounter with the Samaritan woman at the well, of whom he makes a request for water. He drinks from the well of and the vessel of the Samaritan woman. Samaritans were among the despised in Palestinian society of the time. Christ's interaction with the Samaritan woman emphasizes his empathy and relatedness with the lowly.

Clearly, Paraiyar Christianity cannot be fixed by a particular reading of the Bible. Theirs is largely an oral theology and it takes from literary traditions, selectively and creatively, what it identifies with and what it can make its own. Among Dalit traditions, their use of the drum and accompanying songs have been highlighted as modes of expression of Dalit liberation. Prabhakar (1988a) speaks of drum-beat songs among Dalits of Guntur in Andhra Pradesh. These songs have been written by a Dalit poet and they bring out the caste exploitation experienced by the Dalits and their struggles for release from suffering. The songs are rendered to the beat of the *dappu*, the same drum made of hide that had been traditionally beaten by Dalits to summon village meetings or used during religious festivals. Thus, an instrument that has been a symbol of Dalit enslavement and pollution is now appropriated as one of liberation.

Clarke (1997b) too focuses on the drum as the bearer of Dalit divinity and emancipation. At one point in time, the Dalits were required to break the drum before they were baptized into the church and were forbidden even from possession of it. As it was a means and symbol of supernatural communication with the non-Christian divine, the breaking of the drum was considered a necessary preliminary to entrance into the Christian faith. Clarke calls for the reinstatement of the drum as a central symbol in Dalit theology.

The drum is at the heart of the religious world of the Paraiyar and is the central vehicle mediating divine power. The immanent presence of God among the Paraiyar is best symbolized by the drum. Christ being that presence, it is Christ as drum that needs reclaiming. The act of drumming obtained for the pariahs, a place within the social world, thus establishing their human identity and the importance of their control over certain functions necessary in collective ritual performances. It also separated them from caste society, capturing their difference and collective identity.

The reverberating sound of the drum, however, resisted separation and breached the geographical and ritual boundaries that kept apart the pure caste people from the pariahs. The drum is therefore a symbol of reconciliation with the social world and separation from and resistance to it. Like the drum, Christ was the ultimate deviant, a boundary breaker par excellence, who violated all rules meant to separate pure Jew and impure Gentile. He came to bring about the reconciliation of the world, but himself stood outside it, among the poor, the marginalized and the disprivileged; in other words, among the Dalits.

Dalit theology is not allowed to be passive. Its role is emancipatory and socially transformative. Japhet's (1988) Dalits near Bangalore continued to perform servile duties for caste Christians well into the latter half of the twentieth century. They dug burial pits, carried dead animals and worked for high-caste Christian landlords. However, they had no rights to draw water from the village well and had to use the water of a filthy canal half a mile from the village. In the 1980s, however, struggles between them and the caste Christians increased over the rights of access to the village well. Dalits openly defied the caste Christians, despite reprisals. The process of their emancipation had been initiated by biblical reflection and the composition and singing of Dalit songs that captured their situation. The Dalits selected their own Christian leader and decided to take up other work and to withdraw from serving and working for the high castes.

CONCLUSION

What can one say in conclusion to a chapter that charts the contemporary upheavals within the Christian community and shows a trajectory that promises more turbulence? It is difficult to stand back and assess the situation. However, anthropological calm must prevail and it is necessary to deconstruct the formulae for revolutionary praxis even if the full picture cannot yet be gleaned. What is clear is that the battle is being waged especially fiercely on the caste front. The Dalit/non-Dalit axis is the one where fortunes are shifting sharply and most of the action is raging. At least, this is the arena most in the public eye.

This is also an arena where the church has seen fit to rouse itself to some action, due in part, perhaps, to the public nature of the struggles. The recent battles centring on conversion saw many criticize Christian missionaries for promising potential tribal and lower-caste converts freedom from hierarchy and oppression but flagrantly failing to deliver on such promises. Whether or not such promises were made, the criticism has further spurred the church's resolve and its efforts to act on issues related to caste discrimination within the fold. Despite the ambivalence and belated reaction of church authorities on many issues related to caste, some support has clearly emerged for Dalit concerns. Theologians, both Dalit and non-Dalit are engaged in a re-reading of biblical Christology that renders Christ a figure akin to the Dalits. Dalits now find they have an ear in national and international church bodies. The pace of reforms is slow and, sometimes, Dalits may choose the option of leaving mainstream churches in favour of sectarian movements.

The task has already been initiated, however, and this is somewhat more than can be said regarding the area of gender relations to which I would like to shift focus. This is an area where the church or churches badly need to do a little re-thinking and reorientation of their procedures and practices. In comparison with caste, gender has remained a largely silent entity in the struggles of the recent decades. However, this does not mean that concerns have not been expressed.

Even in the debates over the Dalit question, the problems of women have emerged as a separate concern. Ruth Manorama (1994) has spoken of Dalit women as being 'thrice alienated' and as being the 'dalits among the dalits'. They are oppressed because of their class identity, their caste and their gender. Most Dalit spokespersons are male, even if they highlight the issue of gender. It is actually in the arena of personal law and rights of divorce and inheritance that the discrimination experienced by Christian women has come to the fore in a major way. Most such battles are individual ones, though now women's organizations are coming forward to assist in the struggles for legal equality and redress.

The first case to rock the conservative boat was the case of Mary Roy whose battle was against the Travancore Christian Succession Act of 1916. Under this Act, in a case of intestate (without a will) property, the daughter was entitled to only a fourth of the son's share of the estate or Rs 5,000, customarily meant for *stridhanam*, whichever was less. In her case, the Supreme Court found it easy to strike down the unjust law, since it had in any case been wrongly applied, having as it did no validity once the Union of Indian States had taken place. The Indian Succession Act, 1925 had to be employed in the case, which made for equal rights in intestate succession.

The other civil cases which are of immense interest and significance revolve around the issue of divorce. Divorce among Indian Christians is legally governed by the Indian Divorce Act of 1869 (see Devadasan 1974). This Act is discriminatory against women in that it allows men to divorce their wives on the grounds of adultery, while demanding that women prove cruelty, incest, bigamy or desertion *along* with adultery for a case for divorce to be admitted. While divorce by mutual consent has since been incorporated in matrimonial laws applying to other Indian communities, the Christian divorce laws remained unchanged.

Women's groups in association with Christians initiated a campaign for change in the 1980s arguing that the civil laws governing the Indian Christian community desperately needed reform. However, the different denominations within Christianity could not come to any consensus regarding the extent and nature of the reforms. In 1995, however, the Kerala High Court in a judgement in the Mary Sonia Zachariah versus Union of India case, struck down the discriminatory sections of the Indian Divorce Act. The sections were deemed to discriminate against women and to be therefore unconstitutional. Later, in a joint judgement applying to the cases of Jessie D'Silva, Ursulla Menezes and Pragati Varghese, the Bombay High Court recognized cruelty and desertion as independent grounds for the dissolution of a Christian marriage.

Recently, a reform Bill, the Christian Marriage and Matrimonial Causes Bill, 1994, drafted by the Christian churches was passed by the government in 2000. The Catholic church, in particular, however, continues to demand that its own canonical decrees regarding marriage and its annulment be granted separate legal recognition. Women's associations are opposed to this position, arguing that ecclesiastical authorities should not be permitted intervention in civil affairs. They also argue that given the church's conservative stance on most aspects of civil life, particularly in relation to women's rights, legal recognition for its decrees would only work to worsen the situation for women. The passage of the bill has not stilled criticism from women's groups which argue that the bill has several lacunae and does not improve matters with regard to issues such as adoption or succession.

It has largely been the spirit of reform rather than of revolution that has animated the struggles of Christian women for equality. It is the cases of individual women that first brought these issues to the fore. The active participation of women's groups came somewhat later. The struggles have not managed to bring about the large-scale organization of Christian women in India. The Dalits have created a strong pressure group within the church, women have not. It is not surprising that the churches have not equally supported the issues raised by women, though they have often had to make the politically correct noises. The Catholic church is still quite unwilling to relinquish completely its hold on matrimonial issues. The government was slow to act on the issues of the new matrimonial Bill, but may simply have been waiting for the right moment.

In any case, the reform of laws on divorce or inheritance does not exhaust what needs to be done for gender equality in the churches. At some point, issues regarding priestly celibacy or the ordination of women may well be raised, particularly within the Catholic church. These are questions also troubling the church in other parts of the world. I am inclined to think that a question that may assume great importance will be that of the church's, especially the Catholic church's, stance on abortion and contraception, both issues which implicate women's lives in fundamental ways. In a developing country like India these issues take on critical significance. It is not necessary though that sustained group activism will result. What may happen is the increase in numbers of those who simply bypass canonical decree.

7

CONCLUSION

Indian Christianity is complex and difficult of easy description. Certainly, this book has shown that. The anthropological and socio-historical material presented here throws into doubt, a number of popular assertions about the nature of Indian Christianity (or about Christians). It also questions mainstream academic understandings of critical issues in the sociology of religion in India. A significant number of themes of some importance have been discussed in the course of the chapters, though an attempt has been made to gel the theoretical concerns with the ethnographic material and so keep the book accessible even to a comparatively unspecialized audience. For instance, footnotes have been kept to the minimum. Most material has been included in the text and a large number of references are given, for anyone wishing to pursue certain ideas or the work of specific authors.

The themes of the book and the concerns they have drawn us towards shall be dealt with in greater detail below. However, something needs to be said about the impulses that led to its writing before moving on. Though I am an Indian Catholic, this book is by no means part of a personal search for roots. It was born of a professional interest, spurred by an initial investigation into the literature, anthropological and sociological, available on India's varied Christian groups. The writing of it though, overlapped in part with a period in recent history that many Indian Christians believe have been their 'darkest days'. Against the background of a spate of killings and attacks on Christians in different parts of the country, the energy to write this essay diminished. The debates initiated on conversion in the media and the increasingly hysterical tone they assumed silenced rather than encouraged the desire to speak. It was fortuitous that I was around the time offered a three-month fellowship at the Queen's

University of Belfast. Far from the 'ignoble strife', as it were, the fellowship enabled the rough drafts and materials for this to come out of the drawers where they had been gathering dust.

The greatest fear at that stage was not of personal security or of being seen to be 'taking sides' in the debate. It was that the terms of the debate were being horribly mangled and that critical rational discourse was becoming increasingly irretrievable. It does irk anthropologists to be asked to talk about current events, perhaps because they believe that not everything is necessarily signal of a stable social pattern and time is needed to understand the full implications of what is happening. However, we will now have to cope with the knowledge that our ideas and concepts are no longer ours alone. Indeed, they are part of current events and current debates. Concepts such as communalism, Sanskritization, feminism and conversion are increasingly debated as much in the media and in the political assembly as in academic circles.

If pluralism of knowledge is going to demand that we listen to all such voices, what legitimacy can we claim for our own views? We will have to demonstrate that we have a better case (if we do) than those out on the streets or in the television studio. Alternative views will have to be critically appraised, when we put out our own against them. This book has no overt political agenda, except that all our writing must be inherently political. It addresses no ideologues, either of the right or the left, but whatever its audience, it locates itself firmly against all kinds of populist understandings of Indian Christian communities. Its material shows the incontrovertible fact of the immersion of Christian communities in regional cultures everywhere. The book might indeed be forgiven for taking for granted, the immersion of Christian communities in regionally specific cultures, since this is brought out so strongly by the literature we have drawn from. However, it makes an attempt to grasp the functions and foundations of what is retained by the Christian communities of the cultures they engage with and to understand the whys and the hows of what is released.

This lengthy essay, if you like, should not be viewed as a summary of the literature on Indian Christians. It is an attempt to cull, out of a great deal of literature that is scattered and not always easily available and that spans academic disciplines like history, anthropology and religious studies, material on certain central themes. The perspective is anthropological, but the material is drawn very eclectically from different sources. The book seeks to counter certain central ideas in the ways in which Christianity has often been studied. It has brought under critical scrutiny, ideas such as 'accommodation', 'assimilation', 'syncretism' and the like and has argued that the manner in which these kinds of concepts have been employed in the study of Christianity in India has led to a seriously flawed perception.

The various 'Christianities' described in this book have been located regionally and historically and attempts have been made to understand the origin and the mode of development of different groups and the kinds of shifts they might have undergone. The success of the effort is bound by the amount and depth of the historical and ethnographic material at hand. But the limits are transcended by the approach of the enterprise, which has been as far as possible, comparative, aimed at understanding resemblance and pursuing differences. The thematic integration of materials better enabled this kind of approach. It also sensitizes the reader (as the writer) to the gaps, to the kinds of questions that need to be explored and have not been so far, and to the troublesome doubts that ethnographies sometimes raise.

To point these out is not to trash what we have but to elicit interest in the potential for future scholarship. Whole areas await a brush with anthropology: gender relations within different Christian communities, the relationship between the priest and the lay people, the contextual interpretation of biblical themes in different regions. The category of the 'sermon', I would argue, simply begs for anthropological exploration. This is the critical territory for the interaction of clergy and congregation, the textual and the oral, the 'universal' and the local. If a sense of a 'world community' of Christianity is communicated to local groups, it is through sermons that the mediation is centrally achieved. The particular inflection that Christian ideas are given in regional contexts is worth analysis.

An entire world of ritual interaction remains barely discovered in the field of the anthropology of Indian Christianity. The ritual of the confession of sins is one that remains untouched in the ethnographies. How do different groups and individuals treat the concept of confession? Is 'sin' understood in a spiritual or social context? As individual or relational? In the closed world of a Christian parish, can confession be employed for the uncovering of *other's* sins or for the settling of individual and community scores? (For a fascinating account of some of these themes in a region outside the subcontinent, see Rafael 1993). Individual, community and family prayer is an area that might respond richly to anthropological exploration. What is the understanding of 'prayer' that people hold? What do they pray for? All kinds of individual and social conflicts and desires are likely to be compressed in prayer.

A forlorn silence prevails over the entire domain of the religious and monastic Orders. Congregations, whether of priests, nuns or religious Brothers, have figured sometimes in historical accounts of missions in India, but have not so far emerged in sociological or anthropological narratives. We are beginning to get some glimpses now (see Forbes 1986; Haggis 1998), but need much more analysis of the roles, the strategies and the professional and personal challenges and dilemmas faced by women (and men), both clerical and lay, involved at different levels in the mission efforts. The rich material on village churches that we have explored briefly, raises the expectation that a wealth of data awaits the person who wishes to delve into the world of Christian cultic centres, shrines and pilgrimages. A Christian pilgrim map of India could well be drawn, including many shrines in the south and some in other parts of the country. Calling and cult, vow and vocation are still to be drawn into the body of writing on Indian Christianity.

The themes I have outlined here do not receive narrative attention in the text precisely because they rarely show up in any of the literature. There are several other ideas that have been pursued here though, and I will spend some time in bringing these together again. These are ideas that need to be explored further and one hopes that future research will turn even more towards them. The theme of interaction between communities as we have noted in the text is an extremely rich and complex one and has received more or less one-sided attention to date. Most of the time, attention is turned to understanding what Christianity and particular Christian communities have taken from Hinduism. It has been argued here that we need to complicate the question further and to seek an understanding of what Christian ideas and practices have given to people of other faiths and how they have been received.

In a heterogeneous, multi-religious environment, it is often insufficient for the anthropological perspective to be limited to the relationship between Hinduism and Christianity. We have already seen the necessity to integrate tribal religions and Islam in the picture. Material from Kerala and the north-east for instance, showed the importance of these traditions for understanding the complex of Christianity in these regions. One might also argue that in certain regions and social environments, it may be important to look at the interplay of other traditions as well, including for instance, Buddhism or Sikhism.

Or perhaps, Judaism? Dempsey (1999: 157–59) relates a fascinating story, again located in Kerala, where Jews, now a handful, were once a thriving community involved in trade and commercial and maritime activities with and alongside groups such as the Syrian Christians. In a Syrian Christian church in Peroor, customary oil lamps and Christian paraphernalia are to be found alongside tables filled with Jewish menorahs. The popular explanation for this is conveyed through a story related about a saintly Iraqi Jewish woman called Marttasmuni, who lived over a 100 years before Christ. Tortured for their faith after her husband's death, she and her seven children died, steadfast to the name of Yahweh. According to the oral tradition, the woman and her children appeared once a year to the believing. In one year, a silk cloth was draped on the wall, where the apparition used to manifest itself. The images stayed on the cloth for five minutes. This cloth was apparently brought by the Archbishop of Iraq to Peroor and enshrined in the local church. The images of the saints still appear to those of real faith and many miracles are said to have taken place. The church is visited by Hindus and Muslims, apart from Christians and Jews. The Jewishness of Marttasmuni seems to present no difficulties for the Christians (or others), who venerate her precisely for her courage and faithfulness to her religion.

Loosely woven into local Christian oral and written accounts, Marttasmuni's story reminds us yet again of the intricate ways in which traditions may be juxtaposed and connected, or sometimes allowed to co-exist in delicate balance in richly plural contexts. Undoubtedly, the diverse contexts we have explored through this book evidence that traditions feed off each other in complex ways, which cannot be captured very well through a linear perspective. A plea for factoring in the dimensions of time and change into the understanding of the ways in which religions have interacted in India, has been integral to all that has been said here.

The idea of conversion was thoroughly complicated by the refusal to reduce it to sameness, wherever and whenever its occurrence. Motive, mode and management inflected mission in myriad ways in the different contexts and at varying periods of time. The motif of violence hangs treacherously over ideas about conversion, but the effort here has been to studiously disentangle the various elements involved, to separate different phases of conversion, to connect motives and means, to ascertain varied interrelationships of power and evangelical purpose. The relation between pressure and resistance cannot be ignored. The intricate ways in which attempts to cope with disruption and the desire for social mobility and for access to various kinds of power and opportunity intertwine in creating possibilities for conversion, have been pointed out.

Internal to communities, are a whole host of community and individual rituals, patterns of hierarchy and systems of differentiation, structures of family and kinship organization. Debates on caste and the joint family, patterns of kinship terminology and ideas of patriarchy are critical to comprehending the social life of different Christian communities. The movement towards the possible break-up of mainstream churches, the challenges posed by Dalits and perhaps, increasingly, by women are subjects with which the book concludes. They map the ways in which social change has impacted on Christians in recent years. Slow to change as it might be, even the church has in recent times understood the need for worship to be in tune with indigenous ways (see Eck 1995). The Catholic church has *officially* begun to promote the indigenization of the form of worship in specific respects. Seating on the floor is encouraged in churches, as is the use of the *aarti* and ritual items such as garlands, *diyas* and *agarbattis*. The limits and possibilities of such forms of indigenization, particularly in south India, have only just begun to be explored (see Harper 1995; Sherinian 1998).

More than anything else, this book is an *introduction* to Indian Christianity, through the anthropology of it. The sociology of religion is a subject taught to students in theological and religious studies courses. It is obviously a subject in graduate and undergraduate courses in sociology and anthropology. Nevertheless, the means to teach the anthropology of religions in India, though not the anthropology of Hinduism, are woefully inadequate. Reference to one or other monograph, the usual way out, though good at an advanced stage, can never capture the richness and complexity of the terrain of Indian Christianity or the diverse forms it takes in different parts of the country. Little sense of the history of the religion can be communicated or its interaction with varied regional cultures. If this book can fill this gap as well as be a source of 'something new' to whet the appetite for further research among more specialized audiences, it will have fulfilled its aim.

REFERENCES AND SELECT BIBLIOGRAPHY

Abraham, K.C. 1994. Emerging Concerns in Third World Theology. *Bangalore Theological Forum* 26, 3 and 4: 3–14.

_____. 1997. Dalit Theology—Some Tasks Ahead. *Bangalore Theological Forum* 29, 1 and 2: 36–47.

Ahmad, Imtiaz. (ed.), 1973. *Caste and Social Stratification among the Muslims.* Delhi: Manohar Book Service.

_____. (ed.), 1978. *Religion and Ritual among the Muslims in India.* Delhi: Manohar Book Service.

Alexander, K.C. 1968. Changing Status of Pulaya Harijans of Kerala. *Economic and Political Weekly* 3, 26–28: 1071–75.

_____. 1972. The Neo-Christians in Kerala, *in* J.M. Mahar (ed.), *The Untouchables in Contemporary India*: 153–61. Tucson: University of Arizona Press.

_____. 1977. The Problem of Caste in the Christian Churches of Kerala, *in* Harjinder Singh. (ed.), *Caste among Non-Hindus in India*: 50–65. New Delhi: National Publishing House.

Almeida, A. 1978. The Gift of a Bride: Sociological Implications of the Dowry System in Goa. Ph.D. thesis. University of Louvain.

Alter, James. P. and **Herbert Jai Singh.** 1961. *The Church in Delhi.* Nagpur: National Christian Council of India.

Amaladoss, Michael. 1997. *Life in Freedom: Liberation Theologies from Asia.* Maryknoll: Orbis Press.

Amaldass, Anand. (ed.), 1988. *Jesuit Presence in Indian History.* Anand: Gujarat Sahitya Prakash.

Amritham, Samuel and **John. S. Pobee.** 1992. *Theology by the People.* Geneva: World Council of Churches.

Amritha Raj, C. 1980. Theologizing by the Diocese of Kottar in the District of Kanyakumari. MA thesis. Institute Catholique de Paris.

Angrosino, Michael. 1994. The Culture Concept and the Mission of the Roman Catholic Church. *American Anthropologist* 96, 4: 824–32.

Appaswamy, Paul. 1923. *Centenary History of the CMS in Tinnevelly.* Palamcottah: Palamcottah Printing Press.

Arasaratnam, S. 1977. The Christians of Ceylon and Nationalist Politics, *in* G.A. Oddie. (ed.), *Religion in South Asia: Religious Conversion and Revival Movements in South Asia in Medieval and Modern Times*:163–82. London: Curzon Press.

_____. 1981. Protestant Christianity and South Indian Hinduism 1630–1730: Some Confrontations in Society and Beliefs. *Indian Church History Review* 15, 1: 7–33.

Arayathinal, T. 1947. The Missionary Enterprise of the Syrian Catholics of Malabar. *Eastern Churches Quarterly* 7, 4: 236–51.

Ayrookuzhiel, Abraham. 1986. Religion and Culture in Dalits' Struggle for Liberation. *Religion and Society* 33, 2: 33–44.

_____. 1988. Dalit Liberation: Some Reflections on Their Ideological Predicament. *Religion and Society* 35, 2: 47–52.

_____. (ed.), 1990. *The Dalit Desiyata: The Kerala Experience in Development and Class Struggle.* New Delhi: Indian Society for the Promotion of Christian Knowledge.

Ayyar, L.K. Ananthakrishna. 1926. *Anthropology of the Syrian Christians.* Ernakulam: Cochin Government Press.

Azariah, V. and **H. Whitehead.** 1930. *Christ in the Indian Villages.* Chennai: Christian Literature Society.

Azavedo, A.E. d'Almeida. 1890. *As Comunidades de Goa.* Lisbon: Viuva Bertrand and Company.

Baago, K. 1965. *A History of the National Christian Council of India, 1914–1964.* Nagpur: The National Christian Council.

_____. 1967. The First Independence Movement among Indian Christians. *Indian Church History Review* 1, 1: 65–78.

Baden-Powell, B.H. 1900. The Villages of Goa in the Early Sixteenth Century. *Journal of the Royal Asiatic Society of Great Britain and Ireland.* 11: 261–91.

_____. 1908. *The Origin and Growth of Village Communities in India.* London: Swan Sonnenschein and Company.

Bailey, F.G. 1963. Closed Social Stratification in India. *European Journal of Sociology* 4, 1: 107–24.

Bayly, Susan. 1981. A Christian Caste in Hindu Society: Religious Leadership and Social Conflict among the Paravas of Southern Tamilnadu. *Modern Asian Studies* 15, 2: 203–34.

_____. 1989. *Saints, Goddesses and Kings: Muslims and Christians in South Indian Society, 1700–1900.* Cambridge: Cambridge University Press.

Beaglehole, J.H. 1967. The Indian Christians—A Study of a Minority. *Modern Asian Studies* 1, 1: 59–80.

Behera, Deepak Kumar. 1989. *Ethnicity and Christianity: Christians Divided by Caste and Tribe in Western Orissa.* Bangalore. Christian Institute for the Study of Religion and Society.

Beyreuther, Erich. 1955. *Bartholomaeus Ziegenbalg: A Biography of the First Protestant Missionary in India 1682–1719.* Chennai: Christian Literary Society.

Borges, Charles. 1994. *The Economics of the Goa Jesuits 1542–1759: An Explanation of their Rise and Fall.* New Delhi: Concept Publications.

_____ and **Helmut Feldmann.** (eds), 1997. *Goa and Portugal: Their Cultural Links.* New Delhi: Concept Publications.

Bose, Ashish. 1997. *Population Profile of Religion in India: Districtwise Data from 1991 Census.* Delhi: B.R. Publishing Company.

Boxer, C.R. 1963. *Race Relations in the Portuguese Colonial Empire 1415–1825.* Oxford: Clarendon Press.

_____. 1969. *The Portuguese Seaborne Empire 1415–1825.* London: Hutchinson.

Boyd, R.H.S. 1978. The S.P.G. in Ahmedabad: 1830–51. *Indian Church History Review* 12,1: 54–66.

Boyd, Robin. 1969. *An Introduction to Indian Christian Theology.* Chennai: Christian Literature Society.

Boyd, Robin. 1973. The Gospel as Fulfilment in 19th and Early 20th Century Gujarat. *Indian Church History Review* 7, 2: 83–90.

Bragança Pereira, A.B. 1936–40. de. *Arquivo Português Oriental.* 11 vols. Bastora: Tipografia Rangel.

_____. 1991. *Etnografia da India Portuguesa.* 2 vols. Delhi: Asian Educational Services.

Braudel, Fernand. 1973. *Capitalism and Material Life 1400–1800*, tr. Miriam Kochan. London: Weidenfeld and Nicolson.

_____. 1981. *Civilisation and Capitalism 15th–18th Century (1): The Structures of Everyday Life*, tr. Siân Reynolds. London: Collins.

Brown, I.W. 1956. *The Indian Christians of St Thomas.* Cambridge: Cambridge University Press.

Bugge, Henriette. 1994. *Mission and Tamil Society: Social and Religious Change in South India (1840–1900).* Richmond, Surrey: Curzon Press.

Burghart, R. 1983. Renunciation in the Religious Traditions of South Asia. *Man* (n.s.) 18: 635–53.

Burkhart, G. 1985. Mission School Education and Occupation among Lutherans in a Small South Indian Town. *South Asian Social Scientist* 1, 1: 97–118.

Caldwell, Robert. 1857. *Lectures on the Tinnevelly Mission.* London: Bell and Daldy.

_____. 1869. *Tinnevelly and Tinnevelly Mission.* Chennai: Foster Press.

Caplan, L. Social Mobility in Metropolitan Centres: 'Christians in Madras City. *Contributions to Indian Sociology* (n.s.). 11, 1: 195–217.

_____. 1980a. Caste and Castelessness among South Indian Christians. *Contributions to Indian Sociology* 14, 2: 213–38.

_____. 1980b. Class and Christianity in South India: Indigenous Responses to Western Denominationalism. *Modern Asian Studies* 14, 3: 645–71.

_____. 1984. Bridegroom Price in Urban India: Class, Caste and 'Dowry Evil' among Christians in Madras. *Man* 19,2: 216–33.

_____. 1987. *Class and Culture in Urban India: Fundamentalism in a Christian Community.* Oxford: Clarendon Press.

_____. 1989. *Religion and Power: Essays on the Christian Community in Madras*, Chennai: Christian Literature Society.

_____. 1991. Christian Fundamentalism as Counter-culture, *in* T. N. Madan, (ed.), *Religion in India*: 366–81. Delhi: Oxford University Press.

Capuchin Mission Unit (Maryland). 1923. *India and Its Missions.* New York: Macmillan.

Carvalho, A.A. 1975. *Dalit People: A Socio-political Survey of the Caste Oppressed.* Baroda: Shreyan Publications.

Castets, J. 1925. *The New Madura Mission.* Trichinopoly: St Joseph's Press.

Chatterjee, Partha. 1986. *Nationalist Thought and the Colonial World—A Derivative Discourse.* London: Zed Press Ltd.

Chatterji, Saral. K. 1988. Why Dalit Theology, *in* M.E. Prabhakar. (ed.), *Towards a Dalit Theology*: 9–29. Delhi: Indian Society for the Promotion of Christian Knowledge.

Chikane, Frank. 1990. EATWOT and Third World Theologies: An Evaluation of the Past and the Present, *in* K.C. Abraham. (ed.), *Third World Theologies: Commonalities and Divergences,*: 147–49. Maryknoll: Orbis Press.

Clark, Mary. M. 1907. *A Corner in India.* Philadelphia: American Baptist Publications Society.

Clarke, S. 1973. *Let the Indian Church be Indian.* Chennai: Christian Literature Society.

_____. 1988. Dalit Movement: Need for a Theology, in M.E. Prabhakar. (ed.): *Towards a Dalit Theology*: 30–34. New Delhi: Indian Society for Promoting Christian Knowledge.

Clarke, Sathianathan. 1997a. Constructive Christian Theology: A Contextual Indian Proposal. *Bangalore Theological Forum* 29,1 and 2: 94–111.

_____. 1997b. *Dalits and Christianity: Subaltern Religion and Liberation Theology*, Delhi: Oxford University Press.

Clough, Emma Rauschenbusch. 1914. *Social Christianity in the Orient: The Story of a Man, a Mission and a Movement.* New York: Macmillan.

Conrad, Dieter. 1995. The Personal Law Question and Hindu Nationalism, in Vasudha Dalmia and Heinrich von Stietencron. (eds), *Representing Hinduism: The Construction of a Religious Tradition and National Identity*: 306–37. New Delhi: Sage Publications.

Copley, Antony. 1997. *Religions in Conflict: Ideology, Cultural Contact and Conversion in Late Colonial India.* Delhi: Oxford University Press.

Corbet, Robert. G. 1955. *Century of Faith: The Story of the American Baptist Foreign Mission Society, 1814–1954.* Philadelphia: American Baptist Publications Society.

Cronin, Vincent. A. 1959. *A Pearl to India: The Life of Robert de Nobili.* London: Rupert Hart-Davis.

Cunha Rivara, J.H da. 1992. *Archivo Portuguez-Oriental.* 6 fasciculos em 10 partes. Delhi: Asian Educational Services.

D'Costa, Adelyne. 1977. Caste Stratification among the Roman Catholics of Goa. *Man in India* 57, 4: 283–92.

D'Costa, Anthony. 1962. The Demolition of the Temples in the Islands of Goa in 1540 and the Disposal of the Temple Lands. *Nouvelle Revue de Science Missionaire* 18:161–76.

_____. 1964. Administrative, Social and Religious Conditions in the Goa Islands, 1510–1550. *Indica* 1,1:1–10.

_____. 1965. *The Christianisation of the Goa Islands.* Bombay: St. Xavier's College.

Daniel, E. Valentine. 1984. *Fluid Signs: Being a Person the Tamil Way.* Berkeley: University of California Press.

Das, Sisir Kumar. 1974.*The Shadow of the Cross: Christianity and Hinduism in a Colonial Situation.* Delhi: Munshiram Manoharlal.

Das, Veena. (ed.), 1986. *The Word and the World: Fantasy, Symbol and Record.* New Delhi: Sage Publications.

_____. 1987. *Structure and Cognition.* Delhi: Oxford University Press.

Da Trinidade, Paulo. 1954. *Conquista espiritual do Oriente.* Lisbon: Centro de estudos historicos ultramarinos.

Deliège, Robert. 1999. Demonic Possession in Catholic South India, *in* S.M. Michael. (ed.), *Dalits in Modern India: Vision and Values*: 252–71. New Delhi: Vistaar Publications.

De Mello, C. Mercês. 1955. *The Recruitment and Formation of the Native Clergy in India.* Lisbon: Agência Geral do Utramar.

Dempsey, Corinne G. 1999. Lessons in Miracles from Kerala, South India: Stories of Three 'Christian Saints'. *History of Religions* 39,2: 150–76.

Derret, J.D.M. 1977. Hindu Law in Goa: A Contact between Natural, Roman and Hindu Laws, *in* J.D.M. Derrel. *Essays in Classical and Modern Hindu Law*, 2. Leiden: E.J. Brill.

De Silva, C.R. 1978. The Portuguese and Pearl Fishing off South India and Sri Lanka. *South Asia* (n.s.) 1,1: 14–28.

D'Souza, A.B. 1993. Popular Christianity: A Case Study among the Catholics of Mangalore. Ph.D. thesis, University of Delhi.

D'Souza, B.G. 1975. *Goan Society in Transition: A Study in Social Change*. Mumbai: Popular Prakashan.

De Souza, Francisco. 1978. *Oriente conquistado a Jesus Cristo pelos padres da Companhia de Jesus da Provincia de Goa*. Portô: Lello and Irmão.

De Souza, T.R. 1979. *Medieval Goa: A Socio-Economic History*. Delhi: Concept Publishers.

_____. 1990. Rural Economy and Life, *in* T.R. De Souza. (ed.), *Goa Through the Ages*: 78–116. Delhi: Concept Publishers.

Devadason, (ed.), 1974. *Christian Law in India: Law Applicable to Christians in India*. Chennai: DSI Publications.

Devapackiam, Mary. 1963.The History of the Early Christian Settlements in the Tirunelveli District. Ph.D. dissertation, University of Madras.

Devasahayam, V. 1992. *Outside the Camp: Bible Studies in Dalit Perspective*. Madras: Gurukul.

Diehl, Carl G. 1965. *Church and Shrine: Intermingling Patterns of Culture in the Life of Some Christian Groups in South India*, Uppsala: Hakan Ohlssons Boktryckeri.

Diffie, B.W. and **G.D. Winius.** 1977. *Foundations of the Portuguese Empire 1415–1580*. Vol.1. Minneapolis: University of Minnesota Press.

Downs, Frederick. S. 1981. Administrators, Missionaries and a World Turned Upside Down: Christianity as a Tribal Response to Change in North-east India. *Indian Church History Review* 15, 2: 99–113.

_____. 1994. *Essays on Christianity in North-East India*. New Delhi: Indus Publishing Company.

Dube, Saurabh. 1992. Issues of Christianity in Colonial Chhattisgarh. *Sociological Bulletin* 41, 1 and 2: 97–117.

_____. 1995. Paternalism and Freedom: The Evangelical Encounter in Colonial Chhattisgarh, Central India. *Modern Asian Studies* 29,1: 171–201.

_____. 1999. Cultures of Christianity and Colonialism in Chhattisgarh. *Studies in Humanities and Social Sciences* 6,1: 61–78.

Dube, S.C. 1961. Social Structure and Change in Indian Peasant Communities, *in* A.R. Desai. (ed.), *Rural Sociology in India*. The Indian Society of Agricultural Economics. Mumbai: 258–63.

Dumont, L. 1957. For a Sociology of India. *Contributions to Indian Sociology* 1: 7–22.

_____. 1980. *Homo Hierarchicus: The Caste System and its Implications*. Chicago: University of Chicago Press.

Eaton, Richard. 1984. Conversion to Christianity among the Nagas, 1876–1971. *Indian Economic and Social History Review* 21, 1: 1–44.

Eck, Diana. 1982. *Banaras: City of Light*. New York: Alfred A. Knopf.

_____. 1995. *Encountering God: A Spiritual Journey from Bozeman to Banaras*. Delhi: Penguin Books India Ltd.

Elwin, V. 1955. *The Religion of an Indian Tribe.* Mumbai: Oxford University Press.

Elwood, J.D. (ed.), 1980. *Asian Christian Theology: Emerging Themes.* Philadelphia: The Westminster Press.

Estborn, S. 1959. *Our Village Christians: A Study of the Life and Faith of Village Christians in Tamilnad.* Chennai: Christian Literature Society.

_____. 1961. *The Church among Tamils and Telugus.* Nagpur: National Christian Council of India.

Estevão, Thomaz. 1857. *Grammatica da Lingua Concani.* Nova Goa: Imprensa Nacional.

Fabella, Virginia and **Sergio Torres.** 1993. *Irruption of the Third World: A Challenge to Theology.* Maryknool: Orbis Press.

Fanon, Frantz. 1965. *The Wretched of the Earth.* London: Mac Gibbon and Kee.

_____. 1967. *Black Skin, White Masks.* New York: Grove Press.

Fernandes, Walter. 1981. Caste and Conversion Movements in India. *Social Action* 31: 261–90.

Fernando, S. 1984. The Portuguese Patronage (Padroado) and the Evangelisation of the Pearl Fishery Coast. *Indian Church History Review* 18, 2: 94–105.

Fiddes, Nick. 1991. *Meat: A Natural Symbol.* London and New York:Routledge.

Fishman, A.T. 1941. *Culture, Change and the Underprivileged: A Study of the Madigas in South India under Christian Guidance.* Chennai: The Christian Literature Crusade.

Forbes, Geraldine H. 1986. In Search of the 'Pure Heathen': Missionary Women in Nineteenth Century India. *Economic and Political Weekly* 21, 17.

Forrester, D.B. 1974. Indian Christian Attitudes to Caste in the Nineteenth Century. *Indian Church History Review* 8, 2: 131–47.

_____. 1975. Indian Christian Attitudes to Caste in the Twentieth Century. *Indian Church History Review* 9, 1: 3–22.

_____. 1977. The Depressed Classes and Conversion to Christianity 1860–1960, in G.A. Oddie. (ed.), *Religion in South Asia: Religious Conversion and Revival Movements in South Asia in Medieval and Modern Times*: 35–66. London: The Curzon Press.

_____. 1980. *Caste and Christianity: Attitudes and Policies on Caste of Anglo-Saxon Protestant Missions in India.* New Jersey: Curzon Press Ltd.

Freitag, S. *Collective Action and Community: Public Arenas and the Emergence of Communalism in North India.* Berkeley: University of California Press.

Frykenberg, Robert. 1976. The Impact of Conversion and Social Reform upon Society in South India during the Late Company Period: Questions Concerning Hindu–Christian Encounters, with Special Reference to Tinnevelly, in C.H. Phillips and M.D. Wainwright. (eds), *Indian Society and the Beginnings of Modernisation c. 1830–1850*: 187–243. London: School of African and Oriental Studies.

_____. 1981. On the Study of Conversion Movements: A Review Article and a Theoretical Note. *Indian Economic and Social History Review* 17: 121–38.

Fuller, C.J. 1976. Kerala Christians and the Caste System. *Man* 11,1: 53–70.

_____. 1977. Indian Christians: Pollution and Origins. *Man* 12, 3: 528–29.

_____. 1984. *Servants of the Goddess: The Priests of a South Indian Temple.* Cambridge: Cambridge University Press.

_____. 1992. *The Camphor Flame: Popular Hinduism and Society in India.* New Jersey: Princeton University Press.

Furer-Haimendorf, Christoph von. 1976. *Return to the Naked Nagas.* New Delhi: Vikas Publishing House.

Gehani, T.G. 1966. A Critical Review of the Work of Scottish Presbyterian Missions in India, 1878–1914. Unpublished Ph.D thesis. University of Strathclyde.

Gensichen, Hans-Werner. 1967. 'Abominable Heathenism': A Rediscovered Tract by Bartholomaeus Ziegenbalg. *Indian Church History Review* 6, 1: 29–40.

Gerth, H.H. and **C. Wright Mills.** (eds), 1981. *From Max Weber: Essays in Sociology.* New York: Oxford University Press.

Ghurye, G.S. 1969. *Caste and Race in India.* Mumbai: Popular Prakashan.

Gibbs, M.E. 1972. *The Anglican Church in India: 1600–1970.* New Delhi: Indian Society for the Promotion of Christian Knowledge.

Gladstone, J. W. 1976. 19th Century Mass Movements in South Travancore—A Result of Social Liberation. *Indian Church History Review* 10,1: 53–66.

———. 1984. *Protestant Christianity and People's Movements in Kerala: A Study of Mass Movements in Relation to Neo-Hindu Socio-religious Movements in Kerala, 1850–1936.* Thiruvananthapuram: The Seminary Publications.

———. 1988. Christian Missionaries and Caste in Kerala, *in* M.E. Prabhakar. (ed.), *Towards a Dalit Theology*: 104–12. Delhi: Indian Society for the Promotion of Christian Knowledge.

Godwin, C.J. 1972. *Change and Continuity: A Study of Two Christian Village Communities in Suburban Bombay.* Mumbai and Delhi: Tata McGraw-Hill Co.

Gold, Ann G. 1988. *Fruitful Journeys: The Ways of Rajasthani Pilgrims.* Berkeley: University of California Press.

Gomes, O. 1987. *Village Goa: A Study of Goan Social Structure and Change.* Delhi: S. Chand and Co.

Goody, J. and **S. Tambiah.** 1973. *Bridewealth and Dowry.* Cambridge: Cambridge University Press.

Gough, Kathleen. 1956. Brahman Kinship in a Tamil Village. *American Anthropologist* 58, 5: 826–53.

Grafe, H. 1972. Hindu Apologetics at the Beginning of the Protestant Mission Era in India. *Indian Church History Review* 6,1: 43–69.

Grant, John Webster. 1961. *God's People in India.* Bangalore: The Christian Literature Society.

Gudemann, S. 1972. The Compradazgo as a Reflection of the Spiritual and Natural Person. *Proceedings of the Royal Anthropological Institute for 1971*: 45–71.

Haggis, Jane. 1998. Good Wives and Mothers or Dedicated Workers? Contradictions of Domesticity in the Missions of Sisterhood, Travancore, South India, *in* Kalpana Ram and Margaret Jolly. (eds), *Maternities and Modernities: Colonial and Postcolonial Experiences in Asia and the Pacific*: 81–113. Cambridge: Cambridge University Press.

Hambye, E. and **H. Perumalil.** (eds), 1952. *Christianity in India.* Allepey: Prakasam Publications.

Hardgrave, Robert. L. 1968. Breast Cloth Controversy: Caste Consciousness and Social Change in South Travancore. *Indian Economic and Social History Review* 5, 2: 171–87.

———. 1969. *The Nadars of Tamilnad: The Political Culture of a Community in Change.* Berkeley and Los Angeles: University of California Press.

Hardiman, David. n.d. Christianity and the *Adivasis* of Western India: 1880–1930. Unpublished paper.

Hardiman, David. 1996. *Feeding the Baniya: Peasants and Usurers in Western India.* New Delhi: Oxford University Press.

Harper, Susan. 1995. Ironies of Indigenisation: Some Cultural Repercussions of Mission in South India. *Bulletin of Missionary Research* 19:13–20.

Heesterman, J.C. 1985. *The Inner Conflict of Tradition.* Chicago: University of Chicago Press.

Heras, H. 1935. *The Conversion Policy of the Jesuits in India.* Bombay: Indian Historical Research Institute.

Hollis, A.M. 1962. *Paternalism and the Church: A Study of South Indian Church History.* London: Oxford University Press.

Hooper, J.M.S. 1963. *Bible Translation in India, Pakistan and Ceylon,* 2nd edn. Rev. by W.J. Culshaw. London: Oxford University Press.

Hospital, Clifford. G. 1979. Clothes and Caste in Nineteenth Century Kerala. *Indian Church History Review* 13, 2: 146–56.

Houtart, F. and **G. Lemercinier.** 1981. *Genesis and Institutionalisation of the Indian Catholicism.* Louvain: Université Catholique de Louvain.

Hudson, D. Dennis. 1968. The Conversion Account of H.A. Krishna Pillai. *Indian Church History Review* 2,1: 15–43.

——————. 1970. The Life and Times of H.A. Krishna Pillai (1827–1900). Unpublished Ph.D. thesis. Claremont Graduate School, Ann Arbor, Michigan.

——————. 1972. Hindu and Christian Theological Parallels in the Conversion of H.A. Krishna Pillai, 1857–1859. *Journal of the American Academy of Religion* 40: 191–206.

——————. 1982. Christians and the Question of Caste: The Vellala Protestants of Palaiyankottai, *in* Fred. W. Clothey. (ed.), *Images of Man: Religion and Historical Process in South Asia*: 244–58. Chennai: New Era Publications.

——————. 1986–92. Tamil Hindu Responses to Protestants (Among Nineteenth Century Literati in Jaffna and Tinnevelly). *The Journal of Oriental Research* LVI–LXII: 130–53.

——————. 1993. The First Protestant Mission to India: Its Social and Religious Developments. *Sociological Bulletin* 42, 1 and 2: 3–63.

Hutton, John. H. 1969. *The Angami Nagas.* London: Oxford University Press.

Ifeka, C. 1987. Domestic Space as Ideology. *Contributions to Indian Sociology* 21, 2: 307–29.

——————. 1989. Hierarchical Woman: The 'Dowry' System and Its Implications among Christians in Goa, India. *Contributions to Indian Sociology* 23, 2: 261–84.

Ifeka-Moller, C. 1974. White Power: Social Structural Factors in Conversion to Christianity, Eastern Nigeria 1921–1966. *Canadian Journal of African Studies* 8,1: 55–72.

Inden, R. 1990. *Imagining India.* Oxford: Basil Blackwell.

Irudayaraj, Xavier S.J. 1990. *Emerging Dalit Theology.* Madras: Jesuit Theological Secretariat.

Jain, R.K. 1976. *Text and Context.* ISHI. London: ASA Publication.

Japhet, S. 1986–87. Christian Dalits: A Sociological Study of Post-conversion Experience. Unpublished M.Phil thesis. Department of Sociology, Bangalore University.

——————. 1988. Caste Oppression in the Catholic Church, *in* M.E. Prabhakar. (ed.), *Towards a Dalit Theology*: 176–180. Delhi: Indian Society for the Promotion of Christian Knowledge.

Jay, Edward. 1961. Revitalization Movements in Tribal India, *in* L.P. Vidyarthi. (ed.), *Aspects of Religion in Indian Society*: 282–315. Meerut: Kedar Nath Ram Nath.

Jesudasan, S. 1966. *Unique Christ and Indigenous Christianity*. Bangalore: The Christian Institute for the Study of Religion and Society.

Johnson, I.C. 1971. A Study of Theories and Practices of the Pentecostal Movement in India in the Light of Lutheran Understanding of the Christian Faith. Bachelor of Divinity Thesis. Chennai: Gurukul Lutheran Theological College.

Jordens, J.T.F. 1977. Reconversion to Hinduism, the Shuddhi of the Arya Samaj. *in* G.A. Oddie (ed.), *Religion in South Asia: Religious Conversion and Revival Movements in South Asia in Medieval and Modern Times*:145–61. London: The Curzon Press.

Joshi, Satyakam. 1999. Tribals, Missionaries and Sadhus: Understanding the Violence in the Dangs. *Economic and Political Weekly* 34, 37: 2667–675.

Juhnke, J.C. 1979. *A People of Mission: A History of General Conference Mennonite Overseas Mission*. Newton: Faith and Life Press.

Karnanaikil, Jose. 1983. *Christians of Scheduled Caste Origin*. Delhi: Indian Social Institute.

————. 1990. *Scheduled Caste Converts and Social Disabilities*. Delhi: Indian Social Institute.

Karve, Irawati. 1961. *Hindu Society: An Interpretation*. Poona: Sangam Press.

Kaufmann, S.B. 1979. Popular Christianity, Caste and Hindu Society in South India, 1800–1915: A Study of Travancore and Tirunelveli. Ph.D. thesis. University of Cambridge.

Kaye, John William. 1859. *Christians in India: A Historical Narrative*. London: Smith and Elder.

Kent, Eliza. F. 1999. Tamil Bible Women and the Zenana Missions of Colonial South India. *History of Religions* 39, 2: 117–49.

Khare, R.S. 1976. *The Hindu Hearth and Home*. Delhi: Vikas Publishing House.

Klostermair, K.K. 1967. *Kristvidya: A Sketch of an Indian Christology*. Bangalore: Christian Institute for the Study of Religion and Society.

Koilparambil, George. 1982. *Caste in the Catholic Community in Kerala*. Ernakulam: St Francis de Sales Press.

Kolenda, P.M. 1968. Region, Caste and Family Structure: A Comparative Study of the Indian 'Joint' Family, *in* M. Singer and B.S. Cohn. (eds), *Structure and Change in Indian Society*, 339–96. Chicago: Aldine Press.

Kooiman, Dick. 1989. *Conversion and Social Equality in India*. Delhi: Manohar Publications.

Koshy, Ninan. 1968. *Caste in the Kerala Churches*. Bangalore: The Christian Institute for the Study of Religion and Society.

Kulandran, S. 1958. Christian Attitude to Non-Christian Faith. *Religion and Society* 5,4: 7–21.

Kulkarni, A.R. 1992. Christianity: Proselytisation and Purification Movement in Goa and Konkan. Paper presented at the Xavier Centre of Historical Research Seminar on Discoveries, Missionary Expansion and Asian Cultures.

Kurien, C.T. 1981. *Mission and Proclamation: The Church in India Today and Other Pieces*. Chennai: Christian Literature Society.

Lehmann, Arno. 1956. *It Began at Tranquebar: A History of the First Protestant Mission in India*. Chennai: Christian Literature Society.

Liankhohau, T. 1994. *Social, Cultural, Economic and Religious Life of a Transformed Community.* Delhi: Mittal Publications.

Luke, P.Y. and **J.B. Carman.** 1968. *Village Christians and Hindu Culture: Study of a Rural Church in Andhra Pradesh, South India.* London: Lutterworth Press.

McGavran, D. 1979. *Understanding the Church in India.* Bombay: Gospel Literature Society.

Madan, T.N. 1975. Structural Implications of Marriage in North India. *Contributions to Indian Sociology* 9, 2: 217–43.

_____. 1987. *Non-renunciation.* Delhi: Oxford University Press.

Mallison, F. 1991, *in* Diana Eck and Françoise Mallison. (ed.), *Devotion Divine: Bhakti Traditions from the Regions of India.* Chennai: John Benjamin's Publishing Company.

Manickam, S. 1977. *The Social Setting of Christian Conversion in South India: The Impact of the Wesleyan Methodist Missionaries on the Trichy-Tanjore Diocese with Special Reference to the Harijan Communities of the Mass Movement Area 1820–1947.* Wiesbaden: Franz Steiner Verlag.

Manor, James. 1971. Testing the Barrier between Caste and Outcaste: The Andhra Evangelical Lutheran Church in Guntur District 1920–40. *Indian Church History Review* 5, 1: 27–41.

Manorama, Ruth. 1994. Dalit Women: Downtrodden among the Downtrodden, *in* James Massey. (ed.), *Indigenous People: Dalits—Dalits Issues in Today's Theological Debate.* New Delhi: Indian Society for the Promotion of Christian Knowledge.

Marques, A.H. de Oliveira. 1971. *Daily Life in Portugal in the Late Middle Ages,* tr. S.S. Wyatt. Madison, Milwaukee and London: The University of Wisconsin Press.

Marriott, M. (ed.), 1955. *Village India.* Chicago: University of Chicago Press.

_____. 1989. Constructing an Indian Ethnosociology. *Contributions to Indian Sociology* (n.s.) 23: 1–39.

_____. (ed.), 1990. *India through Hindu Categories.* New Delhi: Sage Publications.

_____. 1998. The Female Family Core Explored Ethnosociologically. *Contributions to Indian Sociology* (n.s.) 32: 279–304.

Mascarenhas-Keyes, S. 1987a. Migration and the International Catholic Goan Community. Ph.D. thesis. University of London.

_____. 1987b. The Native Anthropologist: Constraints and Strategies in Research, *in* A. Jackson. (ed.), *Anthropology at Home*:180–95. London: Tavistock Publications.

_____. 1990. Migration, 'Progressive Motherhood' and Female Autonomy: Catholic Women in Goa, *in* L. Dube and R. Palriwala. (eds), *Structures and Strategies: Women, Work and Family in Asia*:103–27. New Delhi: Sage Publications.

_____. 1994. Language and Diaspora: The Use of Portuguese, English and Konkani by Catholic Goan Women, *in* P. Burton, K.K. Dyson and S. Ardener. (eds), *Bilingual Women: Anthropological Approaches to Second Language Use*: 149–66. Oxford: Berg Publishers.

Massey, James. 1988. Ingredients for a Dalit Theology, *in* M.E. Prabhakar. (ed.), *Towards a Dalit Theology*: 57–63. Delhi: Indian Society for Promoting Christian Knowledge.

Massey, James. 1990. Christian Dalits in India: An Analysis. *Religion and Society* 37, 3: 40–53.

—————. 1991. Scheduled Caste: A Special Reference to Scheduled Caste Origin. *Religion and Society* 48, 3: 30–38.

—————. 1994a. The Role of the Churches in the Whole Dalit Issue. *Religion and Society*. 41, 1: 44–50.

—————. (ed.) 1994b. *Indigenous People: Dalits—Dalits Issues in Today's Theological Debate*. New Delhi: Indian Society for the Promotion of Christian Knowledge.

—————. 1995. *Dalits in India: Religion as a Source of Bondage or Liberation with Special Reference to Christians*. New Delhi: Manohar Publications.

Mathew, C.P. and **M.M. Thomas.** 1967. *The Indian Churches of Saint Thomas*. Delhi: Indian Society for the Promotion of Christian Knowledge.

Mathur, K.S. 1964. *Caste and Ritual in a Malwa Cillage*. Mumbai: Asia Publishing House.

Mayaram, Shail. 1997. *Resisting Regimes: Myth, Memory and the Shaping of a Muslim Identity*. Delhi: Oxford University Press.

Menachery, George. (ed.), 1982. *The St Thomas Christian Encyclopaedia of India*. Trichur: St Thomas Christian Encyclopaedia of India.

Miller, Roland. E. 1990. Religious Interaction in Kerala with Special Reference to the Impact of European Medieval Christianity, *in* Michael Gervers and Ramzi Jibran Bikhazi. (eds), *Conversion and Continuity*: 437–48. Toronto: Pontifical Institute of Medieval Studies.

Mills, J.P. 1926. *The Ao Nagas*. London: Macmillan and Co.

Minz, N. 1962. The Impact of Traditional Religions and Modern Secular Ideologies in the Tribal Areas of Chota Nagpur. *Religion and Society* 9, 4.

Montemayor, J.M. 1970. A Sociological Study of a Village Community in Goa, Ph.D. thesis. University of Delhi.

Miri, Sujata. (ed.), 1980. *Religion and Society of North-east India*. Delhi: Vikas Publishing House.

Moraes, George. M. 1964. *A History of Christianity in India: From Early Times to St Francis Xavier: A.D. 52–1542*. Mumbai: P.C. Manaktalas and Sons.

More, J.B.P. Hindu–Christian Interaction in Pondicherry, 1730–1900. Unpublished Manuscript.

Mosse, D. 1986. Caste, Christianity and Hinduism: A Study of Social Organisation and Religion in Rural Ramnad. Ph.D thesis. University of Oxford.

—————. 1994a. Idioms of Subordination and Styles of Protest among Christian and Hindu Harijan Castes in Tamil Nadu. *Contributions to Indian Sociology* 28,1: 67–106.

—————. 1994b. The Politics of Religious Synthesis: Roman Catholicism and Hindu Village Society in Tamilnadu, India, *in* Charles Stewart and Rosalind Shaw. (eds), *Syncretism/Anti-syncretism: The Politics of Religious Synthesis*: 85–107. New York: Routledge.

—————. 1994c. Catholic Saints and the Hindu Village Pantheon in Rural Tamil Nadu, India. *Man* (n.s.) 29, 2: 301–32.

—————. 1996. South Indian Christians, Purity/Impurity and the Caste System: Death Ritual in a Tamil Roman Catholic Community. *Journal of the Royal Anthropological Institute* (n.s.). 2, 3: 461–83.

Mullens, J. 1848. *Brief Sketch of the Present Position of Christian Missions in Northern India and of their Progress During 1847.* Calcutta: Baptist Missionary Press.

_____. 1852. *Revised Statistics of Missions: India and Ceylon.* Calcutta: Baptist Missionary Press.

_____. 1854. *Missions in South India.* London: W.H. Dalton.

Mundadan, A. Mathias. 1984. *Indian Christians: Search for Identity and Struggle for Autonomy.* Bangalore: Dharmaram Publications.

Murdoch, J. 1895. *Indian Missionary Manual: Hints to Young Missionaries in India.* London: James Nisbet.

Mylne, L.G. 1908. *Missions to Hindus: A Contribution to the Study of Missionary Methods.* London: Longmans, Green and Co.

Natarajan, Nalini. 1977. *The Missionary among the Khasis.* Delhi: Sterling Publishers.

Nehru, J. 1998. *The Discovery of India.* Delhi: Jawaharlal Nehru Memorial Fund.

Neill, Stephen. 1970a. *A History of Indian Missions.* London: Penguin.

_____. 1970b. *The Story of the Christian Church in India and Pakistan.* Chennai: Grand Rapids, MI: William B Eerdmans Publishing Co.

_____. 1984. *A History of Christianity in India: The Beginnings to AD 1707.* Cambridge: Cambridge University Press.

_____. 1985. *A History of Christianity in India II. 1707–1858.* Cambridge: Cambridge University Press.

Nelson, A. 1975. *A New Day in Madras: A Study of Protestant Churches in Madras.* South Pasadena. California: William Carey Library.

Nevett, A.M. 1980. *John de Britto and his Times.* Delhi: Gujarat Sahitya Prakash Anand.

New American Bible. 1970. Washington DC: United States Conference of Catholic Bishops.

Newbigin, L. *The Holy Spirit and the Church.* Chennai: Christian Literature Society.

Newman, R. 1981. Faith is All: Emotion and Devotion in a Goan Sect. *Numen* 28, 2: 216–46.

_____. 1984. Goa: The Transformation of an Indian Region. *Pacific Affairs* 57,3: 429–49.

_____. 1987. The Umbrellas of Cuncolim: A Study of Goan Identity. *Proceedings of the Eighth International Symposium on Asian Studies 1986* 4: 1105–17.

_____. 1988. Konkani Mai Ascends the Throne: The Cultural Basis of Goan Statehood, *South Asia* 11, 1: 1–24.

_____. 1990. Vision at Velim: The Political and Cultural Meanings of a Miracle in Goa, Paper Presented at the Eleventh Conference on Modern South Asian Studies. Amsterdam.

_____. 2001. *Of Umbrellas, Goddesses and Dreams: Essays on Goan Culture and Society.* Mapusa: Other India Press.

Nirmal, Arvind. P. 1988. A Dialogue with Dalit Literature, *in* M.E. Prabhakar. (ed.), *Towards a Dalit Theology*: 64–82. Delhi: Indian Society for the Promotion of Christian Knowledge.

_____. (ed.). 1989. Towards a Common Dalit Ideology: Papers presented at the National Seminar on Dalit Ideology Organised by the Department of Dalit Theology, Gurukul Lutheran Theological College and Research Institute. Chennai.

Nirmal, Arvind. P. (ed.), 1991. *A Reader in Dalit Theology*. Chennai: Gurukul Lutheran Theological College and Research Institute.

_____. 1992. Towards a Christian Dalit Theology. *Asia Journal of Theology* 6, 2: 297–310.

_____. 1994. Toward a Christian Dalit Theology, *in* R.S. Sugirtharajah. (ed.), *Frontiers in Asian Christian Theology: Emerging Trends*. Maryknoll: Orbis Press.

Nongbri, Tiplut. 1980. Religion and Social Change among the Khasi. Ph.D. thesis. University of Delhi.

Oberoi, Harjot. 1994. *The Construction of Religious Boundaries: Culture, Identity and Diversity in the Sikh Tradition*. Delhi: Oxford University Press.

Oddie, G.A. 1969. Protestant Missions, Caste and Social Change in India, 1850–1914. *The Indian Economic and Social History Review* 6,3: 259–91.

_____. 1975. Christian Conversion in the Telugu Country, 1869–1900: A Case Study of One Protestant Movement in the Godavery-Christian Delta. *The Indian Economic and Social History Review* 12: 61–79.

_____. 1977a. Introduction, *in* G.A. Oddie. (ed.), *Religion in South Asia: Religious Conversion and Revival Movements in South Asia in Medieval and Modern Times*: 1–12. London: The Curzon Press.

_____. 1977b. Christian Conversion among Non-Brahmans in Andhra Pradesh, with Special Reference to Anglican Missions and the Dornakal Diocese, c.1900–1936, *in* G.A. Oddie. (ed.), *Religion in South Asia: Religious Conversion and Revival Movements in South Asia in Medieval and Modern Times*: 67–99. London: The Curzon Press.

_____. (ed.), 1977c. *Religion in South Asia: Religious Conversion and Revival Movements in South Asia in Medieval and Modern Times*. Delhi: Manohar Book Service.

_____. 1979. *Social Protest in India: British Protestant Missionaries and Social Reform, 1850–1900*. New Delhi: Manohar Publications.

_____. 1981. Christianity in the Hindu Crucible: Continuity and Change in the Kaveri Delta, 1850–1900, *Indian Church History Review* 13: 48–72.

_____. 1982. Anti-missionary Feeling and Hindu Revivalism in Madras: The Hindu Preaching and Tract Societies, c. 1886–1891, *in* Fred W. Clothey. (ed.), *Images of Man: Religion and Historical Process in South Asia*: 217–43. Chennai: New Era Publications.

_____. 1991. *Hindu and Christian in South-East India: Aspects of Religious Continuity and Change, 1800–1900*. London: Curzon Press.

O'Flaherty, Wendy. D. 1973. *Asceticism and Eroticism in the Mythology of Miva*. London: Oxford University Press.

_____. 1980. *Women, Androgynes and other Mythical Beasts*. Chicago: University of Chicago Press.

Oommen, George. 1993. The Struggle of Pulaya Christians for Social Improvement. Unpublished Ph.D. thesis. University of Sydney.

_____. 2000. The emerging Dalit Theology: A Historical Appraisal. *Indian Church History Review* 34, 1: 19–37.

Palriwala, R. 1996. Negotiating Patriliny: Intra-household Consumption and Authority in Northwest India, *in* R. Palriwala and Carla Risseeuw. (eds), *Shifting Circles of Support: Contextualizing Gender and Kinship in South Asia and Sub-Saharan Africa:* 190–217. New Delhi: Sage Publications.

Pandey, G. 1990. *The Construction of Communalism in Colonial North India.* Delhi: Oxford University Press.

_____. 1993. Which of Us are Hindus?, *in* Gyanendra Pandey. (ed.), *Hindus and Others: The Question of Identity in India Today*: 238–72. Delhi: Viking Penguin India.

Parry, J. 1974. Egalitarian Values in a Hierarchical Society. *South Asian Review* 7, 2: 95–121.

_____. 1979. *Caste and Kinship in Kangra.* London: Routledge and Kegan Paul.

_____. 1994. *Death in Banaras.* Cambridge: Cambridge University Press.

Pathak, S.M. 1967. *American Missionaries and Hinduism.* Delhi: Munshiram Manoharlal.

Paul, R.D. 1958. *The First Decade: An Account of the Church of South India.* Chennai: Christian Literature society.

_____. 1961. *Chosen Vessels.* Chennai: Christian Literature Society.

_____. 1967. *Triumph of his Grace.* Chennai: Christian Literature Society.

Pearson, M.N. 1981. *Coastal Western India: Studies from the Portuguese Records.* Delhi: Concept Publishers.

_____. 1987. *The Portuguese in India.* Cambridge: Cambridge University Press.

Penny, Frank. 1904. *The Church in Madras, Being the History of the Ecclesiastic and Missionary Action of the East India Company.* London: Smith and Elder.

Pereira, Rui Gomes. 1978. *Goa (1) Hindu Temples and Deities.* tr. Antonio Victor Conto. Panaji: Rui Gomes Pereira.

Pettigrew, J. 1995. *The Sikhs of the Punjab: Unheard Voices of State and Guerilla Violence.* London: Zed Books.

Pickett, J.W. 1933. *Christian Mass Movements in India: A Study with Recommendations.* Lucknow: Lucknow Publishing House.

_____. 1956. et al. *Church Growth and Group Conversion.* 3rd edn, Lucknow: Lucknow Publishing House.

Plattner, F.A. 1950. *Jesuits Go East: A Record of Missionary Activity in the East, 1541–1786.* Dublin: Clonmore and Reynolds Ltd.

_____. 1964. *The Catholic Church in India Yesterday and Today.* Allahabad: St Paul Publications.

Pocock, D.F. 1973. *Mind, Body and Wealth: A Study of Belief and Practice in an Indian Village.* Oxford: Blackwell Publishers.

Podipara, Placid. 1947. The Social and Socio-ecclesiastical Customs of the Syrian Christians of India. *Eastern Churches Quarterly* 7, 4: 222–36.

Ponniah, J.S. 1938. et al. *An Enquiry into the Economic and Social Problems of the Christian Community in Madura, Ramnad and Tinnevelly.* Madurai: American College.

Prabhakar, M.E. 1988a. Introduction, *in* M.E. Prabhakar. (ed.), *Towards a Dalit Theology*: 1–8. Delhi: Indian Society for the Promotion of Christian Knowledge.

_____. (ed.), 1988b.*Towards a Dalit Theology.* Delhi: Indian Society for the Promotion of Christian Knowledge.

_____. 1997. *Christology in Dalit Perspective, in* V. Devasahayam. (ed.), *Frontiers of Dalit Theology*: 419. Chennai: Gurukul Lutheran Theological College.

Prabhu, George Soares. 1994. Jesus of Faith: A Christological Contribution, *in* K.C. Abraham and Bernadett Mbuy-Beya. (eds), *Spirituality of the Third World*: 139–64. Maryknoll: Orbis Press.

Priolkar, A.K. 1961. *The Goa Inquisition.* Mumbai: A.K. Priolkar.

Quarishi, Ferdaus. A. 1987. *Christianity in the North Eastern Hills of South Asia: Social Impact and Political Implications*. Dhaka: University Press Ltd.

Radcliffe-Brown. A.R. 1964 (1922). *The Andaman Islanders*. Glencoe III: The Free Press.

Rafael, Vicente. L. 1993. *Contracting Colonialism: Translation and Christian Conversion in Tagalog Society under Early Spanish Rule*. Durham: Duke University Press.

Raj, H. 1958. Persistence of Caste in South India—An Analytical Study of the Hindu and Christian Nadars. Ph.D. thesis. Washington. DC: American University.

Rajarigam, D. 1958. Tamil Churches and Caste: A Historical Sketch. *Religion and Society* 5,3: 19–24.

Ralston, Helen. 1987. *Christian Ashrams: A New Religious Movement in Contemporary India*. Lewiston, New York: Edwin Mellon.

Ram, Kalpana. 1991. *Mukkuvar. Women: Gender, Hegemony and Capitalist Transformation in a South Indian Fishing Community*. London and New Jersey: Zed Books Limited.

Rao, R.P. 1963. *Portuguese Rule in Goa 1510–1961*. London: Asia Publishing House.

Rayan, Samuel. 1992. Outside the Gate, Sharing the Insult, *in* Wilfred Felix. (ed.), *Leave the Temple: Indian Paths to Human Liberation*: 131–50. Maryknoll: Orbis Press.

Reddy, G. Prakash. 1987. Caste and Christianity: A Study of Shudra Caste Converts in Rural Andhra Pradesh, *in* V. Sudarsen, G. Prakash Reddy and M. Suryanarayana. (eds), *Religion and Society in South India*. Delhi: B.R. Publishing Corporation.

Redfield, Robert. 1956. *Peasant Society and Culture: Anthropological Approach to Civilisation*. Chicago: University of Chicago Press.

Richter, J. 1908. *A History of Missions in India*. Edinburgh: Oliphant, Anderson and Ferrier.

Rivenburg. 1941. *The Star of the Naga Hills*. Philadelphia: Judson Press.

Robinson, R. 1993 . Some Neglected Aspects of the Conversion of Goa: A Sociohistorical Perspective. *Sociological Bulletin* 42,1–2: 65–84.

_____. 1994. The Cross: Contestation and Transformation of a Religious Symbol in Southern Goa. *Economic and Political Weekly* 29, 3: 94–98.

_____. 1995. Two Ritual Calendars in Southern Goa. *Cambridge Anthropology* 18,1: 23–39

_____. 1997. Cuncolim: Weaving a Tale of Resistance. *Economic and Political Weekly* 32, 7: 334–40

_____. 1998. *Conversion, Continuity and Change: Lived Christianity in Southern Goa*. New Delhi: Sage Publications.

_____. 1999. Interrogating Modernity, Gendering Tradition: Teatr Tales from Goa. *Contributions to Indian Sociology* 33, 3: 503–39.

_____. 2000. Taboo or Veiled Consent?: Goan Inquisitorial Edict of 1736. *Economic and Political Weekly* 35, 27: 2423–431.

Robinson, R. 2001. Negotiating Boundaries and Identities: Christian 'communities' in India, *in* Surinder S. Jodhka. (ed.), *Communities and Identities: Contemporary Discourses on Culture and Politics in India*: 219–38, New Delhi: Sage Publications.

Roche, Patrick. 1984. *Fishermen of the Coromandel*, Delhi: Manohar Publications.

Sahay, Keshari N. 1963. Impact of Christianity on the Uraon of Three Villages in Chotanagpur. Unpublished Ph.D. thesis. University of Ranchi.

_____. 1968. Christianity as an Agency of Tribal Welfare in India, in L.P. Vidyarthi. (ed.), *Applied Anthropology in India.* Allahabad: Kitab Mahal.

_____. 1976. *Under the Shadow of the Cross.* Calcutta: Institute of Social Research and Applied Anthropology.

_____. 1986. *Christianity and Culture Change in India.* Delhi: Inter-India Publications.

Said, Edward. W. 1995. *Orientalism: Western Conceptions of the Orient.* London: Penguin.

Saulière. 1947. *Red Sand: A Life of St John de Britto S.J., Martyr of the Madura Mission.* Madurai: de Nobili Press.

Schmalz, Mathew N. 1999. Images of the Body in the Life and Death of a North Indian Catholic Catechist. *History of Religions* 39, 2: 177–201.

Seybold, Theodore C. 1971. *God's Guiding Hand: A History of the Central Indian Mission 1868–1967.* Philadelphia: The United Church Board for World Ministries of the United Church of Christ.

Shah, A.M. 1974. *The Household Dimension of the Family in India,* Berkeley, Los Angeles and London: University of California Press.

Sharma, Ursula. 1984. Dowry in North India: Its Consequences for Women, in Renèe Hirschon. (ed.), *Women and Property: Women at Property:* 62–74. London: Croom Helm.

Sharrock, J.A. 1910. *South Indian Missions.* Westminster: Society for the Propagation of the Gospel in Foreign Parts.

Sherinian, Zoe. 1998. The Indigenisation of Tamil Christian Music: Folk Music as a Liberative Transmission System. Unpublished Ph.D. dissertation. Wesleyan University.

Sherring, M.A. 1875. *The History of the Protestant Missions in India from their Commencement in 1706 to 1871.* London: Trubner Press.

Shiri, G. 1977. *Karnataka Christians and Politics.* Madras: The Christian Literature Society.

Shulman, David. 1980. *Tamil Temple Myths: Sacrifice and Divine Marriage in the South Indian Saiva Tradition.* Princeton: Princeton University Press.

Singarayar, J. 1978. A Survey of Christians of Scheduled Caste Origin: Discrimination in Society and Church. *National Christians Council Review* 98,: 389–91.

Singer, M. 1972. *When a Great Tradition Modernises.* New York: Praeger.

Singh, Harjinder. (ed.), 1977. *Caste among Non-Hindus in India,* Delhi: National Publishing House.

Silva Rego, A. da. (ed.), 1947–58. *Documentaço para a Historia das Missoes do Padroado Portugues do Oriente* vols.1–13. Lisbon: Agência Geral das Colonias.

Skaria, Ajay. 1999. *Hybrid Histories: Forests, Frontiers and Wildness in Western India.* Delhi: Oxford University Press.

Sorpotael and **Feni.** 1988. The Role of Food and Drink in Catholic Goan Ethnic Identity. Paper presented at the Institute of Social Anthropology, Oxford.

Srinivas, M.N. 1942. *Marriage and Family in Mysore.* Mumbai: New Book Company.

_____. 1952. *Religion and Society among the Coorgs of South India.* Oxford: Clarendon Press.

Stephens, Thomas. 1907. *The Christian Puranna.* Reproduced by Joseph L. Saldanha. Mangalore: Simon Alvares.

Stirrat, R.L. 1992. *Power and Religiosity in a Post-colonial Setting: Sinhala Catholics in Contemporary Sri Lanka*. Cambridge: Cambridge University Press.

Studdert-Kennedy, Gerald. 1998. *Providence and the Raj: Imperial Mission and Missionary Imperialism*. New Delhi: Sage Publications.

Subrahmanyam, Sanjay. 1990. *The Political Economy of Commerce: Southern India 1500–1650*. Cambridge: Cambridge University Press.

_____. 1993. *The Portuguese Empire in Asia 1500–1700: A Political and Economic History*. London and New York: Longman.

Thangaraj, M. Thomas. 1994. *The Crucified Guru: An Experiment in Crosscultural Christology*. Nashville: Abingdon.

Thangasamy, D.A. 1969. Some Trends in Recent Theological Thinking in Madras city. *Indian Church History Review* 3,1: 55–74.

Thapar, R. 1993. *Interpreting Early India*. Delhi: Oxford University Press.

_____. 1997. Foreword, *in* T. Trautmann, *Aryans and British India*: xi–xvi. New Delhi: Vistaar Publications.

Tharamangalam, J. 1996. Caste among Christians in India, *in* M.N. Srinivas. (ed.), *Caste: Its Twentieth Century Avatar*: 263–91. Delhi, Viking: Penguin India.

Thomas, M.M. and **R. W. Taylor.** (eds), 1965. *Tribal Awakening*. Bangalore: Christian Institute for the Study of Religion and Society.

Thomas, P. 1954. *Christians and Christianity in India and Pakistan*. London: George Allen and Unwin.

Tisserent, Eugene. 1957. *Eastern Christianity in India: A History of the Syro-Malabar Church from the Earliest Times to the Present Day*. London: Longman Green and Co.

Tiwari, Ravi. 1988. The Role of Theological Colleges in the Emergence of Dalit Theology, *in* M.E. Prabhakar. (ed.), *Towards a Dalit Theology*: 140–45. Delhi: Indian Society for the Promotion of Christian Knowledge.

Trawick, Margaret. 1990. *Notes on Love in a Tamil Family*. Berkeley: University of California Press.

Trautmann, T. 1997. *Aryans and British India*. New Delhi: Vistaar Publications.

Troisi, Joseph. 1979. *Tribal Religion: Religious Beliefs and Practices among the Santals*. Delhi: Manohar Publications.

Van der Veer. P. 1994. The Foreign Hand: Orientalist Discourse in Sociology and Communalism, *in* Carol. A. Breckenridge and Peter van der Veer. (eds), *Orientalism and the Postcolonial Predicament*: 23–44. Delhi: Oxford University Press.

Vatuk, S. 1969. A Structural Analysis of Hindu Kinship Terminology. *Contributions to Indian Sociology* 3: 94–115.

_____. 1975. Gifts and Affines in North India. *Contributions to Indian Sociology* 9, 2: 155–96.

Visvanathan, S. 1989. Marriage, Birth and Death: Property Rights and Domestic Relationships of the Orthodox/Jacobite Syrian Christians of Kerala. *Economic and Political Weekly* 24, 24: 1341–46.

_____. 1993a. *The Christians of Kerala: History, Belief and Ritual Among the Yakoba*. Chennai: Oxford University Press.

_____. 1993b. *Missionary Styles and the Problem of Dialogue*. Simla: Occasional Paper 6. Indian Institute of Advanced Study.

_____. 1995. The Legends of St Thomas in Kerala. *India International Centre Quarterly*. Summer-Monsoon.

Vitebsky, P. 1993. *Dialogues with the Dead: The Discussion of Mortality among the Sora of Eastern India.* Cambridge: Cambridge University Press.

Wadley, Susan. 1975. *Shakti: Power in the Conceptual Structure of Karimpur Religion.* Chicago: University of Chicago Press.

Waghorne, Joanne. P. 1999. Chariots of the God/s: Riding the Line between Hindu and Christian. *History of Religions* 39,2: 95–116.

Walker, A. 1986. *The Toda of South India: A New Look.* Delhi: Hindustan Publishing Corporation.

Warner, Marina. 1976. *Alone of All Her Sex. The Myth and Cult of the Virgin Mary.* London: Weidenfeld and Nicolson.

Warren, M. 1965. *The Missionary Movement from Britain in Modern History.* London: SCM Press.

Webster, John C.B. 1976. *The Christian Community and Change in Nineteenth Century North India.* Delhi: Macmillan.

_____. 1990. *The Dalit Christians: A History.* New Delhi: Indian Society for the Promotion of Christian Knowledge.

Westcott, A. 1897. *Our Oldest Indian Mission: A Brief History of the Vepery (Madras) Mission.* Chennai: Madras Diocesan Committee of the Society for the Promotion of Christian Knowledge.

Whitehead, Henry. 1913. The Mass Movements towards Christianity in the Punjab. *International Review of Missions* 2: 442–53.

_____. 1921. *The Village Gods of South India.* Calcutta: Association Press.

Wicki, J. (ed.), 1940–72. *Documenta Indica.* 12 vols. Rome: Institutum Historicum Societatis Iesu.

Wiebe, P.C. 1970. Protestant Missions in India: A Sociological Review. *Journal of Asian and African Studies* 5: 293–301.

_____. 1975. Religious Change in South India: Perspectives from a Small Town. *Religion and Society* 22, 27–46.

_____ **and P. John.** 1972. The Catholic Church and Caste in Tamil Nadu. *Eastern Anthropologist* 25: 1–12.

_____ **and S. John-Peter.** 1977. The Catholic Church and Caste in Rural Tamil Nadu, *in* Harjinder Singh. (ed.), *Caste among non-Hindus in India*: 37–49 New Delhi: National Publishing House.

Xavier, F.N. 1852. *Collecçao das Leis Peculiares das Comunidades Agricolas das Aldeas dos Concelhos das Ilhas, Salcete e Bardez.* 2 vols. Nova Goa: Imprensa Nacional.

_____. 1907. *Bosquejo Historico das Comunidades dos Concelhos das Ilhas, Salcete e Bardez.* Vol. 2. Bastora: Tipografia Rangel.

Yesudas, R.N. 1975. *A People's Revolt in Travancore: A Backward Class Movement for Social Freedom.* Trivandrum: Kerala Historical Society.

Younger, Paul. 1989. Hindu–Christian Worship Setting in South India, *in* Harold Coward. (ed.), *Hindu–Christian Dialogue: Perspectives and Encounters.* Maryknoll: Orbis Press.

Zelliot, Eleanor. 1972. *From Untouchable to Dalit.* New Delhi: Indian Society for the Promotion of Christian Knowledge.

INDEX

About the Author

Rowena Robinson is Associate Professor at the Department of Humanities and Social Sciences, Indian Institute of Technology, Mumbai. She has previously taught at the Department of Sociology, Delhi School of Economics, and at Miranda House, Delhi University.

Dr Robinson has previously published *Conversion, Continuity and Change: Lived Christianity in Southern Goa* (Sage, 1998), and is currently editing (with Dr Sathianathan Clarke) a book on conversions in India.